The Logic of Discipline

The Logic of Discipline

*Global Capitalism and the
Architecture of Government*

Alasdair Roberts

OXFORD
UNIVERSITY PRESS
2010

OXFORD
UNIVERSITY PRESS

Oxford University Press, Inc., publishes works that further
Oxford University's objective of excellence
in research, scholarship, and education.

Oxford   New York
Auckland   Cape Town   Dar es Salaam   Hong Kong   Karachi
Kuala Lumpur   Madrid   Melbourne   Mexico City   Nairobi
New Delhi   Shanghai   Taipei   Toronto

With offices in
Argentina   Austria   Brazil   Chile   Czech Republic   France   Greece
Guatemala   Hungary   Italy   Japan   Poland   Portugal   Singapore
South Korea   Switzerland   Thailand   Turkey   Ukraine   Vietnam

Copyright © 2010 by Oxford University Press, Inc.

Published by Oxford University Press, Inc.
198 Madison Avenue, New York, New York 10016

www.oup.com

Oxford is a registered trademark of Oxford University Press.

Library of Congress Cataloging-in-Publication Data
Roberts, Alasdair (Alasdair Scott)
The logic of discipline : global capitalism and the architecture of government / Alasdair Roberts.
    p. cm.
Includes bibliographical references and index.
ISBN 978-0-19-537498-8
1. Capitalism—Political aspects.   2. Democracy—Economic aspects.
3. International finance—Political aspects.   4. Democratization.   I. Title.
HB501.R57 2010
330.12'2—dc22   2009028994

9 8 7 6 5 4 3 2
Printed in the United States of America
on acid-free paper

The past couple of decades have witnessed a major shift in the attitude of many policymakers around the world. They have become increasingly aware of the importance of markets and market-friendly policies. They have also come to realize—many of them for the first time—the benefits that the discipline of the markets can bring.

—Anne O. Krueger, first deputy director of the International Monetary Fund, 2003

These guardians of our state, inasmuch as their work is the most important of all, will need the most complete freedom from other occupations and the greatest amount of skill and practice.

—Plato, The Republic, Chapter 7

Acknowledgments

The ideas in this book have been percolating for several years. Many of the topics contained within it were discussed in a class on public services reform that I taught at Queen's University in Canada from 1996 to 2001 and then at Syracuse University from 2002 to 2008. Some of these chapters were also presented as lectures at the Lal Bahadur Shastri National Academy of Administration in Mussoorie, India, in 2007 and 2008. I've benefited from the comments of participants in these classes and lectures.

Suffolk University Law School gave me the opportunity to write this book in 2008–2009, and several of my new colleagues at Suffolk helped me to refine the manuscript. Thanks are due as well to Jerry and Phyllis Rappaport, whose generosity has made possible the establishment of the chair which I now hold.

My editor at Oxford University Press, David McBride, gave valuable advice and encouragement throughout the process of writing and revision. I'm also indebted to three students in the MPA program at Syracuse University who assisted with the research for this book in 2007–2008: Guillaume Lechasseur, Fernando Pavon, and James Puckett.

Finally, I'm grateful for the enduring and indispensable support of my wife, Sandra, and my children, John and Constance; my parents, James and Nancy Roberts, and my parents-in-law, Guntis and Inta Sraders.

Contents

Figures

The Logic of Discipline

The Logic of Discipline

This is a book about an era in governmental reform that spanned thirty years. Call it the era of liberalization. It began, roughly, in 1978–1980 with the advent of market reforms in China, led by Deng Xiaoping; the election of British prime minister Margaret Thatcher and her subsequent assault on the British planned economy; and the election of U.S. president Ronald Reagan and his own program of economic deregulation. Economic liberalization was at first a revolutionary doctrine, but after three decades it became an orthodoxy promoted by center-left politicians (Democratic president Bill Clinton and Labour prime minister Tony Blair, for example) as well as those on the right. This epoch ended in 2007–2008, as the consequence of a global financial crisis that threatened to plunge the world into depression. This is not to say that the crisis threatened to unravel all of the policy changes of the preceding three decades. However, faith in the ideas that had propelled reform was shattered.

This era will be remembered as one in which markets were liberated and the role of government was constrained. Major businesses that were once operated as government enterprises—airlines, electricity and telephone companies, mining and steel manufacturers, among others—were sold to private investors. Government regulations that limited competition within major industries were pruned and sometimes completely eliminated. Barriers to international trade (such as tariffs on imports and rules designed to discriminate against foreign goods) were reduced, as were constraints on international investment. All of these policy changes led to a dramatic transformation in the structure of the global economy. In some advanced economies, the relative power of different sectors shifted: for example, finance flourished while manufacturing declined. The cross-border flow of goods, services, and money exploded.

In these years, the market reigned over the state. Markets were booming; they were dynamic; they were hotbeds of innovation. A vast amount of intellectual energy was dedicated to the challenges of organizing new methods of commerce: devising new financial instruments, new mechanisms for matching buyers and sellers, and new methods of organizing globally dispersed production chains.

Government, by contrast, seemed to have a more limited assignment: to get out of the way. It was generally agreed that the primary goal for the public sector was to have less of it, and the critical tactical question was how government could make an orderly retreat by either trimming or abandoning its now-redundant appendages.

Or so we sometimes thought. In fact, governmental reform was more complicated than a simple exercise in downsizing. In many critical areas, policy makers felt compelled to invent new ways of performing basic governmental functions. Sometimes they were looking for institutional arrangements that would promote key parts of the pro-market creed, such as the need for sound money and fiscal discipline. And sometimes they were responding to the pressures of the new globalized economy—the need to expand ports so that they could handle the boom in trade, to improve other forms of infrastructure to keep pace with growth, or to modify regulatory and judicial systems to reassure foreign investors.

We can combine these various efforts at governmental reform and say that, taken together, they constituted a distinctive program of state renovation. This program was not aimed simply at dismantling or shrinking the state but also at rebuilding government so that it would complement a liberalized and globalized economy. We will examine many of these reforms throughout this book. And we will find that each of these reform projects had more in common than the shared objective of making the global economy run smoothly. They also shared a design philosophy that I will call *the logic of discipline.*

The logic of discipline is a way of thinking about the organization of governmental functions that has been applied in many different areas over the past three decades. Briefly, the logic has two components. The first component makes the case for reform. This argument usually begins with an expression of deep skepticism about the merits of conventional methods of democratic governance, which are thought to produce policies that are shortsighted, unstable, or designed to satisfy the selfish concerns of powerful voting blocs, well-organized special interests, and the bureaucracy itself. This argument ends with a call for reforms that will promote policies that are farsighted, consistent over time, and crafted to serve the general interest.

(For convenience, I will call this last attribute the virtue of public-spiritedness.)

Allied to this argument about the need for reform is a second argument, one concerned with tactics—that is, the best way of changing governmental processes to promote the virtues of farsightedness, consistency, and public-spiritedness. The tactical argument says that it is important to impose constraints on elected officials and voters so they cannot make ill-advised decisions. This might involve a simple ban on certain kinds of ill-advised decisions or the transfer of certain critical functions so that a designated group of technocrat-guardians can make decisions on the public's behalf. Broadly, the task is sometimes called "depoliticization," because it involves removing certain subjects from the realm of everyday politics. Depoliticization is accomplished through legal instruments—laws, treaties, and contracts—that purport to transfer authority to technocrat-guardians or proscribe certain policy choices entirely.[1]

Here is an example of the logic of discipline at work. As we shall see in chapter 2, one of the most important governmental reforms of the past three decades has been the reorganization of central banks, which are responsible for setting monetary policy. Previously many central banks were under the control of finance ministers, who are members of popularly elected governments and accountable to popularly elected legislatures. Under these old arrangements, it has been argued, central banks faced pressure to stimulate short-term economic activity, despite the long-term inflationary effects, and also to fiddle with monetary policy too frequently. The virtues of farsightedness and consistency in policy were ignored. In many countries, the prescription for fixing this problem was to adopt laws that recognized the formal independence of central banks so that central bankers were free to make sound but politically inexpedient decisions about monetary policy. So here was a case for reform that was predicated on an argument about both the underlying problem (myopia and instability) and the appropriate remedy (legislative change in order to shield the central bank from everyday politics).

Central banking was hardly the only area in which the logic of discipline was deployed, as we shall see in subsequent chapters. The same reasoning was applied in fiscal policy—that is, the business of taxing and spending. Here the attempt was made to bolster the power of Treasury bureaucrats, with the aim of curbing the impulse to over spend; and, simultaneously, to increase the independence of tax collectors so that they could get on with the politically unpopular business of raising revenue. Also, laws were adopted to promote the autonomy of ports and airports so that they could expand their operations to accommodate the boom in international trade and travel.

This was again justified as a way of discouraging interference by politicians who lacked business judgment, cared little about operational efficiency, and suffered from an unhealthy habit of poaching revenues from shippers and airlines to fund politically popular programs elsewhere.

The abysmal state of public infrastructure—roads, bridges, schools, hospitals, prisons, and so on—was said to provide further evidence of the shortsightedness of politicians. Spending on new infrastructure and the maintenance of existing infrastructure seemed to get shortchanged because its benefits were largely enjoyed by voters in the distant future—unlike spending on current programs, whose full political benefits were realized immediately. The remedy for this shortsightedness, it was argued, was to delegate the function of infrastructure development to private consortia while also providing legal guarantees that politicians would not try to interfere in their work.

Similarly, if investors in critical utilities (electricity, telecommunications, or water) are worried about political manipulation of regulations that affect their profitability, the remedy is to create independent regulatory agencies structured much like independent central banks. And if foreign investors are worried that national courts might bend to political pressure and refuse to uphold contracts, then the remedy is to sign treaties that create new super-courts that also are buffered from the influence of politicians and voters.

Advocates of reform in each of these areas were certainly not engaged in a unified campaign, but a common thread did run through all of their reform projects. It was the logic of discipline: skepticism about the performance of democratic processes combined with faith in the curative power of new laws, treaties, and contracts.

Democratization or Discipline?

It might seem peculiar to claim that a major theme of governmental reform over the past three decades was built on skepticism about democratic processes and the desire to transfer authority to new groups of technocrat-guardians. This seems to be at odds with the widely accepted view that the era of liberalization was also one of democratization—that is, a time in which the principle of popular sovereignty was firmly entrenched.

There is a great deal of evidence that would bolster this alternative point of view. During the past three decades we witnessed the collapse of authoritarian regimes in Latin America, South Korea, the Philippines, and Indonesia; the end of apartheid government in South Africa and of one-party rule in

Mexico; the collapse of the Soviet Union and the integration of many of its former satellite states into the European Union. The 1990s were hailed as a decade in which democracy enjoyed an "unabashed victory" over rival forms of government. Pollsters reported a global surge in popular support for democracy as the ideal form of government. At a World Forum on Democracy held in Warsaw in 2000, representatives of one hundred governments affirmed that it is "the will of the people [that is] the basis of the authority of government." "At long last," the U.S. State Department asserted on the eve of the Warsaw meeting, "democracy is triumphant."[2]

Indeed, one could argue that a considerable amount of governmental reform over the previous three decades was actually occupied with the task of giving effect to the proposition that "the will of the people" should guide governments' behavior. New democracies were given advice on running fair elections. Parliamentarians were told how to organize legislative processes so that executives could be held properly accountable. A panoply of watch-dog agencies was created to help legislators: audit offices to scrutinize revenue and spending, ombudsmen to hear complaints about bureaucratic misconduct, and commissions to investigate corruption and human rights abuses.[3]

Many nations also shifted power downward so that governments would be responsive to local needs. "Decentralization was so widely adopted," says Merilee S. Grindle, "that it amounted to a structural revolution in the distribution of public responsibilities and authority in a large number of countries." Local leaders were now elected, where once they had been appointed. They were given substantial responsibilities, such as education and economic development. Decentralization, it was hoped, would allow more people a role in policymaking, increase accountability, and entrench democratic virtues in everyday life.[4]

Governments were in the throes of a "transparency revolution" as well. Laws to reduce governmental secrecy quickly spread around the globe. Legal recognition of the public's right to government information was closely linked to the democratization project, as the Supreme Court of India explained: "Where a society has chosen to accept democracy as its creedal faith, it is elementary that its citizens ought to know what their government is doing....It is only if people know how government is functioning that they can fulfill the role which democracy assigns to them." Other mechanisms also were used to increase openness, such as laws to protect employees who reveal information about waste and misconduct.[5]

"Citizens and organizations have become increasingly vocal in recent years," a 2001 report by the Organization for Economic Cooperation and

Development (OECD) warned. "Governments are under pressure to relate to citizens in new ways." Many governments overhauled mechanisms to improve public participation in decision making; some even conducted experiments in which random samples of "ordinary citizens" were selected to debate and resolve contentious issues. In the developing world, citizens were encouraged to collaborate with watchdog agencies in "participatory audits" of government bureaucracies.[6]

Citizens also challenged the state's monopoly over provision of critical services. "The relationship between state and citizen has changed," British prime minister Tony Blair told his Labour Party supporters in 2004. "People have grown up. They want to make their own life choices." The idea of creating options in the fields of elementary and secondary education, health care, and pension provision acquired increasing popularity. This shift in policy was said to be propelled by demographic change. "Today's young people," Andrei Cherny argued in 2000, "[have] a central unifying ethic all their own: that of *choice*. . . . [They were] born at a time when they had more choices to make with fewer restrictions than ever before in history and bred with an overwhelming desire to make these decisions for themselves in every part of their lives."[7]

Here, then, was a substantial bundle of governmental reforms being promoted in the name of popular sovereignty. They advanced the democratic virtues—participation, transparency, accountability, responsiveness, personal choice. And in addition to this they built upon a deep skepticism about the trustworthiness of traditional governing elites—including political executives and legislators, senior bureaucrats, and experts within government agencies. It was widely argued that we had entered a new age of populism in which "the wisdom of crowds" rather than the special knowledge of elites deserved to be celebrated. "Groups are remarkably intelligent," observed James Surowiecki in 2004, "and often smarter than the smartest people in them. . . . There's no reason to believe that crowds would be wise in most situations but suddenly become doltish in the political arena."[8]

Indeed, populist rhetoric became so intense that it alarmed some observers. In 2007 Andrew Keen lamented the rise of the "the cult of the noble amateur," which he said was encouraged by the leveling effect of information technologies and marked by extreme hostility toward any claims of expertise. The real challenge of modern governance, John Lukacs argued in 2005, was contending with a virulent new form of populism, one no longer channeled within the established institutions of liberal democratic government. "Democracy," Lukacs complained, "has become unlimited, untrammeled, universal." This was held to be a problem outside the developed world as well. "India is no longer a constitutional democracy but a *populist* one," said Ramachandra Guha, regretting "the decline of Parliament and of reasoned public discourse in general."[9]

Anyone who wants to tell a story about the logic of discipline must confront this daunting body of evidence, all of which tends to support the view that the prevailing winds favored a contrary dogma, a logic of popular sovereignty rooted in distrust of governing elites. How do we square an argument about discipline with all of this evidence about democratization?

We begin by recognizing that the era of liberalization was marked by contradictions. Throughout this era, these two logics—discipline and popular sovereignty—operated simultaneously, and often in opposition to one another. In some instances, attempts to pursue the logic of discipline were compromised precisely because of the failure to anticipate the strength of an opposing movement dedicated to the advancement of popular sovereignty. In other cases, however, it was the principle of popular sovereignty that gave way, as power was shifted to technocrat-guardians and new constraints were imposed on the exercise of discretion by elected officials and voters.

The clash between these two reform agendas reflected a deeper collision of ideas about the virtues and limitations of democratic systems. One camp of intellectuals celebrated the capacity of citizens and their elected leaders to govern properly. The other camp, more skeptical, acknowledged the importance of democratic values but warned that they had to be managed carefully if social and economic order was to be preserved.

For these skeptics, the low point for the major liberal democracies came in the mid-1970s. All of the major democracies were struggling, unsuccessfully, to reverse stagnant economies. Several were struggling to manage the demands of newly enfranchised groups, pressures for the devolution of power to minority populations, and problems of domestic and international terrorism. The United States itself had been traumatized by a string of political assassinations, a sharp rise in domestic terrorism and crime, and a constitutional crisis that ended with the resignation of its president.

"Liberal democracy is in serious trouble," Scotty Reston wrote in 1975. Reston was an editor and columnist for the *New York Times* and at that time one of the most influential journalists in the world. "We are living in a time of widespread doubt about the capacity of free societies to deal with the economic, political, and philosophical problems of the age.…There is a kind of counter-revolution against liberal democracy now going on in the world."[10]

This was a grim assessment of the state of liberal democracy. But it was affirmed in the same year in an expansive report by three prominent political scientists—Samuel Huntington, Michel Crozier, and Joji Watanuki. "The crisis of democracy," as their 1975 book called it, was in an odd way the product of its success. Traditionally, the effective operation of democratic political systems depended on "apathy and non-involvement" on the part of many individuals and groups. In the preceding decades, however, a resurgence of faith in democratic and egalitarian ideals had stirred many of these marginalized individuals and groups to action. "The democratic expansion of political participation," Huntington and his coauthors argued, "generated a breakdown of traditional means of social control, a delegitimation of political and other forms of authority, and an overload of demands on government, exceeding its capacity to respond." The overload thesis, as it came to be known, gained popularity among conservative thinkers as an explanation of the malaise of the 1970s.[11]

While conservative political scientists such as Huntington led an assault on one flank of the liberal democratic state, conservative economists mounted a charge on another. Their method consisted largely of asking what sort of behaviors would be expected if individuals in the public sector—politicians, bureaucrats, interest groups, and voters—were assumed to behave just like individuals in the marketplace—that is, with an acute sense of their own self-interest and a sharp understanding of how the game should be played to improve their position. ("The basic behavioral postulate," one scholar wrote, "is that man is an egoistic, rational, utility maximizer.") The body of academic work that applied economists' tools to problems of governance became known as Public Choice theory, and it gained a wide readership in the 1970s and early 1980s.[12]

The Public Choice perspective on political action was not flattering. Politicians, it was assumed, are fixated narrowly on maximizing votes in the next election rather than on the pursuit of broad programs or ideologies. To win elections, politicians must cater to voters who are themselves fixated on their material interests but who vary in their ability to protect those interests. It is typically easier to mobilize a small number of individuals, each of whom are sharply affected by government policy, than to mobilize a large number of individuals who are mildly affected. The result is that politicians give disproportionate aid to the well-organized few. To deliver on their promises, politicians must rely on government agencies. But the bureaucrats who lead these agencies are themselves preoccupied with maximizing their budgets and perquisites, and they often collude with their clients to pressure politicians for more money than they really need.[13]

The Public Choice diagnosis proceeded from premises that were different from those of conservative political scientists—the former group looking at the motivations of players within the system while the latter looked at broad societal transformations—but in the end it produced a similarly bleak view of the predicament of liberal democracies. The governmental system was myopic—largely because of the fixation of politicians on elections. It was biased toward constant expansion—mostly because of pressure from organized interests and pandering by elected leaders. And it was ossified—primarily because of resistance from powerful bureaucrats and the political influence of their clients. Public Choice theorists were not inclined to use the political scientists' terms, but their view was also one in which liberal democracies wrestled with problems of overload and declining "governability."

The two camps also agreed that the best way of restoring the health of liberal democracy was to impose firm checks against the destructive tendencies that were inherent within it. If Huntington and his colleagues were right in concluding that "an excess of democracy means a deficit in governability," then the survival of the political order clearly required "more self-restraint on the part of all groups"—or, in the alternative, the establishment of "limits to the indefinite extension of political democracy." Public Choice theorists, meanwhile, also favored similar constraints—such as new laws to limit spending and taxing so that government budgets would not be left "adrift in the sea of democratic politics." Constraints were also needed to control self-aggrandizement by bureaucrats and public service unions and to minimize "political micro-management" aimed at distributing patronage to powerful constituencies.[14]

It is clear, therefore, that enthusiasm for popular sovereignty in the last quarter of the twentieth century was hardly unabashed. There was, at the same time, a sharp appreciation of the perceived dangers of unconstrained sovereignty—of what we might call the "systemic risks" inherent in the liberal democratic system of governance. The collision of these two viewpoints produced a new understanding of how liberal democracies should be constructed if they were to avoid problems of ungovernability. It was still possible, therefore, to say (as the U.S. Department of State did in 2000), that democracy had finally "triumphed" in the last quarter of the twentieth century. But our understanding of what democracy *meant* also shifted significantly in those years.

The clash of ideas seemed to produce a result that we might describe as enhanced sovereignty within a more limited space. Mechanisms for participation and oversight of the state would be improved, but at the same time the sphere within which public opinion had a direct effect on the content of policy would be reduced. This was most obviously true with regard to state intervention in the economy. Government's role in economic affairs was now understood to be strictly confined. It no longer operated major industries such as steel, energy, or transport—the sectors that politicians of the Left had once called the "commanding heights" of a planned economy. Nor did it regulate other sectors rigorously. Economic intervention was understood to be forbidden territory.[15]

There is also a second way in which sovereignty was limited. Even within the state apparatus itself constraints were imposed. There were certain things that would be put above popular influence. For example, we established rules to force discipline in spending, and we strengthened finance ministries to enforce those rules. We created independent central banks to control monetary policy, independent agencies to administer what is left of the regulatory function, autonomous organizations to collect revenue and to run ports and airports, private consortia to provide basic infrastructure, and new international super-courts to enforce trade and investment rules. These reforms, by imposing limits on choice, empowering new groups of technocrat-guardians, and deliberately buffering certain arms of the state from the mechanisms that provide leverage to popular opinion, repudiated the language of popular sovereignty.

The way in which the influence of popular sovereignty was constrained was not indiscriminate. The aspects of governmental activity that I have just described have something in common. In one way or another they all relate to tasks that must be performed properly if a nation is to survive, and thrive, in a globalized economy. A nation that cannot maintain discipline in fiscal and monetary policy will lose the confidence of globalized financial markets. A nation that cannot demonstrate its impartiality in regulating businesses or adjudicating investment disputes will find itself unable to lure foreign investors. A nation whose ports and airports are decrepit cannot participate in the global trade of goods and services.

One study of recent governmental reform in the United Kingdom observes that the Labour government in power since 1997 "has been unable to explain why depoliticization has been accepted as a legitimate model of governance in some sectors but not others. This has resulted in a typically British patchwork of asymmetrical depoliticization." But it is neither a patchwork nor unique to the United Kingdom. The logic of discipline is most likely to be applied to those aspects of government whose performance is critical to the smooth functioning of globalized markets. (We might say, in an inversion of the socialists' phrase, that the logic is applied to the "commanding heights" of the state structure itself.) If this test is not met, the logic of discipline is less likely to be applied, and reforms that are wholly antithetical to the logic of discipline might be pursued. In education and health care, for example, recent reforms have often been concerned with the extension of political control over service delivery and the weakening of the power of professionals within those domains—a program of politicization rather than depoliticization.[16]

In the United States, it is often argued that the national government is "bifurcated"—that is, essentially two discrete systems combined into one government. The conventional way of thinking about this split is to suggest that there is one part, in which policy influence is broadly diffused, that deals with domestic policy and another part, in which power is concentrated in the hands of the president and the national security apparatus, that deals with foreign and defense policy. The latter part is "deliberately shielded from the effects of democratic debate," argues Eric Alterman, "with virtually no institutionalized democratic participation."[17]

The analogy will be clear. The advance of global capitalism has had a comparable effect on the administrative structures of many national governments. In a sense, all governments are now divided: there are certain tasks, essential to the operation of globalized markets, that are organized in distinctive ways so that they will be buffered from popular influence or the vagaries of political judgment.

The Limits of Discipline

The preceding discussion might create the impression that there was a neat settlement about the way in which government should be organized in the era of global capitalism. This is not the case. The question of how government should be structured, and where the logic of discipline should be applied, is the subject of ongoing political debate. Or perhaps we should say debates, because there is not one single grand argument about the need for discipline. There are, instead, a series of arguments about the need for reform in a particular sector or about the need to preserve reforms already undertaken. In each sector we can find different stakeholders advancing the same logic. Financial institutions apply it in the field of monetary policy; Treasury officials and international lenders, in the field of fiscal policy; shippers and airlines, in the field of transportation; private utilities, in the field of regulation and investment protection; and so on. The logic of discipline is advanced by powerful interests in the areas that matter most to them.

Similarly, we should not overstate the coherence of the rhetoric that is deployed by advocates of discipline in different fields. My argument is that there are strong substantive commonalities in the way that reform is justified.

But the commonalities sometimes go unrecognized by the stakeholders themselves, and certainly none would refer to a "logic of discipline" itself. Arguments about reform are usually messy. Elsewhere I have argued that the process of building such arguments is one of bricolage, the cobbling together of already familiar ideas in order to bolster the case for some new reform.[18]

And there is certainly ample material for bricolage. Arguments about the dangers of amateurism in government go back to Plato's *Republic* (see the epigraph to this book). The Progressive movement in the United States in the early years of the twentieth century also was concerned with the depoliticization of core governmental functions, especially in local government. And many constitutional democracies rely on autonomous bodies to monitor elections, safeguard human rights, and assure the rule of law. So the case for constraints on sovereignty in certain areas is not unfamiliar. The challenge for the stakeholders I described earlier was to make the argument for similar limitations in the field of economic affairs. And they were required to do this in the face of stiff resistance from organizations and individuals who felt empowered by the apparent renaissance of democratic values in the waning years of the past century.[19]

In short, the campaign for discipline has not been a monolith: it has been dispersed in structure and often varied in form of argument. Moreover it has often failed to accomplish its goals. A major aim of this book is to examine the instances in which the logic of discipline has been defeated, compromised, discredited, or rendered irrelevant by changed economic conditions.

In thinking about the setbacks that advocates of discipline have encountered, it is useful to break recent history into two periods. We can say something about the troubles that the campaign for discipline encountered *before* the advent of the global financial crisis, the beginning of which can roughly be placed in the summer of 2007. And we can say something about the distinct set of troubles that the campaign for discipline encountered *during* the crisis itself.

Before 2007, advocates of discipline had learned something about the limits of a reform strategy that put heavy emphasis on the reform of governmental systems through legal change. I said earlier that the logic of discipline contained a tactical argument that the best way to promote the virtues of farsightedness, consistency, and public-spiritedness was to impose constraints on democratic processes, either by foreclosing certain choices entirely (as balanced-budget rules do) or by transferring authority over certain choices to specialists who are protected from political interference. We shall see that these constraints were often contained in new statutes, treaties, and contracts. Advocates of discipline had great faith in the ability to reform governmental processes through the adoption or modification of legal instruments.

Many of these advocates described themselves as institutionalists. In adopting this label, they meant to convey the message that they understood the critical importance of "governing institutions" to long-run economic development. Before the 1990s, many development specialists, particularly those affiliated with major organizations like the World Bank, paid little attention to the ways in which the design of state institutions affected economic growth. But this changed in the 1990s. The World Bank in particular developed an enthusiasm for the improvement of "institutional capability" in poorer nations. This shift was encouraged by scholarly work, such as that done by the economist Douglass North, who emphasized the ways in which institutions influenced long-run economic performance.[20]

However, there was a critical difference between North and many groups that were directly engaged in the campaign for discipline. North defined the term "institution" broadly, to include informal constraints, such as norms of behavior, codes of conduct, and conventions that are "part of the heritage we call culture." Many other scholarly proponents of the "new institutionalism" (as it came to be known) took a similarly broad view of what an institution is. A skeptical view about the possibility of institutional change flowed naturally from this broad definition. "Formal rules may change overnight," North warned in 1990, but "informal constraints embodied in customs, traditions and codes of conduct are much more impervious to deliberate policies."[21]

Advocates of discipline purported to march under the banner of "new institutionalism" but often took a much narrower view of their assignment. They were concerned with the formal–legal aspects of governance: constitutions, treaties, laws, and contracts. They were not much concerned with informal constraints on behavior. As Dani Rodrik recently said, there was "a tendency to oversimplify the issues at stake…by identifying 'institutions' solely with the formal, legislated rules in existence." And because the advocates of discipline had a reduced view of what institutions were, they took a relatively upbeat view about the ease with which institutions could be changed. For reasons that will shortly become obvious, I will call this *naive institutionalism*.[22]

This attitude was not entirely new. In its early decades, the field of political science was dominated by a similar way of thinking about governance, sometimes known as formal-legalism: "a preoccupation with formal structures and legal strictures" and "the organized and evident institutions of government." But formal-legalism was largely abandoned within political science in the years following the Second World War, as scholars in that field realized its limitations as a means of understanding patterns of political behavior.[23]

During the era of liberalization, naive institutionalism had advantages for three key constituencies: advocates of reform, target governments, and scholars interested in studying the effects of reform. For proponents of reform, the formal–legal approach had the advantage of efficiency and simplicity. Legal reforms can be communicated easily from one country to another, and adoption can be a quick process, if executives and legislators are properly motivated. Governance reform becomes a matter of "technology transfer" from among countries. By contrast, any reform approach that takes informal constraints seriously is bound to require more time for assessing the particular conditions of a particular country and also more likely to require the invention of a tailor-made remedy involving a long-term commitment of effort to execute. Reformers who face time and resource constraints are unlikely to find this an appealing prospect. Hence the reversion to naive institutionalism, which offers the false promise of change in the "short to medium-term perspective."[24]

Also, formal–legal changes are observed more easily than changes to informal constraints. This has advantages for reform advocates, including those in development aid agencies, who may face pressure to demonstrate success in advancing reform. For the same reason, target governments will emphasize formal–legal changes if their primary purpose is to signal to other governments or investors that they are serious about reform. Finally, observability creates temptations for scholars interested in undertaking studies of the ways in which reforms are diffused among countries, or the impact of reforms. Scholars often acknowledge the limitations of formal–legal reform. But as we will see, there is still an urge to focus on easily measured aspects of the governmental process.[25]

Despite its attractions, there was ample evidence even before the era of liberalization that a strategy of reform that emphasized only the formal–legal aspects of governance was unlikely to succeed. In the United States, an extensive scholarly literature was produced in the 1970s to explain why the legislative initiatives of the Great Society era failed to produce significant social change. The prevailing theme was that good intentions expressed in law can easily be defeated in the "implementation phase" by powerful political, bureaucratic, and socioeconomic forces. In this same period, the American legal community undertook a substantial campaign to modernize the legal systems of poorer countries by exporting techniques of legal education, legal practice, and judicial administration. The program was bolstered by money provided by the U.S. government, which was eager to build alliances with developing states during the Cold War. By the mid-1970s, however, this reform program was widely regarded as a failure, flawed by a lack of understanding of political, economic, and social conditions in the targeted countries.[26]

Advocates of discipline, apparently unaware of this history, were doomed to repeat it. As we shall see, attempts at formal–legal transformation often were affected by political or sociocultural factors whose power had not been anticipated. In a few instances these factors actually favored reform by providing a buttress that went unacknowledged in analyses of the reform process. More often, however, these factors frustrated reform or defeated it entirely.

Ex post analyses of failed reforms rarely defined these factors with precision. The usual tactic was to throw them into a residual category of considerations, sometimes labeled as "the political and cultural context" or "the wider framework for governance," that appeared to affect the prospects for institutional reform. But this residual category was clearly important, and by the mid-2000s many development specialists seemed ready to abandon a narrow, formal–legal conception of reform. "Merely adopting some other country's laws and formal regulations is no guarantee of achieving the same institutional performance," a chastened World Bank report concluded in 2005. "[W]e need to get away from formulae and the search for elusive 'best practices'…[and acquire] a better understanding of non-economic factors—history, culture, and politics—in economic growth processes." A 2008 Bank report agreed, in language that would have been familiar to a student of the Great Society reforms thirty years earlier: "Policy design and implementation is a complex, multi-directional, fragmented and unpredictable process."[27]

Effect of the Crisis

Before August 2007, it could still be argued that the logic of discipline had the benefit of favorable headwinds, even if particular efforts at the imposition of discipline were encountering "problems of implementation." The case for discipline still had tremendous power. The engine of economic globalization appeared to be running smoothly, and skepticism about the competence and rationality of governments relative to markets was still broadly shared.

Within two years, the conventional wisdom was completely reversed. Global commerce had collapsed and, along with it, faith in the power of markets. The role of the state was expanded substantially. And in many of the areas that we will canvass in this book, the campaign for discipline had suffered substantial setbacks.

We must briefly describe the arc of the global financial crisis. It is now agreed that the United States, and some other major economies, experienced a substantial bubble in the housing market that started roughly in 1995, expanded even more rapidly after 2001, and burst after 2006 (see fig. 1.1). A combination of factors contributed to the bubble. Low interest rates made it possible for home buyers to make larger offers to home sellers. At the same time, lenders became less rigorous in deciding whether prospective buyers were qualified for mortgages. Bubble psychology drove lenders and buyers: if prices were always increasing, there was little risk involved in approving bigger mortgage loans or bidding extravagantly on property.[28]

There was more than bubble psychology at work, however. The business of mortgage lending had itself been transformed in ways that encouraged inflation in housing prices. Many lenders were less careful because they quickly sold mortgages to third parties, who pooled these mortgages to create new assets, known as mortgage-backed securities. Securities like these became popular investments for a variety of loosely regulated financial

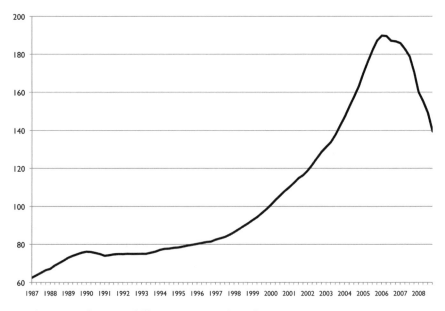

Figure 1.1 The Case–Shiller U.S. Home Price Index, 1986–2008.

Source: Standard & Poors: http://www2.standardandpoors.com.

institutions that were themselves highly leveraged: they took advantage of low interest rates to borrow trillions of dollars that could be invested in these securities and, thereby, channeled into mortgage lending. Executives in these financial institutions were motivated by salary schemes that encouraged them to maximize short-term profits with scant regard to cumulative long-term risks. They were abetted by credit rating agencies that, partly because they were paid by the institutions that were selling the securities, understated the riskiness of the securities in which financial institutions were investing and also by insurers who, assuming that losses would never be incurred, sold the investing institutions cheap protection against that possibility.

Then the housing bubble burst. Overbuilding and an unexpected rise in interest rates led to a decline in house prices and wave of defaults on lower quality mortgages. This, in turn, raised doubts about the value of mortgage-based securities and other instruments connected to them. Losses to financial institutions were estimated to exceed $3 trillion. Financing schemes were so complex that financial institutions could not be sure whether their business partners were still reliable, and lending between financial institutions seized up, pushing weaker institutions into insolvency. Panic spread globally because of the tight interconnection of financial markets. Major firms were dissolved or taken into state ownership.

The collapse in house prices meant that American households were poorer than they had imagined they were. Households became poorer still after the stock market collapsed in October 2008. The net worth of U.S. households declined 20 percent, or $13 trillion, in just eighteen months. Distressed financial institutions also tightened their lending to households and businesses. For all of these reasons, spending for consumption or investment purposes declined sharply. The interconnection of markets meant that the effect of reduced spending was again globalized, and by 2009 the world economy had fallen into its deepest recession in modern history. Central bankers and finance ministers were taking extraordinary measures to stimulate demand and avert a full-scale depression.

In many ways, the financial crisis upended the logic of discipline. Consider, for example, the role of central banks. Over the previous two decades, dozens of central banks were given formal independence on the argument that this was the only way of assuring that monetary policy would be firmly anti-inflationary. Only a few years ago, this reform was hailed as a great success. But it can now be argued that central bank independence was a sort of Maginot Line: a massive structure that was heavily fortified against the wrong threat. Independence entrenched a doctrine about the role of central banks that included a blindness to systemic vulnerabilities and the dangers raised by asset bubbles. When a financial crisis did occur, central bankers were caught flatfooted; collaborating closely with elected leaders to avoid a collapse of the financial sector, they quickly compromised the show of independence.

The campaign for discipline was compromised in other respects as well. The appeal of independent regulatory agencies waned as they, too, began to look like mechanisms for entrenching flawed policies. The virtues of fiscal discipline were quickly forgotten as trillions of dollars were committed to prevent the collapse of financial sector and to compensate for the decline in private consumption and investment. The case for creating autonomous ports and airports weakened as trade and travel collapsed: the problem for these ports and airports was now underutilization, not congestion. Similarly, the argument for private investment in infrastructure collapsed as investors themselves abandoned the field. The urgency of establishing safeguards to reassure investors in less stable regions diminished as they fled to safer markets.

Recall that the case for discipline had been predicated on an argument that democratic political processes were prone to three vices: myopia, instability, and selfishness. The assumption was that a free market would not be prone to the same frailties. The financial crisis disproved this thoroughly. It arose because of a breakdown of discipline within the financial sector itself.

The crisis also showed that the case for discipline within the public sector was contingent on the assumption that the financial sector itself would not require aid from government. When the financial sector itself became distressed, the logic of discipline in monetary and fiscal policy was quickly put aside. The logic of discipline, it now appears, always applied with a large asterisk—an unspoken qualification that it would be suspended when required by the needs of capital.

Is the logic of discipline dead? It is too soon to say. We can imagine, for example, a scenario only a few years down the road when the case for discipline is revived. At that time, governments may be struggling with the inflationary and budgetary effects of policies adopted during the crisis, and arguments may again be made about the virtues of central bank independence and firm fiscal rules. We might return to normalcy, as that condition was defined in the era of liberalization. But this is not a certain outcome. The logic of discipline might be so firmly discredited that it will be politically impossible for elected leaders to apply it in practice. We might insist that it is markets, rather than governments, that are prone to myopia, instability, and greed and therefore in need of discipline.

This would be a complete turnabout, but it would not be unprecedented. In his *General Theory*, published in 1936, John Maynard Keynes argued that it was the state, rather than the market, that was better able to take the long view in matters of economic management. By the end of the Second World War it was "highly respectable doctrine" that strict controls had to be imposed on capital, rather than governments, precisely because of its erratic behavior. The logic of discipline was invoked against markets rather than voters and politicians. In the era of liberalization, the logic was turned on its head. But the financial crisis suggests the need for another recalibration. Even if the institutional substructure built during the era of liberalization is not completely dismantled, enthusiasm for extending the logic of discipline should certainly be tempered.[29]

The Quiet Revolution
Central Bank Independence

Can a democracy discipline itself? What is it that creates this sense of helplessness? It's clearly something that has to do with the lack of social discipline.... The problem in our economy is we have these persistent, well-organized pressures by each individual and group to preserve his or her absolute position regardless of what happens to the country as a whole.

—*Alfred Kahn, chairman, U.S. Council on Wage and Price Stability, 1980*

Why does the Fed grow hysterical over a 2.5 percent inflation rate but think that $10 trillion financial bubbles can be ignored?

—*Dean Baker, Center for Economic and Policy Research, 2008*

When it is completed in 2014, the new headquarters of the European Central Bank will rise seven hundred feet over the Main River in the eastern suburbs of Frankfurt, Germany. It will tower over industrial buildings and homes on the river's north bank. Imagine two mirrored slab-block skyscrapers built in close parallel; then slightly twist the two, as though wringing a towel, so that they begin a corkscrew into the sky. Next, add a glass atrium between the two twisted slabs. The effect is remarkable. It is as though the entire building is trying to wrench itself from the earth.

The European Central Bank (ECB) was created in 1998 by most of the countries that constitute the European Union (EU). Like all central banks, it is a governmental institution that has responsibility for making decisions about the supply of money. In the ECB's case, the object of attention is the euro, introduced in 1999 to replace the older currencies of eleven nations. Sixteen countries now use the euro; together they constitute the Eurozone.

The importance of the ECB's decisions to citizens of the Eurozone cannot be easily overstated. Every citizen who uses euros has a stake in ECB decisions that affect their value. If the ECB fails to restrain inflation, millions of Europeans who have made long-term investments in euro-denominated assets will suffer a substantial loss. But if the ECB is too zealous in restraining inflation, European businesses will retrench and workers will lose their jobs. The effect of ECB policies can be very uneven. Although long-term investors are harmed by inflation, borrowers benefit because it corrodes the real value of their debts. And because Eurozone is large and diverse, the effects of ECB policies will be felt unequally across its expanse: decisions that seem appropriate for the Germany economy may appear misguided to citizens in Spain.

All of the countries in the Eurozone are democracies. The 1992 Treaty on European Union, which mandated the establishment of the ECB, also says that the aim of the EU is to "consolidate democracy" and strengthen "the democratic nature" of member institutions. Because the ECB is an EU institution that has such a profound and uneven effect on citizens, we might expect that it would be one place where the concern about democratic control would be pronounced. We would expect it to be one of the primary centers of political contestation. We would expect to see, in the institutional design of the ECB, the usual array of mechanisms for facilitating democratic politics: a mandate that is vague enough to allow debate over the aims of policy; top managers who are directly accountable to elected officials, or who at least think like politicians; extensive mechanisms for public consultation; and tough rules to assure the disclosure of information to politicians and citizens.

When we look at the actual design of the ECB, however, our expectations are dashed. The ECB is carefully sheltered from everyday politics. The president and other members of the ECB executive board are appointed for eight-year terms and can be removed only if a court determines they are guilty of serious misconduct. The ECB president is not a politician; rather, he or she must be an individual recognized for professional banking experience. (The current president, Jean-Claude Trichet, was a French bureaucrat and head of France's central bank.) The treaty stipulates that deliberations within the ECB on monetary policy are confidential. ECB employees are bound by an obligation of secrecy even after they retire from the bank.[1]

The ECB also maintains a careful distance from elected officials. It is explicitly forbidden from taking instructions from the European Council, which represents member states, and from the popularly elected European Parliament. It is "normal" for elected officials to have a view about monetary policy, the ECB's first president, Wim Duisenberg, conceded in 1998, but it would be "abnormal if those suggestions were listened to." The ECB says it must be guided by the treaty alone, which states that inflation control is the bank's main objective. Duisenberg was firm in resisting demands from Eurozone ministers to shift its policy during an economic slowdown in 2001. "I am polite," Duisenberg told journalists at the time. "You might say, I hear, but I don't listen."[2]

In a sense, the design of the ECB as an institution is much like the design of its new Frankfurt headquarters. Just as the Frankfurt tower twists to escape everyday life on the surrounding streetscape, the ECB itself twists to escape the crosscurrents of everyday politics. It operates under a set of rules intended to place it above politics. In a decade that was ostensibly dedicated to the opening up of decision-making processes, the leaders who designed the ECB decided that the difficulty with the formulation of monetary policy was quite different: too much politics rather than too little. The ECB is a monument to the logic of discipline. And the ECB is not unusual. By the turn of the millennium, most of the world's central banks were structured so that they also would have formal independence from political executives and legislators.

This near-universal adherence to the idea of central bank independence is relatively new. Three decades ago, most central banks were agents of their national finance ministries. John Kenneth Galbraith, then one of the world's best-known economists, dismissed the idea of central bank independence as an eccentricity. He took it to be self-evident that political leaders must retain control over monetary policy, precisely because it involved difficult judgments about the distribution of benefits and costs across society. Central bank independence, Australia's finance minister agreed, was "completely at odds with our traditions requiring public officials to be in the end accountable."[3]

Over those three decades, however, there has been a "quiet revolution" in central bank governance, in the words of Alan Blinder, a Princeton University economist and former vice chairman of the Federal Reserve's board of governors. It is now regarded as self-evident that formal rules are necessary to take monetary policy "outside the realm of party politics." Today's central bank, as described by Paul Bowles and Gordon White, is "a modern embodiment of the Platonic guardian. . . . [S]uch a bank operates in effect as a fourth branch of government and yet, by virtue of its 'independence' and 'apolitical' character, it is deemed to be above and outside the normal political pressures and requirements of democratic societies."[4]

Trauma and Reform

There are two reasons why central bank independence should be regarded as an application of the logic of discipline. First, it is a reform that is clearly aimed at correcting the perceived deficiencies of conventional democratic processes. And second, it is an expression of naive institutionalism—that is, the idea that defective processes can be fixed through changes in law. There also is a close connection between this reform and the conservative reaction to the political and economic traumas of 1968–1982, a period remembered by many economists as the Great Inflation.[5]

The seeds of the Great Inflation were planted in the United States in the late 1960s. With the expansion of the Vietnam War, federal spending on defense increased until it reached 9 percent of the gross domestic product (GDP)—more than double its level today. Federal spending on domestic programs also increased as a result of the establishment of Medicare, the expansion of Social Security and other income support programs, and the undertaking of new federal initiatives in the areas of education and transportation. Increased federal expenditures led to inflationary pressures that might have been reduced through tax increases, but these were politically unpalatable.[6]

One significant check on inflationary policies had traditionally been the Bretton Woods Agreement, which allowed other governments to present their U.S. currency to the United States Treasury for exchange into gold at a fixed rate. As inflation corroded the value of the dollar, many governments did this, so that the U.S. supply of gold rapidly depleted. In 1971, President Richard Nixon responded by abandoning the promise of convertibility. The dollar dropped in value against other currencies, thereby raising the price of imports and adding to inflationary pressures. The U.S. central bank, the Federal Reserve, which could have taken steps to stanch inflationary pressures, failed to act decisively. Many believed that then Federal Reserve chairman Arthur Burns was pressured into not acting by Nixon, who feared that firm action would cause an economic slowdown just prior to the 1972 presidential election.[7]

This sequence of policy missteps was then compounded by bad luck. In 1973, major oil-producing states formed a cartel that quickly quintupled the price of oil. This, combined with sharp rises in the prices of other commodities, stoked inflation further: in 1974 consumer prices rose by 12 percent. Moreover, the economy began to slow, and unemployment increased. Other

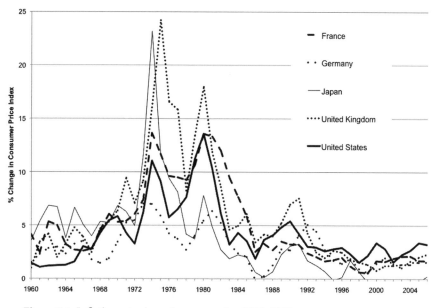

Figure 2.1 Inflation rates in major economies, 1960–2006.
Annual percentage change in consumer price indices for major economies.
Source: Organization for Economic Cooperation and Development: http://stats.oecd.org.

advanced economies soon suffered the same combination of high inflation and economic stagnation (fig. 2.1).

Throughout the 1970s, Western governments struggled to find an appropriate response to this predicament: sometimes increasing government spending to boost growth; sometimes imposing controls on wages and prices to restrain inflation; and alternating between loose monetary policy (to spur growth) and tight monetary policy (to restrain inflation). The result (aggravated by a second oil price shock in 1979) was deeper economic and political turmoil. Labor unrest grew as unions struggled to keep wages in line with rising prices. Leaders of several countries were ousted by electorates angry over their inability to restore economic stability. In the United States, the journalist Theodore White observed that "the Great Inflation had become the obsession of common talk.... [N]o other issue could rival inflation as a pressure on the American mind." Inflation was "the central economic issue and...a national anxiety."[8]

The question was how to restrain inflation. It was conceivable, from a technical point of view, that the Federal Reserve could induce a sharp recession that would reduce the inflation rate. But it seemed unlikely that elected leaders would accept this. "Inflation is likely to linger," the economist Edward M. Gramlich predicted in 1979, because the "staggering human costs" of a strict monetary policy were politically unbearable. Theodore White agreed. "The cruelty necessary to halt an inflation has everywhere been beyond the reach of any government elected freely by its people.... To stop inflation, many must suffer." In modern history, White observed, only autocrats had succeeded in grappling with inflation.[9]

In fact, though, the Great Inflation *was* broken by a strict monetary policy. Paul Volcker, appointed as Federal Reserve chairman in 1979, was a long-time central bank professional with close ties to the international financial community. Two months after his appointment, the Federal Reserve began an aggressive effort to reduce inflation. Short-term interest rates doubled from 10 to 20 percent, and the country slid into a deep recession. Volcker and the Federal Reserve were excoriated, and Congress threatened to trim the central bank's powers, but the Federal Reserve's policy did not change for the next three years, until price stability was restored and the economy began to recover.[10]

After 1982, the story of the Great Inflation was polished until it acquired the quality of a moral tale. The story fit neatly into the conservative critique of liberal democracy. The advanced democracies had stumbled into trouble because voters and special interests pressed their leaders to spend more without taxing more. Politicians gave way to these demands, ignored the first signs of trouble, allowed problems to fester, and shifted course erratically and fruitlessly in pursuit of painless solutions. The trauma was overcome only after central bankers applied a strict remedy. Volcker and his colleagues were not autocrats, but neither were they easily deterred by protests. In the end, the public benefited from their firmness.

A policy prescription was drawn from this moral tale: governments should assure the independence of their central banks so that they are free to maintain firm anti-inflationary policies without regard to the political reactions that might be generated by their decisions. A central bank that is not "subservient to central government," and preferably led by conservative elements of the financial community, would serve as a "commitment device"— in the sense that it committed a country to a consistent and rigorously anti-inflationary path.[11]

Advocates of central bank independence went further by defining exactly what independence meant in practice. These definitions typically emphasized the laws that defined the relationship between elected leaders and a central bank. (This was known as the degree of de jure independence.) For example, a central bank was more likely to be counted as independent if the law contained a guarantee that bank heads would be appointed for fixed terms, with removal only for serious misconduct; a proscription against government directions to the bank on monetary policy; and a mandate to focus on inflation control, to the exclusion of other objectives. Statutory restrictions on the capacity of governments to finance deficits by selling bonds to the central banks (who would then pay for them with newly created currency) also were taken as an important sign of bank autonomy.[12]

By reducing the definition of central bank independence to a matter of law, economists were engaging in a form of naive institutionalism. Several conceded that there might be "informal arrangements" that could undercut the actual freedom of a bank with de jure independence. But these informal arrangements were usually discounted, and for a practical reason: they could not be easily measured. To determine empirically whether there was a robust relationship between central bank independence and low inflation, economists needed a concrete, easily observed indicator of autonomy. Legal status seemed to provide such a measure.

Furthermore, early research seemed to show a connection between the de jure independence of a country's central bank and its record on inflation control. In 1988, economist Alberto Alesina found a significant relationship between formal bank independence and the inflation rate in twelve advanced economies, but he was careful to note that the correlation did not imply that independence itself had led to lower inflation. A 1991 study of eighteen advanced economies was bolder, concluding that independence did contribute to lower inflation. In 1992, a study of seventy-two countries supported by the World Bank also concluded that de jure independence contributed to low inflation in advanced economies; although the evidence was equivocal for developing countries. And in 1993, Alesina and his coauthor, Lawrence Summers, found a "near perfect negative correlation between inflation and central bank independence" in sixteen advanced economies. Alesina and Summers were now much more confident about the policy implications, saying their research showed "the economic performance merits" of central bank independence.[13]

A large body of later work challenged these early findings, arguing that the formal definition of independence was too simplistic. For example, a 1997 study that included rough measures of other potential factors—such as public "distaste for inflation" caused by episodes of high inflation—concluded that central bank independence was a "relatively unimportant" determinant of inflation performance in high-income states. Evidence about the relationship between independence and inflation in developing countries also remained ambiguous. A 2005 study by International Monetary Fund

(IMF) researchers of twenty-four Latin American countries conceded a correlation between de jure independence and low inflation but could not find a causal relationship running from the former to the latter. A 2006 IMF study of seventy-one developed and developing countries simply concluded that formal independence "does not play an important role" in deterring inflation.[14]

These studies came too late to influence elite opinion. By the early 1990s it was settled wisdom that formal bank independence was a prerequisite for achieving price stability. Charts showing the simple correlation between formal independence and inflation rates in advanced economies were often published in the popular press in the early 1990s. The academic evidence was "unequivocal," a columnist in Britain's *Independent* newspaper opined in 1993. "The intellectual case for central bank independence," the *Economist* declared at the same time, "is more or less won."[15]

All of the major central banks were soon granted formal independence. The Federal Reserve was already regarded as an institution with a high degree of autonomy. And as we have seen, the 1992 Treaty on European Union made an even firmer commitment on autonomy for the new European Central Bank. In 1997, the Japanese government revised its law to strengthen the formal autonomy of the Bank of Japan, which had previously been criticized for being "subject to the general directions of the government." The reform reflected the "general consensus that formally independent central banks are more likely to produce better policy outcomes." And in that same year, the United Kingdom's newly elected Labour finance minister, Gordon Brown, startled observers with a surprise announcement that the law governing the Bank of England would also be overhauled to assure its formal independence. A wave of similar reforms rolled through other countries as well (fig. 2.2). By the end of 1990s, central banks had gone through a "global process of institutional transformation."[16]

The rationale for independence also shifted. Initially, autonomy had been justified as a way of checking the wayward impulses of politicians and voters in the advanced economies. As international financial markets were liberalized, however, formal bank autonomy also became a way of reassuring foreign investors about a country's commitment to a policy of price stability. The attraction of reform was greatest for developing countries that were dependent on foreign capital and also democratic—because, as one analysis observed, "democracy...permits a cacophony of voices to influence economic and social policy; [and] central bank independence helps to rule out the most populist of alternative strategies, at least on the monetary side." Legal reform to establish bank independence had the virtue of being an

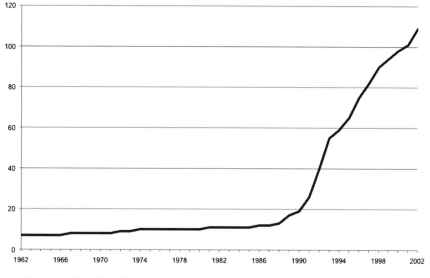

Figure 2.2 Number of independent central banks, 1962–2002.

Source: Provided to the author by Martin Marcussen, Centre for European Politics, University of Copenhagen.

easily observed signal to capital markets about the trustworthiness of new democratic states.[17]

This global transformation in the status of central banks coincided with a dramatic lowering of inflation rates around the world. Among advanced economies, the inflation rate dropped from about 9 percent at the start of the 1980s to only 2 percent between 1995 and 2003 (fig. 2.1). Among developing countries, the inflation rate dropped from nearly 50 percent in the 1980s to only 6 percent in the early years of the new millennium. Economists dubbed this the Great Moderation and considered it cause for self-congratulation. "The global taming of inflation," IMF economist Kenneth Rogoff asserted in 2003, was a "huge success.... Inflation has dropped to levels that, only two decades ago, seemed frustratingly unattainable." It seemed possible to think of inflation as we once thought of smallpox—as an exterminable scourge that could be "tamed (if not virtually eradicated) within a decade."[18]

There were many competing explanations for this success. However, there was broad agreement that the movement toward central bank autonomy had played a key part. As Rogoff wrote in 2003: "Institutional changes have made a huge difference.... More independent central banks... [have] unquestionably played a central role in the overall reduction of inflation." It appeared that the central bank reform was one of those rare cases in which an unambiguous link could be drawn between formal–legal change and improved policy outcomes.[19]

More Than Law

Later in this book we will see circumstances in which a naive–institutionalist view of reform was pursued but failed to produce the expected results. We can easily imagine how this could happen: a well-intentioned reformer proposes the adoption of a law hoping it will improve governance in some way, but this hope is dashed because the effect of the law is blunted by powerful political, economic, or bureaucratic forces. In this sort of case, it is obvious that the naive–institutionalist prescription is fatally incomplete because it fails to account for these other critical factors.

However, this is not the only way in which a naive–institutionalist view of reform can be incomplete. Suppose, for example, that a formal–legal change is followed by a favorable outcome: reformers might wrongly think that the legal change produced the result because they overlook the ways in which powerful forces had been operating in their favor.

This is the error that was made by many proponents of central bank reform. Their understanding of what happened in the field of monetary policy was pinched. Governments had been told to alter their central bank laws on the premise that this would encourage long-run price stability. A long period of price stability followed and was treated as confirmation of the premise. But this conclusion was unjustified for three reasons. First, it overlooked changes in *political context* that made it feasible for central banks to pursue a tougher anti-inflationary policy. Second, it neglected important changes in the *internal structure* of central banks that tended to bolster their autonomy and anti-inflationary tendencies. And third, it neglected the significance of new *external accountabilities* that also regulated bank behavior.

Changes in political context

There were two significant changes in political context that bolstered the authority of central banks. The first was a change in attitudes about the significance of inflation and the best means of controlling it. This attitudinal shift was evident in many quarters. Political leaders, for example, were now prepared to give up control over monetary policy and resist demands that they recover that control, even though they might still protest the pain caused by central bank policies.

Indeed, in the United States it was this shift, and not structural reform, that was critical in producing the change in monetary policy. The Federal Reserve of 1983 was not significantly different in legal structure from the Federal Reserve of 1968. "In the abstract," former Federal Reserve chairman Arthur Burns said in September 1979, "the Federal Reserve system had the power to abort inflation at its incipient stage fifteen years ago, or at any later point." Until 1979, however, the "political environment"—as Burns called it—would not tolerate firm action. In 1979, conditions changed. One president (Jimmy Carter) was prepared to appoint a tough chairman, and a second (Ronald Reagan) was willing to protect him as the economy slowed.[20]

The shift in attitude among political leaders was the practical consequence of a decade of policy failure. Delegation of control over monetary policy became tolerable because politicians no longer believed that the tool was worth controlling directly—that, as a matter of practice, their ability to stimulate short-term growth through loose monetary policy was overrated. Moreover, it was clear that alternative methods of controlling inflation—such as wage and price controls—were ineffectual and deeply unpopular. Expert opinion about inflation control shifted as well, affirming that what political leaders had learned from practice was also right in theory.

Equally critical was a shift in mass opinion. Even Volcker conceded that central bankers were compelled "to operate...within the range of understanding of the public and the political system." But public attitudes shifted as the Great Inflation scarred a generation of voters in many advanced democracies. Inflation ceased to be an abstraction or mild inconvenience. The corrosive effects of price instability were evident in daily life—in the rising cost of essentials, extraordinary nominal mortgage rates, and high unemployment. By the end of the 1970s, inflation had been constructed as a problem, to borrow a phrase from sociology: many voters understood its importance and were prepared to tolerate firm action to reduce it.[21]

Over time, the politics of inflation control also changed in a second way, through a shift in the power of constituencies likely to oppose or favor the principle of central bank independence. On the one hand, constituencies that resisted a tough anti-inflationary policy were weakened. Traditionally, organized labor opposed tight-money policies that had the short-term effect of increasing unemployment. The United Auto Workers (UAW), for example, fought the Federal Reserve's policies after 1979 and even argued that the Volcker should be replaced by someone who was directly accountable to voters. "You have to think in terms of restructuring the Federal Reserve Board," said UAW president Douglas Fraser in 1981. "Should one man like Volcker have awesome power—and not be elected?" But the UAW was at the peak of its strength in 1979, with 1.5 million members; by 2007 it had only 465,000.[22]

The UAW's collapse was part of a broader decline in the political power of organized labor. In the United States, union membership as a proportion of the U.S. workforce dropped steadily, from 24 percent in 1970 to 12 percent in 2003. The trend was paralleled in most other advanced economies. In Australia and New Zealand, union membership dropped from more than 50 percent to near 20 percent in the same period; in France, from 22 percent to 8 percent; in Japan, from 35 percent to 20 percent. The United Kingdom provided a particularly stark example of the decline of unions. Membership dropped from 45 percent in 1970 to 30 percent by the mid-1990s. The Labour Party, the traditional channel for political action by organized labor, revised its constitution to end the dominance of unions in its internal affairs. The Labour government elected in 1997 was thus liberated to pursue a range of policies, including formal autonomy for the Bank of England, that organized labor had traditionally opposed.[23]

The decline of organized labor was accompanied by the growing influence of constituencies that favored a rigorous anti-inflation policy. It was the U.S. financial sector, for example, that immediately benefited from the aggressive anti-inflationary policies of Volcker's Federal Reserve because high inflation threatened the industry's profitability and share prices. The industry was also the Federal Reserve's most vigorous ally during the recession that followed, when there were many calls to limit the autonomy of the central bank. Intense lobbying by the financial sector saved Volcker from replacement by President Reagan at the end of Volcker's first term in 1983. In the United Kingdom, meanwhile, leaders of the financial sector played a key role in making the case for independence of the Bank of England.[24]

The power of the financial sector obviously varies from one country to another, just as the power of organized labor varies. In general, though, the power of the financial sector in leading economies grew as the influence of organized labor declined. In the United States, the share of total economic activity accounted for by the financial sector, broadly defined, grew from 15 percent in 1979 to 20 percent in 2005. In the same period, the financial sector's share of corporate profits increased from roughly 20 to 45 percent. There was a comparable shift in the economic role of the financial sector in the United Kingdom and other advanced economies. Financialization, as it is called, was not simply a process of economic transformation: it is also a cultural and political phenomenon. The standing and power of the financial sector grew throughout the 1980s and 1990s, indirectly bolstering the position of central banks.[25]

Changes in the internal structure of central banks

The naive–institutionalist view also overlooks transformations in the internal organization of central banks that have bolstered their autonomy and sharpened their anti-inflationary biases. There have been three significant changes.

The first was in the method of staffing senior positions within central banks. There is good evidence that central banks are more likely to pursue stringent anti-inflationary policies if their top ranks are dominated by former private sector bankers or businessmen, economists, or central bank careerists and are less likely to do so if there is heavy representation of former trade unionists and politicians. The anti-inflationary professions have historically dominated the leadership of central banks, although their hold weakened during the 1960s and early 1970s. But the profile of the upper levels of central bank hierarchies in advanced economies shifted again during the era of liberalization. Representation of private finance increased markedly, as did the representation of scholarly economics. In most advanced economies, central banks are now more likely to be led by individuals whose professional background predisposes them to firmer anti-inflationary policies.[26]

Central banks also shifted internal procedures for making decisions about monetary policy. A tradition in many central banks of concentrating authority in the hands of a single individual has given way to a practice of decision making on key issues by committee. As Alan Blinder observed in 2004, decision making by committee "has now become the rule." In a sense, there has been a double delegation: first to the independent central bank and then *within the bank* to a collective body. "We are entering a time," agrees Robert Shiller, "when central bankers administer policies that come not just from their own individual minds but instead from the interaction of many minds." This procedural change has the effect of anchoring monetary policy because of the inertial tendencies of group decision making.[27]

There is a third significant change in internal structure. Throughout the 1990s, banks in the advanced economies increased their spending on internal research departments staffed by professional economists. In 1990, these banks employed roughly 300 researchers with PhDs; by 2003, they employed 700. (This growth occurred at a time when governments facing budget deficits were mainly concerned with *reducing* public payrolls.) For advanced-economy central banks, it was increasingly important to have internal research capabilities that could rival the economics faculty of a well-established university.[28]

Like their university counterparts, researchers within central banks were careful to defend their prerogatives. Researchers at the ECB emphasized that they worked within an "autonomous" department within the bank and required "a good deal of freedom" to do high-quality work. A committee of academics hired to scrutinize the research department of the Bank of Canada actually chastised its leadership for attempting to guide research "to meet the objectives set out in [the bank's] medium-term plan for policy relevant research." Researchers, they said, "should be given more freedom to select their own topics and manage their own research agendas." Research departments insisted that the main measure of their effectiveness was set externally, by the number of papers accepted in highly regarded academic journals. In fact, the research departments of central banks (like academic faculties) were frequently scorecarded according to their productivity, as defined in this narrow way.[29]

The expansion of research capabilities within central banks was undertaken with the expectation that it would improve the quality of bank decision making. But it also had the incidental effect of bolstering central bank independence. It contributed to the "scientization" of central banking—that is, to the perception that the field of monetary policy was one where finding the right course of action required the application of scientific, rather than practical, knowledge. Direction on monetary policy by elected officials became doubly problematic—not only because they were judged to have incentives to skew policy in the wrong direction but also because they were judged to be unskilled in scholarly economics.[30]

New external accountabilities

There is a third consideration that has reinforced the ability of central banks to make a claim of independence from political executives and legislators. This is the growth of counterbalancing accountabilities to peer networks and financial markets. For example, the global community of central banks is now more tightly interconnected than ever before, with the result that each central bank is more susceptible to scrutiny and influence from others. There is no possibility of direction or sanction by the network on any one bank, but peer pressure can be applied to conform to norms about sound policy that prevail within the community. This creates a counterweight to domestic political pressures.

Interbank coordination is not entirely new. Even in the decades before the Second World War, the leaders of the dominant central banks collaborated closely on economic policy, and in 1930 they created a new institution, the Bank for International Settlements (BIS), to facilitate cooperation. (Montagu Norman, a long-serving governor of the Bank of England in the prewar era, called the BIS "a club for central bankers.") But mechanisms for interbank coordination have become much more complex over the past three decades. Leading central bankers participate in the International Monetary and Financial Committee, a key policy group within the International Monetary Fund. Since 1987, there have also been regular meetings of central bank governors and finance ministers from the G7 economies. Ten other multilateral forums for discussion among central banks have been added since 1990. In the view of Martin Marcussen, we are witnessing the emergence of a "transgovernmental governance network" of central bankers—a "more or less formalized institutional framework" for development of central bank policy whose core is "small, coherent, and tightly interconnected." Anne Marie Slaughter agrees, arguing that central banks have constructed a "dense web of relations" that serve as a conduit for policy deliberations and also for information about central bankers' "reputations . . . concerning competence, quality, integrity, and professionalism."[31]

The development of this transnational network of central bankers was made easier by the extraordinary degree of continuity and conformity within the community of central bank governors. A 2001 study found that the average tenure for the world's central bank governors was seven years; to put it another way, the community loses only 14 percent of its numbers in an average year. In 2001, the population of governors was almost exclusively male. Four-fifths had degrees in economics or finance, and well over half attended university in the United States or the United Kingdom. One-third had once worked with the International Monetary Fund or the World Bank. "Central bankers in the global central bank network look like each other in objective terms," Marcussen observed, concluding that "they will probably also look at and analyze the world in very similar ways."[32]

Not only are central banks more tightly connected to one another; they are also linked more closely to the community of scholarly economists. Of course, we have already seen evidence of this in the growth of research capabilities within central banks. This was matched by an explosion of interest in central banking within academia itself. In the first decade of the new millennium, scholars produced more work that touched on central banks in an average month than was published in total in the two decades between 1970 and 1989. Academics also became more likely candidates for the leadership of central banks. Ben Bernanke, chairman of the Federal Reserve after 2006, was previously a professor of economics at Princeton University; Mervyn

King, governor of the Bank of England after 2003, had been a professor at the London School of Economics.[33]

The integration of central banking into scholarly networks also means that the banks face new accountabilities. Again, these are not formal lines of responsibility; scholars cannot dictate the policy of central banks. But integration does create new norms and incentives for the leaders and staff of central banks. We have seen this, already, in the application of scholarly norms about independence and productivity to the research units of central banks. Researchers and senior staff within central banks who want to move into academia—or preserve the option of doing so or use the threat of relocation to extract higher wages from their employers—have strong incentives to pay attention to these norms. The incentive is heightened by the growth in academic scrutiny of central bank operations. Bank officials who deviate from academic norms are more likely to incur a significant reputational cost.[34]

Finally, there is a third form of external accountability. In the era of liberalization, central banks became increasingly aware of the extent to which their decision making is subject to close surveillance by financial markets. Before the liberalization of global financial markets, the opinion of investors did not matter so much: they had fewer remedies if governments pursued inflationary policies that corroded the real value of their capital. After controls on cross-border investment were dismantled, investors had the option of exit—that is, moving their money to countries that were less likely to impose an "inflation tax."

In one sense, financial markets are friends of independent central banks because they have the capacity to punish politicians who meddle in bank decision making. But economists observe that markets also have a "disciplinary effect" on newly independent banks: the threat of capital flight hangs over banks that deviate from an anti-inflationary policy. Legal independence is therefore combined with a loss of "policy autonomy." For increasingly open economies, the decline in discretion may be severe. "Since early this decade," former Federal Reserve chairman Alan Greenspan claimed in 2008, "central banks have had to cede control of long-term interest rates to global market forces."[35]

The Anti-Inflation Regime in Crisis

The transformation of the role of central banks thus involved much more than adoption of new laws to recognize their formal independence. As we have seen, it involved a sea change in elite and mass opinion about the dangers of inflation and the most effective techniques for fighting it as well as a shift in the distribution of political power away from those skeptical of rigorous anti-inflationary policies and toward those favorable to such policies. It also involved alterations in the internal organization of central banks themselves. At the same time, central banks have been tightly integrated into professional, peer, and market structures.

All of these elements combined over the past three decades to constitute an extraordinary new regime for the formulation of monetary policy. We can see that in important ways it is misleading to describe this regime as one that is concerned primarily with central bank autonomy. While voters and elected leaders delegated authority to central banks, the delegation was contingent on the assumption that central banks would apply their powers to the specific task of avoiding another Great Inflation. At the same time, central banks were subjected to greater control by peers, academics, and markets. To borrow a phrase used by Karl Polanyi, reformed central banks are now more deeply embedded in social and market structures that regulate their behavior. In some respects, central banks are like courts, another class of institutions that are embedded in juridical, scholarly, and professional networks: even though they are formally autonomous, their discretion is still tightly bound in practice.[36]

This complex anti-inflation regime seemed to be a great success before the global financial crisis that began in August 2007. But its credibility was badly damaged afterward, largely because of the perception that leading central banks—the Federal Reserve in particular—had contributed to the onset of the crisis. Three charges could be made against the Federal Reserve. The first was that it had simply failed to acknowledge evidence of a housing bubble or anticipate the damage that would be done to the financial system and economy when the bubble inevitably burst. The second was that it had failed to use its regulatory powers to control mortgage lending and the booming market for complex financial instruments. The third was that the central bank had failed to use its influence over interest rates to deflate the bubble, or at least slow its growth, by raising the cost of borrowing by homeowners.[37]

In the popular press, blame for these errors was often put on the shoulders of Alan Greenspan, chairman of the Federal Reserve from 1987 to 2006. Greenspan, one writer said, "is the leading villain in this story." But it is simplistic to explain a massive policy failure only as the result of one man's errors in judgment. We have already established that the system for crafting monetary policy was radically transformed in the era of liberalization. Advanced economies built an elaborate new regime for determining monetary policy.

It is reasonable to ask whether this complex system contributed to the failure as well.[38]

This is not an unusual question to ask. On the contrary, it is routinely posed in the wake of policy debacles. After the 9/11 attacks, for example, the U.S. Congress established a special commission to consider why the country's national security apparatus failed to "connect the dots" about imminent terrorist attacks. Its report dwelt heavily on the weaknesses of a bureaucracy "built in a different era to confront different dangers." A similar commission was created to examine the decision making that led to the invasion of Iraq in 2003. It too found systemic problems, including "a tendency to adhere to a prevailing view," in this case about Iraqi military capabilities, in spite of mounting evidence to the contrary. A third commission struck in 2003 found "cultural traits and organizational practices" within the National Aeronautics and Space Administration that led staff to ignore risks that resulted in the destruction of the space shuttle Columbia. And congressional inquiries undertaken after Hurricane Katrina concluded that "systemic failures" caused decision makers to ignore long-term warnings about the threat to New Orleans.[39]

Common themes connect these four investigations. One theme is the tendency of complex systems to remain fixated on the crisis that led to their emergence. (The aphorism is that armies are always ready to fight the last war.) Another is the tendency of bureaucratic systems to dismiss evidence that contradicts conventional wisdom about the character and severity of threats they are likely to face. A final theme is the inability of bureaucracies to respond intelligently to new threats, either because those threats had not been anticipated or because an appropriate response would require heavy investment in new capabilities. These are all variations on the same central point: complex governmental systems can remain preoccupied with old dangers and oblivious to new ones.

The renovated system of central banking suffered from the same vulnerability. Once the financial crisis was under way, it became commonplace to say that one of the central functions of any central bank is to maintain the overall stability of the financial system as a whole. But this function was largely subordinated in importance during the preceding three decades. Central bank independence was not justified as a technique for protecting systemic stability. The renovated system of central banking was, above all, an *anti-inflation* regime, constructed to avoid a reprise of the trauma that had afflicted the advanced democracies during the 1970s. The regime was not built to anticipate the new threats to economic order that would arise when the primary goal—a long period of price stability—

had been achieved and businesses and households felt emboldened to take greater financial risks.

The central banking system suffered from doctrinal blindness. Throughout the system there was a "near-consensus view" that the main task of central bankers was to focus primarily on inflation control. Systemic stability was not regarded as the core function. A related difficulty was the unwillingness to acknowledge mounting evidence of a bubble in the housing market or to concede that central bankers could do anything to discourage a bubble, if it existed. The "intellectual assumptions" dominant within the central banking system assumed that markets were rational and efficient; that for this reason bubbles could not persist; and that attempts at intervention would be counterproductive.[40]

A 2009 assessment of the British response to the financial crisis provided a classic statement of goal fixation at work. In the period before the crisis, the assessment concluded, "The Bank of England tended to focus on monetary policy analysis as required by the inflation target, and while it did some excellent analytic work in preparation for [a 2006 IMF review of global financial stability], that analysis did not result in policy responses (using either monetary or regulatory levers) designed to offset the risks identified."[41]

A correlate of doctrinal blindness was hostility to dissenting points of view. According to economist Barry Eichengreen, the "pressure of social conformity" within the economics profession was intense, discouraging attention to scholarship that warned of potential disaster. Fellow economist Robert Shiller—one of the world's most influential economists—described his own experience with "groupthink" within the system: "From my own experience on expert panels, I know firsthand the pressures that people may feel when questioning the group consensus.... While I warned about the bubbles I believed were developing in the stock and housing markets, I did so very gently, and felt vulnerable expressing such quirky views. Deviating too far from consensus leaves one feeling potentially ostracized from the group, with the risk that one may be terminated." IMF research director Raghuram Rajan encountered this problem in 2005 after he warned of "the low probability" of financial catastrophe because of irrational market behavior. Rajan was subjected to an unremitting attack by leading economists and central bankers (including former Treasury secretary Lawrence Summers) for a "nostalgic" and "lead-eyed" analysis that would encourage "misguided policy impulses in many countries." In 2006, William R. White, chief economist for the Bank of International Settlements, also warned that central banks were fixated on price stability and were overlooking risks posed by asset bubbles. White, too, was ignored. He said later that he struggled with an "acceptance problem.... The signs were perfectly clear [but] people didn't want to respond to the warnings.... [T]he analytic framework that you use is crucial and the vast majority of people were not prepared to accept [the danger]."[42]

Even if the danger had been appreciated, however, central banks might have found it difficult to move against it. We have already seen that the actual authority of central banks is hedged by elite and popular opinion: the Federal Reserve had a mandate to avoid another Great Inflation, but it had no mandate to burst asset bubbles. As White observed, any action by central banks to control bubbles would have provoked "vigorous lobbying from many people made rich by the process." For most American households, their home is their major asset; action by the Federal Reserve to cool the housing market would have constituted an overt attempt to reduce its market value. As Federal Reserve governor Laurence Meyer said in 2002, policies aimed deliberately at the destruction of wealth would put the bank in "a politically untenable position."[43]

The financial sector also would have reacted harshly against attempts to restrain a bubble or curb the market in exotic financial instruments. Its support of central bank autonomy was conditioned on the assumption that bank powers would be used to avoid inflation, which undercut financial institutions' profitability. Major financial institutions had lobbied aggressively in the past to avoid regulation and even on the cusp of the financial crisis still resisted attempts to gauge their vulnerability to an economic downturn. In 2009, a senior regulator within the Federal Reserve conceded that it should have shown "firmer resolve" in dealing with financial institutions that were "especially vocal about the costs of regulatory burden and international competitiveness" when regulatory initiatives were proposed.[44]

Major central banks were moved to more radical action as the financial crisis deepened. Their reaction was often spasmodic, but this was a natural consequence of the blindness that afflicted the central banking system before the collapse. Willem Buiter, a former member of the Bank of England's monetary policy committee, laid part of the blame on scholarly economists who now played a key role within many central banks. "The strong representation of academic economists and other professional economists...turned out to be a serious handicap," Buiter said in 2009. "The economics profession was caught unprepared when the crisis struck."[45]

In many ways, the banks' response to crisis upended the orthodoxy about how central banks were supposed to behave. Refined calculations about the long-run inflationary effects of bank decisions on monetary policy were put aside in an urgent effort to avoid a slide into depression. "Inflation," one critic complained in 2008, was now "almost an afterthought." As conventional tools for reducing interest rates lost their effectiveness, the major central banks resorted to the purchase of government-issued debt with newly created money, a tactic described as "quantitative easing." Only a few months earlier, this tactic had been regarded as one of the traits of a central bank that lacked real independence from government. (Indeed, an August 2009 IMF research paper conceded that quantitative easing "exposes the central bank to a possible perception of capture by the fiscal authority... especially during times of high deficits.")[46]

Central banks were also compelled to work closely with Treasury officials in crafting a response to the crisis. The image of independence was blurred as the Federal Reserve coordinated statements with the Treasury and collaborated in implementing programs to rescue failing financial institutions and maintain liquidity in key markets. Critics complained that the Federal Reserve had become an instrument for making risky and politically sensitive commitments to the financial sector that should have been made by the Treasury directly. "Independent central banks don't do what this Fed has done," economist Allan Meltzer complained in 2009.[47]

This tension between the demands of crisis management and orthodox ideas about central bank independence had been seen before. The Bank of Japan encountered a "serious problem" a decade earlier because it was granted de jure independence just at the moment when the Asian financial crisis required it to coordinate closely with the Japanese finance ministry. "Inevitably," the Bank of England's head, Mervyn King, observed in 2004, "the desire to respect the newly won independence of the [Japanese] central bank came into conflict" with the reality that it was "no longer possible to identify clear and distinct responsibilities for the two institutions." Ironically, this became King's own predicament—and also the Federal Reserve's—five years later.[48]

The shift in behavior by the American, British, and Japanese central banks showed that conventional wisdom about the role of central banks was not inviolable after all: it could be bent in moments of crisis. In the words of business journalist David Wessel, the Federal Reserve would do "whatever it takes" to avoid a protracted recession. For Anglo-American policy makers in particular, the ultimate consideration was pragmatism, not doctrinal rigor.[49]

This was manifest in the charges made against the European Central Bank as the financial crisis deepened. The ECB was broadly recognized as the best example of the rigorous application of de jure independence. And the ECB took its mandate seriously. It was less willing to lower interest rates because its mandate required strict attention to long-term price stability. "We have only one needle in our compass," ECB president Jean-Claude Trichet protested. The ECB also hesitated to undertake quantitative easing, arguing that this might jeopardize ECB autonomy. The ECB's position earned it the sort of criticism that is always made by pragmatists: that it was rigid, inflexible, and orthodox in its response.[50]

The Arc of an Idea

The argument for central bank independence mutated substantially over thirty years. It began as a simple application of the logic of discipline: legal reforms were necessary to establish the independence of central banks so that they could make difficult decisions about monetary policy. Formal–legal reforms empowered a new guardian class of central bankers and scholarly economists. Over time the argument for independence was refined to include the claim that de jure independence would be an effective means of reassuring foreign investors about the commitment to price stability.

By 2009, however, this now-conventional argument for central bank independence had been discredited in several ways. The most obvious difficulty was the failure of leading central bankers to anticipate and avoid the crisis of 2007–2009. The sophisticated anti-inflation regime built in the preceding three decades may well have proved effective in avoiding a reprise of the Great Inflation, but this particular virtue was accompanied by a glaring weakness. The regime also institutionalized a vulnerability—a blindness to the new risks engendered by careless liberalization and a long period of growth and price stability. The newly powered class of technocrat-guardians had proved unable to manage those risks properly. This manifest failure of performance made it possible for critics to launch powerful challenges to bank autonomy.

In addition, the argument for central bank autonomy was revealed to be incomplete. Advocates of central bank independence liked the *simplicity* of their prescription: legal changes that affirmed a few clear rules about the role of central banks would produce unambiguously better policy. But the naive–institutionalist notion that de jure independence alone had an impact on policy outcomes could now be discounted. The anti-inflation regime that was constructed in advanced economies over three decades was robust because it was reinforced by important shifts in political conditions, internal structure, and relationships between central banks, scholarly economists, and financial markets. There was much more at work than a simple change in formal–legal arrangements.

And the argument for independence was shown to be incomplete in a second sense. Advocates of central bank independence also liked the *universality* of their prescription: there was little room for debate about when it should be applied. However, it turned out to be a prescription that made certain undeclared assumptions about the state of the world—principally, that the risks of systemic instability were not substantial. When this assumption collapsed after 2007, elite opinion about appropriate bank behavior shifted rapidly.

The fact that the case for central bank independence was revealed to be contingent on these undeclared assumptions about prevailing conditions caused it to lose a significant amount of its rhetorical power. It provided reluctant policy makers in many countries with the opportunity to make the counterargument that the model might not fit their own circumstances either. Anglo-American proponents of bank independence might claim that the crisis of 2007–2009 was truly exceptional, but as we shall see in the next chapter this was not so clear. Financial crises were endemic during the age of liberalization. There was ample opportunity for other governments to argue that they, too, confronted "unusual and exigent" conditions. And if leading economies were permitted to deviate from the orthodoxy in such circumstances, why were others precluded from doing the same?

Treasury Power and Fiscal Rules

Parliament is incapable of exercising its financial
responsibilities. We must do it for them.

—*An anonymous U.K. Treasury official, 1987*

In 1997, the economist and former central banker Alan Blinder had "a nasty
little thought." During his two years as vice chairman of the Federal Reserve,
he had been impressed by the quality of its decision making: its staff were
highly skilled, thoughtful, and largely oblivious to everyday politics. It
seemed strange that in a democratic society important decisions about
monetary policy should be left to technocrats, but the arrangement seemed
to work. Perhaps, thought Blinder, the central bank model could be extended
to other areas. "Would the country be better off," he asked, "if more public
policy decisions were removed from the political thicket and placed in the
hands of unelected technocrats?"[1]

The Business Council of Australia (BCA), an association of that country's
largest companies, took Blinder's question seriously. In 2000, the council
argued that it was time for a fundamental reengineering of the way in which
governments made decisions about taxing and spending. "In a world of free
capital flows," it suggested, "credibility has become a fundamental precondi-
tion of policy effectiveness....Budget deficits undermine market confidence." What was needed was a new institution like an independent central
bank that would force wayward politicians to adjust taxes and spending so
that budgets are balanced.[2]

No government adopted the Business Council's plan exactly. But for some time it attracted the close interest of senior policy makers and academics in many countries. The economist Charles Wyplosz argued that it would be a "natural step" to apply the "highly successful" central bank model to budgeting, by giving a committee of unelected experts the power to see that balance is maintained. "It may seem radical and undemocratic," the *Economist* acknowledged. "But that, remember, is what many governments once said of demands to make their central banks independent."[3]

The BCA's proposal was attractive because it offered a remedy for a disturbing trend: the upward growth of public expenditure in the decades following the Second World War. In the industrialized world, public spending consumed roughly one-fifth of GDP in 1920, scarcely more in 1937, and still only 28 percent in 1960. However, spending accelerated over the next two decades: by 1980 it consumed 42 percent of GDP; by 1996, 45 percent. And governments were not taxing enough to pay for increased spending. The result for most countries was recurrent budget deficits and mounting public debt (fig. 3.1). For many policymakers—especially those in finance ministries—the disturbing aspect of this trend was that it no longer seemed a product of deliberate national policy. It was called "fiscal drift."[4]

As we noted in chapter 1, there were two influential explanations of fiscal drift. One was the overload hypothesis, which suggested that broad cultural

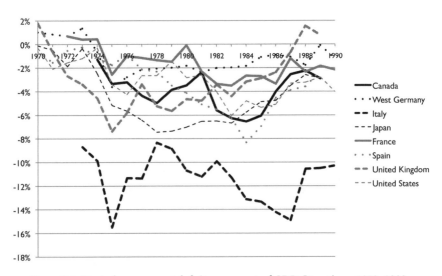

Figure 3.1 Central government deficits as percent of GDP, G7 nations, 1970–1990.
Source: World Bank, *World Tables 1993* (Baltimore: Johns Hopkins University Press, 1993).

and political shifts—such as the enfranchisement of more voters, declining deference to elected leaders, and improvements in the capacity to mobilize fellow citizens—led to a sharp increase in the number of demands placed on government. A second group of arguments were advanced under the banner of Public Choice theory. These emphasized the role of politicians who pander to voters with the goal of reelection; well-organized special interests, seeking special treatment; and civil servants determined to pad their bureaucratic nests. Under either theory, the overall effect is the same: a steady upward ratcheting of expenditure and debt.[5]

The solution was understood to be institutional reform that would curb the unhealthy tendencies of unconstrained democratic processes. Although the Business Council's notion was spurned, two other innovations were widely adopted. In many countries, power was consolidated in the hands of finance ministries, with the expectation that they would control the spending impulses of legislators and other agencies. Many countries also adopted legal rules that were intended to limit spending and borrowing. This was the logic of discipline at work: skepticism about the capacity of democratic institutions to regulate themselves, combined with the naive institutionalist's optimism that institutional reforms would produce significant changes in the behavior of governmental systems.

These attempts at discipline largely failed. The authority of finance ministries could be asserted during crises but faltered afterward, largely because it proved so profoundly hostile to the principle of democratic control. And legal constraints on spending and borrowing proved to be unequal to the impulses they sought to contain. This was evident even before the onset of the global financial crisis in August 2007. The crisis itself did even more damage to the idea of budgetary discipline, as Treasuries themselves became the most activist of spending ministries.

Treasury Power

In 1964, the political scientist Aaron Wildavsky proposed a simple metaphor to describe the process by which governments make decisions about taxing and spending. Government agencies, he said, take on well-defined roles in budget battles. Most behave as advocates, trying to maximize the amount of money allotted for the programs that serve their clients. Opposing these advocates are a few central organs that act as guardians of the public purse. The most important guardian is the finance ministry or treasury. The guardian's "great passion," Wildavsky said, "is to get and hang on to a surplus." But its predicament is difficult. It is outnumbered by spenders who exaggerate the value of their programs and connive with clients and legislators for a larger share of the budget.[6]

The implication is straightforward: if the guardian's power wanes, then fiscal discipline will be jeopardized. To some observers, this seemed a plausible explanation of what had happened in the 1970s. A study prepared for the OECD in 1985 lamented "the growing institutional imbalance between guardians and advocates.... [Guardians] have been outnumbered, overpowered, and outwitted.... Unless the guardians assume a more active role in the budgetary process, the remaining fifteen years of this millennium may well become an age of mega-deficits."[7]

Many economists sympathized with this call for a restoration of guardian power. A decade earlier, William Nordhaus suggested that fiscal drift arose because "myopic" politicians bent on reelection had strong incentives to offer voters a "potlatch" of public expenditure. One remedy for democratic myopia was to turn fiscal policy over to "persons who will not be tempted by the Sirens of partisan politics...a Treasury dominated by civil servants." But Nordhaus recognized the objections that could be raised about the delegation of fiscal authority to "an agency which is not politically responsive to legitimate needs."[8]

As deficits persisted, these qualms evaporated. "The critical economic policy issue" for most countries, Alberto Alesina and Roberto Perotti argued in 1996, "is fiscal consolidation and the maintenance of long-run fiscal balance." A critical first step to the restoration of fiscal discipline was "strengthening of the roles of the executive branch vis à vis the legislature, and of the treasury minister vis à vis the rest of the executive branch, in order to achieve a centralized and 'top-bottom' approach to the budget process."[9]

Other analysts agreed. Institutional reforms that assured a "strong position" for the finance minister relative to spending ministers would create a "commitment device for fiscal discipline." They would also send an important signal to foreign lenders about a nation's seriousness on fiscal restraint. "The consensual view," a World Bank researcher concluded in 2005, "holds that fiscal discipline and budget responsibility are best achieved and preserved by centralizing the budget authority in the executive and, within it, under the tight steering of the finance ministry."[10]

Like the Business Council of Australia, these analysts were also pursuing Blinder's "nasty little thought." Nordhaus drew explicitly on the example provided by central banks in the field of monetary policy. A powerful treasury might not be autonomous, but it would still have much in common with an independent central bank. It, too, would be an elite organization, distinct from other ministries, less bureaucratic internally, and fused by a culture of intellectual rigor and rationality. It would be "driven less by particularistic spending interests than the spending ministers."[11]

By the 1990s, advocates of treasury power could also point to studies that appeared to show the success of central bank reforms. "Relatively few economists dispute the benefits of a certain amount of central bank independence," Alesina and Perotti argued. A similar but limited body of research conducted in the 1990s seemed to suggest that countries with highly centralized budgeting procedures were more likely to maintain fiscal discipline. But these studies, like the central banking studies, suffered from a heavy emphasis on easily observed formal rules and neglect of other societal characteristics that could influence spending. They also overlooked the political turmoil that often followed the consolidation of treasury power.[12]

In any event, elite opinion once again ran ahead of research. Throughout the era of liberalization, there was a trend toward the concentration of authority in the hands of finance ministers. "Budgetary politics," according to Lotte Jensen and John Wanna, "moved upward to an elite strata of decision-makers inside government."[13]

A common trigger for the centralization of power was an economic crisis or plausible evidence of a looming crisis. These were in ample supply during the era of liberalization. "The age of financial liberalization," wrote Martin Wolf, "was an age of crises." (An "epidemic" of crises, according to the French academics Gérard Duménil and Dominque Lévy.) A 2008 IMF study calculates that countries suffered over three hundred crises between 1975 and 2005, whether through default on foreign loans, banking failures, or a plunge in currency value. This was a dramatic change from the preceding two decades, in which crises were relatively uncommon. Carmen Reinhart and Kenneth Rogoff concluded in 2008 that there was a "striking correlation" between the liberalization of capital markets and the number of crises.[14]

Finance ministries often used crises as opportunities to consolidate their influence through changes in law or bureaucratic procedure. These attempts to consolidate power often failed in the long run. This was largely because legislators and voters eventually rebelled against the undermining of democratic values. The mechanism for maintaining discipline recommended by economists—the intensification of treasury power—was not stable. It often produced a painful dynamic of concentration, resistance, and reversal.

The United States briefly saw this dynamic at work as the financial crisis deepened in fall 2008. Decisions on whether to rescue or abandon failing financial institutions that had enormous budgetary and economic consequences were taken by Treasury officials without any opportunity for legislative or public debate. The justification was that the failures demanded an immediate response and that there was no time for public deliberation. However, in September 2008 the Treasury proposed legislation that seemed to confirm this kind of decision making as the new modus operandi. Its draft bill, only three pages long, gave Treasury Secretary Henry Paulson broad discretion to spend $700 billion—roughly 5 percent of GDP—on assistance for the financial sector. Courts would be barred from undertaking any review of Paulson's decisions.[15]

The reaction to this proposal was fierce. Financier George Soros called the plan "the ultimate fulfillment of the Bush administration's dream of a unitary executive." *Newsweek* magazine dubbed Paulson "King Henry." Congress revolted, refusing to approve the legislation until it had been expanded to a 170-page catalogue of conditions and accountability requirements. Nevertheless, the law still gave Paulson wide latitude. Within days, the Treasury announced that it would use the appropriated money for an entirely different purpose—providing capital to financial institutions rather than purchasing "toxic assets." It countered congressional complaints about this shift by saying that the crisis demanded a quick adaptation. Protests about the accretion of Treasury power and the decline of accountability persisted in following months.[16]

This battle over the accumulation of Treasury power was new to the United States, but it was familiar in many other advanced democracies. The United Kingdom was a prominent example. The U.K. Treasury was humiliated by the country's economic failures in the 1970s, which culminated in an appeal by its Labour Party government for aid from the International Monetary Fund in 1976. But Treasury's prestige and influence was restored in the 1980s, as the Conservative government led by Prime Minister Margaret Thatcher undertook a wrenching program of economic readjustment. Treasury staff had a renewed sense of their role as guardians of fiscal discipline.[17]

When the Conservative government of Prime Minister John Major was replaced by New Labour in 1997, the power of Treasury persisted. Prime Minister Tony Blair and his finance minister, Gordon Brown, were determined to assure financial markets that they would not repeat the errors of the Labour government of 1974–1979. The hard lesson learned in intervening years, said former Labour minister Roy Hattersley, was that "Labour governments only enjoy the favours of international finance when they agree not to behave like Labour governments."[18]

Brown quickly became one of the most powerful finance ministers in modern British history. A new committee dominated by Treasury was established to oversee public expenditure. In practice, however, spending authority was even more centralized. The execution of decisions following Treasury's first comprehensive review of government spending was "brutal," according to David Lipsey. Brown and Blair "just called in ministers and told them how much they were getting. There was no appeal." The Treasury soon used its budget power to influence the substance of policies traditionally within the domain of other ministries.[19]

The firm exercise of Treasury power led to rising complaints about the corrosion of other institutions. The idea of cabinet government—that the cabinet should be "the core of the constitutional system" and the forum in which critical decisions are made—was threatened by Treasury's dominance. In 2007, Andrew Turnbull, a recently retired head of the British civil service, offered a scathing criticism of Brown and his department. Brown, said Turnbull, had

> a very cynical view…of his colleagues. He cannot allow them any serious discussion about priorities. His view is that it is just not worth it.…The surprising thing about the Treasury is the more or less complete contempt with which other colleagues are held.…It has enhanced Treasury control but at the expense of any government cohesion and any assessment of strategy. You can choose whether you are impressed or depressed by that, but you cannot help admire the sheer Stalinist ruthlessness of it all.[20]

Turnbull's complaint was echoed by many others, including the House of Commons Treasury Committee, which in 2001 said that the Treasury had come to "exert too much influence over policy areas which are properly the business of other departments." Other parliamentary committees complained that policies in the departments they supervised were in fact driven by the "theological niceties" of Treasury.[21]

Brown succeeded Blair as prime minister in 2007, but his hold on power was tenuous. Public opinion had turned against the party, and Brown confronted several challenges from within its ranks. He suffered from the collective exhaustion built up after years of Treasury dominance and began his term as the most unpopular of Britain's leading politicians. Most voters considered him insensitive to their concerns. Only the onset of another crisis in 2007 provided Brown with a brief respite from attacks on his leadership. By

2009, Brown was again being attacked by his own cabinet ministers for indifference to the priorities of party members.[22]

A similar dynamic was at work in Canada in the 1990s. A newly elected Liberal cabinet was shaken by attacks on the Canadian dollar during the Mexican financial crisis of 1994, speculation that Canada might be unable to refinance its government debt in international markets, and worries that it too might need help from the International Monetary Fund. Attempting to restore confidence, the Canadian government promised deep cuts in federal expenditure. Finance Minister Paul Martin, one senior official later complained, "seized control of the government of Canada."[23]

This was prelude to a half decade in which Canada's Department of Finance "centralized authority in [its] hands...and effectively locked [its institutional rivals] out of the budget-making process." "The prime minister and the minister of Finance," Donald Savoie observed in 1999, "have come to hold in their own hands all major and some minor decisions. They decide...the broad contours of government economic policies. They even decide which spending proposals should go forward, and this with or without Cabinet consent."[24]

Fiscal order was restored but again at a cost: complaints about the concentration of treasury power and the collapse of accountability—to the cabinet, parliament, or the public. The nation had become, in the words of journalist Jeffrey Simpson, "a friendly dictatorship." Like Brown in Britain, Finance Minister Paul Martin also became prime minister but suffered from accumulated anger over the way in which governmental power had been exercised and lost his parliamentary majority after only six months.[25]

Stories such as these were reprised around the world. In Denmark, officials in the Ministry of Finance were bruised by the central government's failure to control expenditure in the late 1970s. However, the widespread understanding that the country had come close to "the abyss" (as the finance minister put it in 1979) laid the groundwork for the ministry's return to a position of dominance. The Danish system of governance is quite distinct from those of the United Kingdom and Canada and is more likely to produce coalition governments. The techniques for guardian influence varied accordingly. The imperative to maintain cohesion on fiscal targets resulted in intensive negotiations on policy among party leaders, often conducted through a new economic committee chaired by the finance minister. By the end of the 1990s, fiscal balance was restored. But the revival of finance ministry power was "neither unchallenged by other actors nor unproblematic," according to Lotte Jensen. Legislators and citizen groups complained that the closed-door negotiations compromised their ability to influence policy and mobilize against unfavorable decisions.[26]

Like Denmark, New Zealand also was a "small state in big trouble" in the early 1980s, and it provided a vivid example of the dynamic of concentration and resistance. New Zealand's moment of crisis arrived in 1984, when a newly elected Labour government faced default on its foreign-held debt. The crisis provided New Zealand's Treasury with the opportunity to impose dramatic changes within the public sector. Treasury staff "were able to seize control" of the policy making process, one official later recalled. "We did not create crises," another said, "but we weren't above taking advantage of them."[27]

"Through its control of the purse and its intellectual leadership," Allan Schick says, "Treasury had a dominant voice in the reform process" in New Zealand. "The New Zealand experiment," as Jane Kelsey calls it, was managed by "a core of politicians committed to the structural adjustment programme, irrespective of the electoral risk, who were able to capture their party machines and steer through the changes with minimal obstruction or effective dissent; [and] a team of technocrats with a common, coherent view, who commanded the instruments of executive power."[28]

Abroad, New Zealand became a model of retrenchment. At home, however, years of centrally driven reform produced growing popular discontent. Trust in government declined throughout the 1980s. By 1992, according to former Labour prime minister Geoffrey Palmer, the nation confronted a constitutional crisis, and the government reluctantly acceded to a referendum on adoption of a new proportional-representation electoral system. The overwhelming vote in favor of the new system was interpreted as an attempt to "to reimpose restraint on government and . . . establish a new tradition of popular consent" after the trauma of the preceding decade. The new system is more likely to produce coalition governments, which means that influence over budget plans is now more widely dispersed. It is unlikely that the political conditions necessary for sweeping reforms that followed the 1984 crisis could ever be reproduced under the new voting rules.[29]

A similar cycle could be seen in Latin America, the region whose economic woes had sparked much of the scholarly interest in the question of how budget institutions should be designed in the 1990s. Two countries in the region undertook major budget reforms during that decade: Argentina and Peru. Concentration of authority was a key feature of both reform projects. Carlos Santiso observes that the Peruvian reforms reflected the "prevailing orthodoxy in economic policy management . . . [which] privileges the insulation of economic policymaking in the executive branch and the building of 'hierarchical budget institutions' to preserve fiscal discipline." And both projects appeared to be effective in restoring fiscal discipline in the short term.[30]

Nonetheless, both reform projects were problematic from the point of view of popular sovereignty. In Argentina, President Carlos Menem relied to an unprecedented degree on presidential decrees to execute his austerity plans, circumventing the congress and raising complaints about the subversion of democratic structures. This technique of governing could not be sustained, and in 1994 Menem agreed to constitutional amendments intended to restrict his power to issue decrees. For this and other reasons, fiscal discipline declined.[31]

In Peru, budgeting reforms were only one part of a parcel of institutional changes introduced by President Alberto Fujimori with the aim of consolidating executive power. In 1992, he executed a military-supported coup, thereby dissolving an uncooperative legislature. A new constitution abolished congress's second chamber and curtailed its authority. The buildup of presidential power and the atrophy of legislative oversight encouraged abuses of power and a backlash that led ultimately to Fujimori's exile in 2000. Fujimori's successor, Alejandro Toledo, paid the price for Fujimori's excesses: he faced a resurgent congress that balked at measures intended to restore budget balance. During Toledo's administration, IMF observers often worried that Peru's "difficult political situation" would compromise fiscal discipline.[32]

In all of these cases, the economists' prescription (increase treasury power) turned out to do significant collateral damage to democratic institutions. It proved to be untenable in the long run precisely because of the failure to provide an acceptable way of reconciling guardian power with the requirements of popular sovereignty.

Experience revealed the extraordinarily primitive quality of the reasoning in favor of treasury power. Economists had jumped from an empirical observation (that concentrated power led to fiscal discipline) to a simple rule for governmental design (that power should therefore be concentrated). There were no caveats: for example, that one might be wary about further concentration of power in systems that were already prone to executive dominance. There was no tactical sense at all: for example, no consideration of how one dealt with resistance from opponents of treasury power. And there was equal indifference to questions of political philosophy: for example, why it should be right for the claims of legislators or citizens to be suppressed in the name of fiscal discipline. When moments of crisis were past, it was questions such as these that determined whether treasury power (and therefore fiscal discipline) could be maintained. The logic of discipline could not answer them.

Fiscal Rules

Increased treasury power was only one of the techniques for promoting fiscal discipline that were recommended to governments during the era of liberalization. Another popular device was the fiscal rule. This was a legal instrument—often contained in a national law but perhaps also in a constitution or treaty—that was intended to impose limits on government budgeting. For example, a fiscal rule might require a balanced budget, or specify the maximum level of spending or taxation, or place a cap on the size of the deficit or debt.

Fiscal rules are explicitly pitched as devices to constrain the sovereignty of democratic institutions. "Such rules," according to one analyst, "remove legislators' discretion in making spending and taxation decisions." (The absence of any hesitancy in this statement should be noted. Advocates of fiscal rules often made assumptions about their impact that proved unrealistic in practice.) The ideal rule was one that constrained "successive governments...over a reasonably long period of time." Limiting discretion seemed reasonable because it was understood that this discretion was usually abused. "The main underlying cause" of fiscal indiscipline, an IMF study reported in 2007, is "the injudicious use of discretion...in the context of competing electoral constituencies and political and redistributive conflicts."[33]

Fiscal rules were another illustration of the logic of discipline at work. They did not create a new guardian organization, as laws on central bank independence did—although they did bolster the position of treasuries. Nonetheless they shared the purpose of restraining democratic processes, on the premise that those processes were prone to misbehavior. And advocates of fiscal rules sometimes hoped that this innovation would reduce political contention about the idea of budget discipline. A well-designed fiscal rule would establish "a depoliticized framework for fiscal policy" just as central bank reforms appeared to depoliticize monetary policy.[34]

Belief that fiscal policy could be depoliticized was accompanied by the naive institutionalist's faith in the power of law to shape governmental behavior. This is evident in the very definition of fiscal rules: as a "permanent constraint" on fiscal policy (according to a European Commission report) or as "permanent institutional devices" to assure discipline (according to an IMF-sponsored study). These were naive definitions because they simply asserted what was, in fact, a highly contestable proposition: that legal instruments could be crafted that would permanently tie the hands of policy makers.[35]

Fiscal rules are often imposed on subnational governments; most U.S. states, for example, are bound by constitutional or statutory balanced-budget requirements. But fiscal rules were rarely established for national governments before the 1980s. Many prominent economists were skeptical about national rules, partly out of distaste for the critique of democratic political processes. The economist Arthur Okun observed in 1972: "One reason people impose rules on themselves is that they do not trust their own rationality. But if the nation's top officials are irrational about their area of professional expertise, then the nation needs better officials rather than a confession of irrationality by the existing ones."[36]

However, such protests were undercut by years of continued deficits. Financial liberalization added another argument for fiscal rules: that they could serve as another easily observed signal to foreign lenders about a government's commitment to fiscal discipline.

And so fiscal rules spread. The U.S. Congress adopted legislation in 1985 (the Balanced Budget and Emergency Deficit Control Act) that set increasingly tough spending restrictions aimed at achieving budget balance in six years. In 1991, Canada adopted a similar law, the Spending Control Act, with multiyear expenditure limits. And in 1992, most countries in the European Union accepted limits on deficits and total debt (contained in the Treaty on European Union) as a condition for entry into Eurozone. By the mid-1990s, the International Monetary Fund and other organizations were actively promoting their advantages. At least thirty-three countries experimented with national rules by 2008 (fig 3.2).[37]

In practice, however, fiscal rules often failed to live up to the expectations of their advocates. One difficulty was that governments proved wary of adopting inflexible constraints on spending and taxing. For example, the economists James Buchanan and Richard Wagner had argued in 1977 that a balanced budget rule should be entrenched in the U.S. Constitution. "Political and public disrespect" for budgetary balance was so pervasive, they said, that discipline could be restored only by incorporating the rule into the nation's fundamental law. But attempts to constitutionalize a fiscal rule failed in the United States. Instead, the country experimented throughout the 1980s and 1990s with fiscal rules that were contained in legislation. Other countries avoided constitutionalized rules as well.[38]

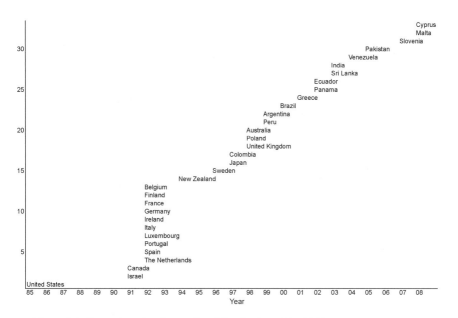

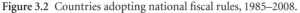

Figure 3.2 Countries adopting national fiscal rules, 1985–2008.

Initial Eurozone countries are included on year of signing of Maastricht Treaty; others, by year of adoption. Some Eurozone countries also have national laws with fiscal rules for central government, which are not included in this chart.

Source: Suzanne Kennedy and Janine Robbins, *The role of fiscal rules in determining fiscal performance*, Department of Finance Working Paper 2001–16 (Ottawa, CA: Department of Finance, 2001), table 1; George Kopits, *Fiscal rules: Useful policy framework or unnecessary ornament?* IMF Working Paper No. 01/145, September (Washington, DC: IMF, 2001), table 1, and "Overview of fiscal policy rules in emerging markets," in *Rules-based fiscal policy in emerging markets*, ed. George Kopits (Houndmills, UK: Palgrave Macmillan, 2004), table 1; Ana Corbacho and Gerd Schwartz, "Fiscal responsibility laws," in *Promoting fiscal discipline*, ed. Manmohan Kumar and Teresa Ter-Minassian (Washington, DC: IMF, 2007), table 5.1.

Legislated (rather than constitutionalized) rules had the advantage of being easily revised—and often were. When it became clear that the target set by the U.S. Congress in its 1985 legislation (a balanced budget by 1991) was politically infeasible, it was deferred until 1993. In 1990, the target was abandoned. Israel's 1991 deficit reduction law initially required that the budget be balanced by 1995. But the targets were reset in 1994 and five additional times over the next decade. (Even so, targets were often exceeded in those years.) Argentina adopted a fiscal responsibility law in 1999 that required budget balance by 2003. The intermediate target for 2000 was quickly overshot. The deadline for balance was delayed in 2001, but the revised requirements also were breached. A new law was adopted in 2004, but targets were again missed in 2005. India's fiscal responsibility law, adopted in August 2003, promised the elimination of the central government's deficit by 2007. Just eight months later the schedule was extended to 2009.[39]

The most prominent example of fiscal rules—those contained in the Treaty of European Union—also were adjusted. Compliance with the deficit and debt limits contained in the treaty was generally good in the period immediately before adoption of the euro in 1999, mainly because countries could be barred from the Eurozone if they failed to meet the treaty's requirements. After 1999, smaller states in the Eurozone continued to remain generally compliant. But major economies, such as those of Germany and France, did not. By 2005, both countries had repeatedly violated the targets. Nevertheless, the European Union's Council of Ministers refused to follow the enforcement procedures contained in the treaty. Instead, it modified the criteria for judging violations to accommodate countries with looser fiscal policies.[40]

Japan made a more radical reversal, foreshadowing difficulties that other major economies would encounter after 2007. With the encouragement of the International Monetary Fund, the Japanese government adopted a law in November 1997 that obliged it to halve the government deficit as a share of GDP in six years. (It was not a coincidence that this was the same year in which Japan also gave de jure independence to its central bank, again at the IMF's urging.) But the reform was ill-timed. The regional financial crisis that began in Thailand in July 1997 pushed Japan into recession and led to the collapse of some of its major financial institutions just as the deficit law was being approved by the Diet. The Japanese government quickly abandoned the law and increased spending on aid to the financial sector and economic stimulus. Government debt shot from 110 percent of GDP in 1997 to 160 percent in 2003.[41]

Legislated fiscal rules that survived intact were often drafted to preserve substantial discretion. For example, New Zealand's 1994 fiscal responsibility law requires only that the government reduce total debt to "prudent levels"— and after achieving this goal, that it maintain budget balance "on average, over a reasonable period of time." The United Kingdom's 1998 law is similarly vague. It requires the Treasury to provide Parliament with a fiscal policy code that respects the principles of "transparency, stability, responsibility, fairness and efficiency" but preserves the Treasury's prerogative to deviate from the code under extenuating circumstances. The fiscal policy code provided to Parliament in 1998 did not contain firm targets either: it promised only that fiscal policy would be managed "in a prudent way." This, yet another treasury statement explained, meant that government would maintain budget balance "over the economic cycle."[42]

Deciding when an economic cycle has started or stopped is extraordinarily difficult, and by crafting the fiscal rule in this way the U.K. Treasury gave itself leeway to decide whether it was in compliance. (As an IMF study put it: "There may be a perception of a conflict of interest in the way the cycle is currently defined.") In 1997, the finance minister, Gordon Brown, promised that the Labour government would avoid "accounting tricks, dubious figures, or rigging of the rules." But critics claimed that Labour's commitment waivered as its electoral prospects weakened. In 2005, for example, the Treasury announced that the current economic cycle had actually started in 1997 rather than 1999, as it had said earlier. This seemed like a minor technical adjustment. But the government banked a surplus in the intervening year, 1998. Moving the start of the economic cycle to 1997 allowed the government to offset a deficit in the election year of 2005. In 2007, the International Monetary Fund questioned the credibility of the United Kingdom's procedure for judging compliance with its budget rules.[43]

By 2007, expectations about the effectiveness of fiscal rules were substantially reduced. The naive institutionalists' assumption that rules could impose hard constraints on policy makers, or serve as a powerful mechanism for signaling to financial markets, was largely put aside. This is not to say, however, that fiscal rules have no effect at all. Governments seem to incur some costs when they violate or change fiscal rules, and this may discourage them from doing so readily. Rules might also anchor political debate by giving more weight to budget balance as the norm for judging fiscal plans. These are important considerations, but they fall short of the binding effects that advocates of fiscal rules initially anticipated.[44]

Experience also raises a bundle of important and related questions. The first is whether it is possible to describe the political, economic, or cultural conditions that determine whether a government is likely to comply with a fiscal rule. This is the same question that we posed regarding central bank independence. Indeed, we could contrast experience with fiscal rules against experience with central bank independence and ask a second question: why did one effort to impose discipline (via fiscal rules) generally meet with failure while efforts to establish bank autonomy met with what might be described as mixed success? One explanation might be that the effects of monetary policy are diffused and hard to trace, whereas the effects of spending and tax changes are concentrated and easy to see. But this is not the only explanation. There are many other possibilities, most of which again require some consideration of broader political, economic, and cultural conditions.

We could go further and ask a third question: do fiscal rules matter at all? Naive institutionalists begin with the assumption that rules matter and then concede (through hard experience) that other factors might affect the extent to which rules matter. But it might even be possible to turn this viewpoint on its head. Perhaps a bundle of other considerations are the real determinants of a commitment to fiscal discipline and the rule is only an indicator that these other factors are at play. This would explain cases like New Zealand, where retrenchment actually preceded the adoption of a legislated fiscal rule, or Canada, where restraint continued even after the legislative rule lapsed.[45]

The common aspect of all three questions is that they are important, and the logic of discipline has nothing to say about them. Advocates of discipline asserted firmly that formal–legal reforms would change the behavior of complex governmental systems, and the experience with fiscal rules proved them wrong. There was more to the story than the language of treaties and laws.

The Effect of Crisis

With the advent of the global financial crisis, immediate concern about fiscal discipline largely evaporated. Governments opened the public purse to provide support to failing financial institutions and then to provide stimulus for economies that were sliding into recession. The amounts were massive and, in the countries at the center of the crisis, largely committed to stabilization of the financial sector. In the United States, for example, it was expected in March 2009 that the net cost of programs to stabilize the financial sector would equal 13 percent of GDP over three years; by contrast, the total cost of stimulus programs was about 4 percent of GDP. In the United Kingdom, stabilization costs were expected to equal 9 percent of GDP, roughly seven times the cost of stimulus.[46]

The effect on public finances was substantial. In the United States, the federal deficit for 2009 equaled 10 percent of GDP—far higher than in any other year since the Second World War. The United Kingdom's deficit for 2009–also was expected to reach 10 percent of GDP, again a postwar high. The International Monetary Fund projected that the crisis would cause general government deficits to widen by about 5 percent on average for the group of twenty major economies. It followed that the total debt-to-GDP

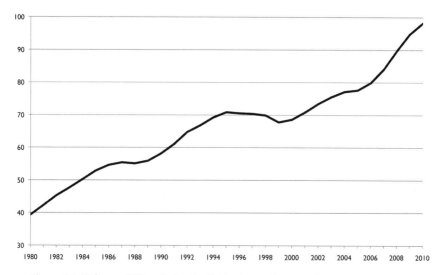

Figure 3.3 Debt-to-GDP ratio for the G-20 advanced economies, 1980–2010.

Source: International Monetary Fund, *The state of public finances: Outlook and medium-term policies after the 2008 crisis* (companion paper), March 6 (Washington, DC: IMF, 2009), 24.

ratio also jumped dramatically for this group of nations (fig. 3.3). The jump in indebtedness caused by the financial crisis provides a sad coda to a three-decade-long struggle to reverse fiscal drift.[47]

This burst in spending also had a devastating effect on the integrity of fiscal rules in many countries. Although the United States no longer has a federal balanced-budget law, after the 2006 midterm elections, Democratic legislators did adopt new legislative procedures intended to discourage deficit spending. ("Enough is enough with running up the debt of this country," Representative Rahm Emanuel said at the time.) By 2008, these rules were forgotten. Within the Eurozone, meanwhile, by mid-2009 thirteen of sixteen member countries had exceeded deficit limits stipulated in the Treaty of European Union. The European Commission announced its intention to begin disciplinary action against most of the offenders, including France, and threatened action against Germany as well. But commission officials suggested that they were unlikely to pursue stringent punishment for the rule breakers. India, facing both a national election and an economic slowdown, abandoned targets in its fiscal responsibility law and in 2009 incurred a deficit equal to 7 percent of GDP.[48]

The United Kingdom provided the most dramatic example of the undoing of fiscal rules. The "tough rules" established by Gordon Brown in 1997 came under added strain in February 2008 when the Office for National

Statistics concluded that debt of the just-nationalized Northern Rock bank had to be included in the government's accounts. Stabilization and stimulus spending dealt the final blow. By the end of 2008, the U.K. Treasury was arguing that it would be "perverse...to apply the rules in a rigid manner." "We are in unique times," Brown told reporters as he defended the suspension of deficit and debt restrictions. By 2009, the British government seemed to question the validity of rules at all, warning against a fixation on "single measures" of fiscal responsibility. Sometimes, it said, the right way to assure budgetary health is to incur large deficits that stimulate long-run economic growth.[49]

The argument for fiscal rules was undermined during the crisis because it, too, was revealed to be contingent on never-articulated assumptions. When the financial sector was in dire straits it was taken for granted that discipline should be set aside. A different mode of reasoning was applied, which said that short-term deficits could be tolerated if they were essential to the long-run health of the economy. Skeptics could be forgiven for questioning whether arguments about the broader public interest actually camouflaged programs that compensated major financial institutions for the consequences of their bad judgment. And they could question why the same mode of reasoning had never been tolerated to justify other kinds of expenditure that produced long-run benefits—such as spending on education, or infrastructure, or environmental protection.

The crisis briefly heightened treasury power, as crises always do. But the role of treasuries could also be challenged. Wildavsky's formulation portrayed treasuries as guardians, untainted by "particularistic spending interests," and mainly occupied with the job of restraining other "advocate" agencies. But in an important sense the financial crisis turned this model on its head: treasury officials were now the advocates, seeking massive aid for financial institutions with which they had extensive and close entanglements. The question could reasonably be asked—were treasury officials being sufficiently tough in deciding precisely how much was needed, and how it should be used? It was Plato who, in his *Republic*, had touted the virtues of a guardian class. But Plato also grappled with the ensuing question, brought to the fore once again by the financial crisis: *Quis custodiet ipsos custodes*—Who will guard the guardians?

Islands in the Public Sector

Tax Collectors

4

The prescription ... is to increase—perhaps even to maximise—
the degree of autonomy that the revenue authority has in relation
to politicians and government.... It signals to business people and
to potential investors that the power to tax will not be abused.

—Odd-Helge Fjeldstad and Mick Moore, 2008

One had to create an institution independent of the public sector,
an island in the public sector. It was necessary to create an
institution similar to the central bank.

*—Luis Alberto Arias Minaya, former adjunct superintendent
of the Peruvian tax authority SUNAT, 1998*

While advanced economies worried about control of expenditures, many
developing countries confronted a more basic problem: collecting taxes.
This was another area in which Blinder's "nasty little thought" was vigorously applied. The 1980s and 1990s constituted a decade of "radical reform"
in tax administration within the developing world, again built on the logic
of discipline. But the naive–institutionalist approach to reform again proved
vulnerable to counterattacks by well-entrenched bureaucratic, political, and
social forces.[1]

Ghana was a test bed for reform of tax administration in the era of liberalization. By the early 1980s, its economy was in ruins because of political
unrest and a series of misguided efforts to manage the economic turbulence
of the 1970s. The public sector also was in a shambles. One result was that

tax collection collapsed. The tax ratio—the proportion of GDP collected by the state—declined from 13 percent in 1973 to 5 percent in 1983. The country suffered chronic deficits as well as a breakdown of essential services. The interest rate hikes of 1980–1983 added to Ghana's budget woes. It defaulted on foreign loans in 1983 and became one of the International Monetary Fund's biggest clients.[2]

In Ghana, as in other developing countries, tax collection can be undermined in several ways. Like other public agencies, the tax administration often lacks adequately skilled staff and appropriate computer systems. Because it is directly involved in the collection of money, it is prone to corruption as well. And political leaders may view the tax administration as a useful tool for advancing their immediate political interests. They can hand out jobs as political favors, as they can in any other agency. They can also provide tax exemptions to powerful friends or use tax collecting powers to harass opponents.

As part of a recovery program negotiated with the IMF, Ghana improvised a solution to its tax collection woes. Its two existing tax collection bureaus—one for customs and excise taxes, the other for income taxes—were removed from the Ministry of Finance and placed in a new, separate authority, the National Revenue Secretariat. Heads of the two bureaus, although accountable to an oversight board, were given "absolute control" over spending in their organizations and allowed to create personnel rules "completely divorced from the structure…for the core civil service." Revenues that exceeded a target level were to be used for employee bonuses and better facilities. The results of this reform appeared to be dramatic: by the end of the 1980s, the tax ratio had grown from 5 to 17 percent of GDP, and the deficit had been eliminated.[3]

Ghana became a model for Uganda, another poor country that experienced a collapse in tax revenues in the 1980s. In Uganda, though, all collection functions were merged into a single body, overseen by an independent board. Workers were screened before receiving an appointment in the new organization, and those who survived the screening earned wages that were sometimes nine times higher than in the civil service they left behind. Again, the reform seemed to yield substantial benefits. Uganda's tax ratio rose from about 6 percent of GDP in the late 1980s to 12 percent by 1995.[4]

Peru, meanwhile, was suffering through a similar crisis. Mismanagement and corruption contributed to a drop in the tax ratio from 16 percent in 1980 to 5 percent in 1991. Its new independent tax authority, SUNAT, fired most of the government's tax employees and gave the remaining workers a two thousand percent raise. Unlike the African agencies, SUNAT had no board—only a superintendent appointed by the president. It also had an unusual funding scheme: SUNAT was guaranteed 2 percent of all revenue that it collected. In Peru, too, the reform appeared to improve performance. The country's tax ratio revived to 15 percent by 1997.[5]

All of these reforms had been characterized by a large degree of improvisation, but by the mid-1990s the core ideas were synthesized into an ideal type, labeled the Autonomous Revenue Authority (ARA). Under the ARA model, tax collection functions would be "extracted" from ministries of finance and established as separate bodies. These bodies would then be endowed with "a number of autonomy-enhancing features" designed to protect them from the threat of political interference, the rigidities of civil service rules, and the vagaries of budget allocation processes. Through appropriate institutional design, an IMF study explained, the ARA would be "isolated from external influences" and thus able to execute its responsibilities professionally.[6]

The template for reform was the independent central bank. This was evident to Glenn Jenkins, a tax specialist at Harvard University's Institute for International Development, who was an early advocate of the ARA model. "When one compares various central banks with the tax administration in their respective countries," Jenkins said, "it is clear that the banks operate with greater efficiency and effectiveness. The proposal...is to restructure the tax administration very much in the same manner as central banks have been established around the world."[7]

The analogy to central banking was explicit in the case of the Peruvian reforms. The first head of SUNAT was transferred from Peru's central bank, and he brought a core group of administrators with him. This "focused the reform in a unique way," according to Robert Talierco Jr. "These public servants...shared a common vision of a professional bureaucracy.... [T]hey were used to working in an autonomous agency, and expected to carry over their conceptions of autonomy to SUNAT." A former Peruvian minister of finance explained: "SUNAT was genetically born from the central bank."[8]

Like central banks, ARAs were justified through the logic of discipline. As we have seen, central bank independence was defended as a way of constraining political leaders who might otherwise abuse their discretion over monetary policy for short-term political gain. A comparable argument was made in favor of ARAs. The political leader's problem, in Taliercio's view, "is essentially one of too much discretion" over the enforcement of tax laws. Political leaders can see the immediate political benefits from control over the tax authority. In the long run, however, political leaders pay a substantial price for such practices. Patronage corrodes enforcement capabilities, and this in turn reduces the probability that citizens will comply with tax laws. Similarly, citizens are less likely to reveal information about their income and wealth if they think that disclosure will make them targets for extortion.[9]

If the problem is too much discretion, the solution is to structure the tax administration function so that discretion is eliminated. The hands of political leaders are tied for their own long-term benefit. It is important that governments are seen as taking bold steps to limit their own control over collection so that citizens are persuaded that it will be done competently (thus raising the risk that their evasion will be detected) and fairly (thus lowering fears of extortion). The creation of an ARA becomes an effective way of signaling that the rules of the game have changed. It serves as a "commitment technology": elected leaders are seen to have made "a credible commitment to taxpayers that tax administration will be more competent, effective, and fair."[10]

The ARA model followed the logic of discipline also in its approach to institutional change. ARA reform schemes emphasized the centrality of legislative changes as a means of assuring the independence of tax collectors. In other words, the naive–institutionalist conception of reform was repeated here as well. "There is…a relatively coherent package of formal measures that is likely to achieve this goal [of autonomy]," one study concluded:

1. Give the revenue agency a separate legal status, as a corporate body with clear legal responsibilities and duties, and wide powers to own assets, borrow money etc.;
2. Put it under the control of a management board whose members are independent of government by virtue of (a) being nominated from a diversity of sources, both inside and outside government; (b) having long, fixed periods of tenure, revocable only on clear criteria and through open and legal processes; and (c) having remuneration arrangements that cannot be affected by the current government;
3. Place all staff clearly and directly under the authority of the chief executive, who will in turn be chosen by and answerable only to the management board; and
4. Provide an operational budget that is independent of the normal annual national budgeting process, either through constitutional provisions or by allowing the authority to fund itself through appropriating a fixed share of the revenues it collects.

Advocates of ARAs probably took a naive–institutionalist approach to reform for the same reasons as proponents of central bank independence. Partly it was a matter of inexperience in reform. In addition, formal–legal changes were easily observed: an important consideration for governments interested in signaling commitments as well as for scholars attempting the study of the diffusion and impact of tax administration reforms. ARA advocates were also encouraged by the early research that appeared to show a relationship between de jure central bank independence and low inflation.[11]

The ARA model, like central bank independence, was an example of an "enclave approach" to public sector reform—that is, it was aimed at improving performance within a particular part of government rather than the entire breadth of the public sector. Enclave reforms always raise a question about the reasons for targeting one component of the public sector over another. For example, educational and health services in developing countries are also undermined because of politicization, corruption, and inadequate staffing. What justified special treatment for tax collectors?[12]

One answer was that more effective revenue collection was a prerequisite for improvement in any other sector. This was a reprise of a very old argument by tax reform specialists. "No underdeveloped country has the manpower resources or the money to create a [governmentwide] high-grade civil service overnight," Nicholas Kaldor argued in 1963. "But the revenue service is the 'point of entry'; if they concentrated on this, they would secure the means for the rest." A complication with this argument is that the ARA model was never followed by plans for similar reforms of "spending" agencies. Some development specialists questioned whether improved revenue collection ever led to increases in spending for the poor.[13]

Another explanation is that tax collection was understood to be one of the core functions that must be performed competently for a nation to survive in a globalized economy. Tax collectors do not simply generate the revenue needed for domestic social programs. They also collect the money needed to service foreign debts and, thus, to maintain credibility in global financial markets. It was default, after all, that triggered the IMF's intervention in Ghana. In the late 1990s, Peru's central government spent more on interest payments to foreign lenders than it did on health services and almost as much as it did on education.[14]

Efficient tax collection is also critical to the flow of trade. In many developing countries, a large part of revenue is still generated by tariffs on imports and exports. The indirect costs imposed by incompetent customs management compound as trade flows rise and globalized production systems become more intolerant of delay. "Customs administration is inescapably an impediment to trade," an IMF report said in 2003. "Although customs administration would wither away in an ideal world, in practice trade taxes are likely to be a significant source of revenue for many of its members, especially developing countries, for the foreseeable future.... [I]f trade taxes are to be levied, it is best that this be in a way that does least collateral damage to international trade flows."[15]

The Failure of Reform

The ARA model spread rapidly among countries in Latin American and anglophone Africa in the 1990s and early 2000s. By 2005, twenty-three developing countries had adopted some variation of the reform (fig. 4.1). The model was actively promoted by the International Monetary Fund and World Bank. The United Kingdom's overseas development agency, the Department for International Development (DFID), was also enthusiastic about ARAs and provided aid to many of the African governments that tried establishing one. A cottage industry of consultants emerged to help developing countries

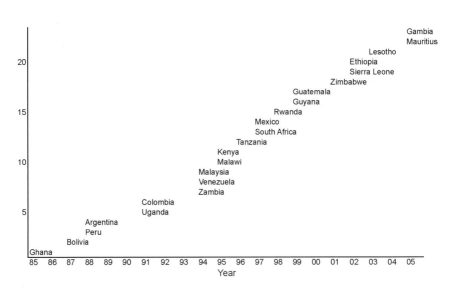

Figure 4.1 Developing countries adopting autonomous revenue authorities, 1985–2005.

Source: Robert R. Taliercio Jr., *Designing performance: The semi-autonomous revenue authority model in Africa and Latin America*, Policy, Research Working Paper series No. 3423, October 27 (Washington, DC: World Bank, 2004); Maureen Kidd and William Crandall, *Revenue authorities: Issues and problems in evaluating their success*, IMF Working Paper No. 06/240, October (Washington, DC: International Monetary Fund, 2006); Odd-Helge Fjeldstad and Mick Moore, *Revenue authorities and state capacity in anglophone Africa*, Working Paper No. 2008/1 (Bergen, NO: Chr. Michelsen Institute, 2008).

establish their new agencies. The ARA, a 1998 DFID report said, appeared to have become the "standard model" for reform of tax administration.[16]

Despite the broad enthusiasm, it remained true that countries engaged in ARA reforms were embarked on a large experiment in administrative design. Certainly, the preliminary results from countries such as Ghana, Uganda, and Peru suggested that the ARA model might help to reverse a revenue collapse. But the rationale behind the model remained "largely intuitive," as researchers at the IMF acknowledged a decade later. Advocates had been captivated by the logic of discipline. The question now was whether experience would validate the logic. ARAs worked in theory—but did they work in practice?[17]

Unfortunately, experience showed that they often did not. No other country reprised the impressive turnaround of the three leaders. Indeed, even the vanguard countries stumbled in later years. Some of the followers failed badly. A few countries saw significant improvements in administration, but it proved difficult to demonstrate that this was the result of ARA reform. The premise that tax administration could be made impervious to "external influences" was badly shaken.

Among the most powerful of these external influences were ministries of finance, who had many reasons for viewing ARAs with distaste. Higher salaries within the ARA created complaints about inequities elsewhere, including the finance ministry itself, while rules that guaranteed a share of revenue to the ARA limited the finance ministry's budget discretion. Most damaging, however, was the tension between the two organizations over the formulation of tax policy. It was easy to propose that finance ministries should make policies and revenue authorities should apply them: in practice this distinction proved untenable.

Thus the ARA model created a situation in which a new organization became the rival of the most powerful player in the bureaucracy. This conflict played out in many countries, never to the advantage of the ARA. In Bolivia, an early attempt at autonomization was quickly undone, and the new organization was reabsorbed into the finance ministry. In Mexico, the finance ministry retrieved a policy unit that had been allocated to the new authority and reasserted its right to issue directions about the authority's internal operations. In Kenya and Malawi, the finance ministry simply refused to provide the ARA with the share of revenue it was entitled to receive by law. In Venezuela, the finance minister secured a presidential decree that restored his ministry's authority over the ARA's personnel system. In Uganda, the finance ministry obtained a legislative change that gave its appointees a majority on the revenue agency's oversight board. And in Peru, the finance ministry—frustrated by instances in which its own advice to Congress on tax policy was contradicted by SUNAT—eventually secured the resignation of its superintendent and a veto on his replacement.[18]

"We can be clear about a point of fact," two specialists asserted in a 2008 retrospection about ARAs. "Despite the rhetoric and debate about 'autonomy,' there has been very little loosening of the political and bureaucratic grip of central executive authorities over the revenue collectors."[19]

Sometimes this power was used to restore patronage or wield improper influence within the ARA. In Kenya, for example, senior ARA officials were removed "on instructions from 'above'" despite the objections of the ARA's head, who had formal authority over the positions. ARA reform in Zambia did not end harassment of opposition politicians or favorable treatment for businesses friendly to the government. Peru's SUNAT was infiltrated by corrupt elements of the nation's intelligence service in the late 1990s, and its powers were used to monitor and harass the government's political opponents.[20]

There also was a resurgence of corruption at the lower levels within many ARAs. This was especially obvious in Uganda, where the performance of the ARA deteriorated after the withdrawal of support provided by DFID. In 2003, the expatriate head of the Ugandan authority, Annebritt Aslund, conceded that corruption was still "problem number one" in her organization. In Tanzania, too, administrative corruption continued to thrive despite ARA reform, undercutting the ARA's authority to collect revenues. In some parts of the Tanzanian authority, job applicants paid "speed money" for special consideration—itself a form of corruption but also a useful signal to insiders about the applicant's willingness to collude in corruption after hiring.[21]

The persistence of corruption led to a reappraisal of the arguments that had been made in favor of ARA reform. For example, one claim was that higher salaries would reduce the incentives for ARA employees to engage in corrupt behavior. But postreform experience showed that the potential gains from corruption could still be much larger than increased salaries. (This was particularly true as inflation corroded the pay hike.) Moreover, a highly publicized salary increase sometimes had the effect of increasing the worker's obligation to support his extended family—resulting in an actual loss to the worker himself and perhaps sharpening the incentive to engage in corruption.

The process of screening employees carefully before hiring also had limited effect. It briefly disrupted, but did not dissolve, patterns of corruption at lower levels of the tax administration. During the transition to ARA status, when jobs were most clearly at risk, employees curbed their behavior. But the limitations of new internal controls were quickly understood by employees, and corrupt practices reemerged. Perversely, the resurgence of corruption was sometimes encouraged by tax collectors who did not survive the transition to ARA status. Dismissed workers found jobs in the private sector, where their task was to bribe former colleagues in return for favorable treatment for their clients. Thus corrupt networks survived.[22]

After two decades of experimentation with ARAs, reformers were chastened about their usefulness in improving tax collection. "Like many similar organizational fashions," a British analyst wrote in 2007, "The autonomous revenue authorities that have been established in many countries have . . . not lived up to the original, highly inflated expectations." There was broad skepticism about the "sustainability" of ARA reforms and an appreciation that formal–legal changes could be unwound easily. As a 2002 World Bank memorandum observed about statutory rules that were supposed to guarantee ARA budgets: "Clearly, having these mechanisms on the books is no guarantee that they will work in practice."[23]

This was a clear recognition of the limitations of the naive–institutionalist view of reform, which I have argued typifies the logic of discipline. The ARA experiment ended with an understanding that something more than formal–legal changes were required for an ARA to be successful. However, there was no clear articulation of what those additional conditions might be. Sometimes it was described simply as "political commitment" or as the presence of an "enabling environment" or a "wider framework for sound governance." It was a matter of understanding the "political economy" of tax reform, according to another study. But the political economy of ARA reform was still largely unexplored territory. This was terrain that typically lay "beyond the scope of a revenue administration project," as a British report observed.[24]

These proponents of the logic of discipline suffered from impoverished theory and therefore did not anticipate the depth and quality of resistance to the changes they proposed. If the organizational change posed a direct challenge to existing bureaucratic, political, and social structures, and there was no strategy for anticipating the points of conflict, then it was likely to fail.

This challenge to the logic of discipline went beyond the assumptions about *how* changes in governance were accomplished. There were also grounds to doubt the anticipated *effect* of change. It was not clear that ARAs worked as a commitment technology that persuaded taxpayers about the rigor and fairness of tax administration and thereby made them more likely to pay taxes. Tax-paying culture (as it is called) is difficult to measure—and to change. Where collections increased, it was more likely

The Gates of Trade
Autonomous Mainports

The flow of money through globalized financial markets may be hard to visualize, but the flow of goods and people that results from economic globalization is not. Its effect is obvious, in the increased number of shipping containers carried through major ports and the increased volume of people and goods embarked at major airports.

The effects of the boom in U.S. consumer spending after 2001 were certainly apparent in San Pedro Bay, the location of the two busiest U.S. ports, Los Angeles and Long Beach. In 2000, those two ports handled 95 million shipping containers, coming mainly from factories in East Asia. By 2006, the number of containers that had to be pushed through the two ports jumped by 63 million, or almost 70 percent (fig. 5.1). This was equivalent to taking all of the container traffic arriving annually at the ports of New York and New Jersey and diverting it into San Pedro Bay.

The result was congestion. By 2004, the San Pedro ports could not keep up with the flow of goods. There were not enough berths for arriving ships, not enough experienced dockworkers to unload them, and not enough trains and trucks to haul away the freight. In October 2004, one hundred ships were anchored at sea, "a huge floating traffic jam" waiting to unload.

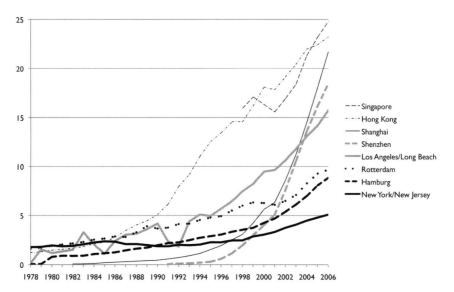

Figure 5.1 Container traffic (in millions of TEUs) through major ports, 1978–2006.

Includes the four busiest Asian ports in 2006 as well as the two busiest ports in North America and Europe.

Source: Containerisation International: http://www.ci-online.co.uk.

A spokesman for Union Pacific Railroad conceded that the surge in trade had "overwhelmed the infrastructure." Independent truckers, frustrated by unpaid hours waiting for their loads, simply quit. Container yards quickly filled. "They just ran out of space," said a dockworker, "They had cans piling up." San Pedro Bay was "effectively maxed out," the *Journal of Commerce* reported.[1]

In fall 2004, many other ports were suffering from congestion problems. Singapore, the world's busiest, was near capacity and warning of delays. Shippers were threatening to remove their business from the Port of Rotterdam, Europe's largest, unless backlogs were resolved. The backlog at Rotterdam was "catastrophic" for barge operators who relayed goods inland because they were no longer able to guarantee delivery times. South American ports were strained too. Ships sometimes anchored for thirty days outside the Port of Santos, Brazil's major trade gateway, waiting to load coffee, soybeans, and other commodities. And India's twelve ports were plagued by delays caused by rapid growth. Container traffic at the Jawaharlal Nehru Port Trust in Mumbai, India's largest port, almost tripled in just five years.[2]

In 1912, at the peak of an earlier boom in global trade, a British economist observed that the business of a port had become "a sensitive thing, a thing dangerous to tamper with or to throw into even temporary disorder." This warning was largely forgotten as global trade collapsed in the middle part of the twentieth century. But it gained new relevance in the era of liberalization. A globalized economy cannot work if ports cannot manage the flow of commodities and merchandise.[3]

In the modern era, the strain was shared by the global air transport system because the world's network of airports also lacked the capacity to keep up with the surge in traffic. (Together, major seaports and airports are sometimes known as mainports.) In the United States, for example, the volume of passengers and cargo loaded onto aircraft roughly tripled between 1980 and 2006, but system capacity did not keep pace. The Federal Aviation Administration said in 2001 that most major U.S. airports routinely had periods in which demand exceeded capacity. In 2007, the U.S. Department of Transportation reported record-breaking flight delays and cancellations. "The system," the U.S. Government Accountability Office concluded in 2008, "is clearly under stress."[4]

In Europe, the number of passengers carried by airlines increased by almost 90 percent between 1995 and 2006. A European Parliament report anticipated that traffic would double again over the next two decades, exceeding the capacity of most European airports even after planned expansions were completed. It suggested that up to twenty-five new airports might be needed to avoid crippling congestion. The global trade association for airports warned in 2007 of a "looming capacity crunch" that would cause "serious and unacceptable delays across much of the developed world."[5]

In the Asia–Pacific region, meanwhile, air passenger traffic jumped by 50 percent between 2002 and 2007. In 2008, the Chinese government announced a bold plan to build almost one hundred new airports during the next decade to overcome congestion problems. In India, passenger traffic increased from 13 million in 2002 to 32 million just five years later. India's busiest airport, Mumbai, was built to handle 14 million passengers a year; in 2007, it managed a flow of 26 million. In the same year, Delhi's airport handled 10 million more than its planned capacity of 13 million. Flights to and from major Indian airports were routinely delayed because of queues for takeoff and landing.[6]

Mounting anxiety about the capacity of mainports to meet the requirements of a globalized economy resulted in organizational reforms that produced "an unprecedented transformation on a global scale." In many countries, ports and airports used to be organized as conventional government bureaucracies, often integrated into a single national ministry or department. These old monoliths were now broken up and replaced by a larger set of organizations, each usually responsible for the management of a single port or airport.[7]

Decentralization was accompanied by autonomization—that is, the creation of legal barriers to protect mainports from political and bureaucratic interference. This could be done in different ways. Sometimes governments were satisfied to create mainport authorities or corporations that are government-owned but with significant operational freedom. Laws were amended so that these authorities are free from civil service laws; free to spend income collected from shippers or airlines; and protected from political interference in management decisions. However, governments sometimes took autonomization a step further—by giving a private operator a long-term contract to manage key parts of a mainport or by completely divesting a mainport to the private sector.[8]

The United Kingdom was one of the forerunners of mainport reform in the era of liberalization. In 1983, the Thatcher government transferred the assets of the national Docks Board, which operated twenty ports, to a new company, Associated British Ports, which it then privatized. The government later privatized several other ports individually. In 1986, the government-run British Airports Authority (BAA), which operated seven major airports, was converted into a publicly traded company. Sixteen locally run airports also were converted into corporations that were freed from direct management by local councillors.[9]

Other Commonwealth countries also transformed mainports. In Canada, major airports were transferred from the federal government to a set of nonprofit corporations; at the same time, major ports were shifted to a string of more independent authorities. Most Australian ports were reorganized as government-owned corporations while a few were sold to private investors, and two dozen government-run airports were leased to private operators. New Zealand's major airports also were transformed into privately run corporations, although local governments continued to own a minority interest. Its ports were shifted to autonomous corporations under a 1988 law intended to stop "marauding politicians fiddling around."[10]

Similar reforms were undertaken elsewhere. The Port of Rotterdam, Europe's busiest, was reorganized as a corporation owned primarily by municipal government but no longer directly controlled by it. Portugal gave responsibility for its major port, Lisbon, to an independent authority while Spain did the same for all of its ports. Policy on the Iberian Peninsula was mirrored throughout Latin America, where many countries adopted laws that made ports and airports more independent. Mexico, for example, dismantled its centralized bureaucracy, creating two dozen authorities to manage its major ports.[11]

Singapore, meanwhile, transferred port operations to an independent but government-owned corporation, and Hong Kong transferred airport activities from a municipal department to a new independent authority. On the Chinese mainland, central government experimented with a policy of "localization" in which decision making over ports and airports was shifted to provincial and municipal officials. Several were incorporated and publicly listed, although with a majority interest retained by government. India came later to reform but eventually experimented with private management of several major airports and ports.[12]

The United States was not a leader in mainport reform, partly because it did not need to be. The two key features of reform—decentralization and autonomization—were already well-established features of the American port and airport networks. For constitutional reasons, its mainports were always run by local or state governments rather than a centralized national bureaucracy. And many of these mainports were already structured as autonomous authorities. To some degree, the world was now reproducing the American method of mainport organization.[13]

In the United States, mainport autonomization was one of the main legacies of the Progressive era, a period in American politics that roughly spanned the first half of the twentieth century. Progressives were reformers who sought to modernize the machinery of American government in many ways. One of their main preoccupations was the corrosive effect of politics on the delivery of basic services in major American cities. For this reason, their reforms were often intended to concentrate authority in the hands of specially trained administrators—"men of business judgment"—who were protected from political influence.[14]

The Progressive impulse led to the creation of several of the country's major mainport authorities. The first was the Port Authority of New York and New Jersey, established in 1921 to overhaul port facilities that were fraught with corruption and inefficiency. The new authority was structurally and financially independent and led by a panel of commissioners appointed for fixed terms. The vision, in the view of Jameson Doig, was one in which a "skilled staff" would be shielded from "the many vagaries of politics... [and] guided only by principles of efficiency and the public interest."[15]

The same reasoning led to the transfer of the region's airports to the authority a quarter-century later. A municipal official explained in 1946 that it was a way to "get the airports out of politics." "The truth," the *New York World Telegram* opined, "is that all too frequently men elected to office are not qualified to tangle with complicated, modern municipal management. They may be overly vote-conscious. They may be hog-tied to political bosses. They may just be plain incompetent. But whatever the reason, time after time when the politicians have gotten in a jam they have had to create an authority and call on successful businessmen to bail them out."[16]

This was the logic of discipline at work, without the more refined language used by economists a half-century later. It was an argument predicated on deep skepticism about the reliability of democratic processes combined with faith in the capacity of professionals to make decisions that would serve the long-term public interest. The method of reform was legal change to buffer those professionals from political influence.

This was also the reasoning that was used to justify mainport reforms in the era of liberalization. Before reform, T. E. Notteboom and W. Winkelmans observed in 2001, mainports had "political" rather than "technocratic" management systems. Political systems, it was claimed, were typified by managerial incompetence, diffuse goals, and a bias toward "community welfare" and "distributional equity" rather than commercial imperatives. Political interference, a spokesman for Australian ports complained in 2000, meant that "short term government agendas" were allowed to undermine projects that were essential to meet "market development needs."[17]

A 1996 World Bank report echoed the lament. "Politicians," it said, often exploit traditional mainport structures "to further goals which may have little to do with corporate efficiency." Particularly in developing countries, mainports sometimes assumed "social functions," such as supplying housing, schooling, and health services for employees and their families. One of the most important of these functions was the provision of employment itself. A World Bank analyst argued in 2001 that mainports often served "as natural shelters for the unemployed."[18]

One of the principal objectives therefore was to limit political control over mainport operations. "A major aim of [port] reform," an Australian commentator explained in 1998, "is to either remove or distance governments from day to day port operations." "If public ports are to operate like market-driven private enterprises," observed the Belgian analysts Notteboom and Winkelmans, "commercial imperatives must be separated from environmental and community interests." Likewise, one of the goals of airport restructuring was to create "autonomous airports...free from state policy constraints" and able to "focus on operational and service improvements." "While innovation is possible at airports where local and regional political leaders exercise some influence over management decisions," another commentator argued in 2000, "increased autonomy for airport administrators will substantially improve the likelihood of innovation and its beneficial impact on productivity and service quality."[19]

The Demands of a Globalized Economy

Critics of Progressivism often disputed its claim that the movement transcended everyday politics. They argued that progressive reforms produced immediate benefits for some segments of society, such as the commercial interests that needed more reliable government services. At the same time, other segments—such as working-class and immigrant communities who relied on political parties to provide a crude social safety net and unions, whose members bore the costs of efficiency drives within government—were disadvantaged. Progressivism, in the view of James Weinstein, was part of a "conscious effort to control the economic and social policies of federal, state, and municipal governments by various business groups in their own long-range interests as they perceived it."[20]

This was certainly true of the ports of Long Beach and Los Angeles, both created in the 1920s. These two Progressive Era ports were "endowed with substantial policy and fiscal autonomy" but also had the backing of a powerful commercial lobby that saw the ports as the engine of the region's economic growth. The ports acquired a "development mentality," as one official described it, and their organizational structure seemed to free them "to invest wholeheartedly in infrastructure without too much interference." For decades, this model appeared to work: the harbor was dredged to handle bigger ships, more berths and terminals were built, and major new rail connections were added.[21]

By the end of the twentieth century, radical changes in the structure of the economy had the effect of widening the range of businesses that worry about mainport efficiency. A series of policy and technological changes—the removal of tariffs, deregulation of air and marine transport, computerization, containerization, and the advent of megaships—transformed the way in which goods are produced and distributed. This led to the emergence of complex networks of overseas production and reliance on "just-in-time" delivery of goods. One consequence of this global logistics revolution is a larger risk of economic disruption because of congestion at mainports; another is a much broader constituency of firms with a keen interest in mainport operations.[22]

This was illustrated in fall 2004, as ships queued outside San Pedro Bay. The delays frustrated retailers across the United States as goods ordered for the Christmas season languished offshore. Problems in San Pedro Bay "really interrupted the just-in-time delivery systems we have in place," one trade specialist complained. At a national textile-and-apparel conference held in Portland, Oregon, in November 2004, three-quarters of the participants said that congestion in San Pedro Bay was the most important issue they faced. An executive with Singapore's Neptune Orient Lines warned that "all of the work of the last fifteen years on building global supply chains is beginning to become unwound."[23]

Shippers such as Neptune Orient Lines were vocal advocates of mainport reform. In 2004, the chief executive of the container line P&O Nedlloyd, Philip Green, warned ports that "it is not acceptable to say nothing can be done" about congestion. He said that P&O Nedlloyd would put ports "under as much pressure as possible" to increase their capabilities; if some ports did not improve, the company "would be forced to consider alternatives." For example, P&O Nedlloyd could shift business from San Pedro Bay to another of the half-dozen major ports along the west coast of the United States and Canada. Or it could move from the Port of Rotterdam to another of the nine major ports within the Hamburg–Le Havre range, which girds the coast of northwest Europe.[24]

Concentration within the shipping industry increased its power to make such threats. P&O Nedlloyd itself was the product of a 1996 merger that made it the largest containership fleet in the world; in 2005, it was absorbed by a major rival, Maersk Sealand. By 2007, the top five carriers accounted for more than 40 percent of the market. As a result of concentration, major container lines "are in a position to push port authorities to the limit," one analyst observed in 2006. Although the pace of airline consolidation has been less intense, concentration in that industry has also put pressure on airports that are worried about losing their status as hubs. In 2007, the head of British Airways warned that the United Kingdom would be "throwing in the economic towel" if plans to expand London's Heathrow Airport were not approved.[25]

International institutions also have helped the transport industry apply pressure on governments for mainport reform. In 2007, for example, the World Bank launched its Logistics Performance Index, which ranked 150 countries according to shippers' perceptions of their "logistical friendliness," a measure that included perceptions of mainport capacity. In 2007, Singapore ranked first; Afghanistan, last. Indian journalists lamented that the country stood at a "dismal" thirty-ninth place, well behind its rival China.[26]

Industry threats to shift business from one mainport are calculated to play on the anxieties of government officials. Historic rivalries between mainports have been intensified because of improvements in road and rail infrastructure that undermine the ability of mainports to claim a comparative advantage as the gateway to a region's interior. And in countries that previously had highly centralized mainport bureaucracies, reform itself has intensified competition by freeing individual mainports to make improvements that lure business away from others.

The result is a world in which mainports, encouraged by commercial interests, prey on their peers. In the United States, for example, the head of the Minneapolis–St. Paul airport cheered when its rival, Chicago's O'Hare, seemed to have its expansion plans frustrated throughout the 1990s: "Chicago is completely bottled up.... There's an opportunity for the Twin Cities to become the dominant city in the Midwest." And when plans for expansion of Heathrow Airport seemed to be thwarted, airports on the Continent—Amsterdam, Paris, Frankfurt—were poised to displace it as a major European hub.[27]

Ports competed in a similar way. San Diego port officials quickly exploited the troubles in San Pedro Bay in 2004. "Our goal is to get these ships to come here on a permanent basis," San Diego's port commissioner said at the time. "This is our opportunity to show the shipping industry that we are a viable port and we'd like to do business." Similarly, in the 1990s, community leaders in the French port of Le Havre were fixated on the health of the neighboring Belgian port of Antwerp; Antwerp, in turn, was fixated on its northern neighbor, the Dutch port of Rotterdam. Municipal leaders in Antwerp were elated in 2005 when they opened a new dock that doubled their port's capacity. Port managers in Rotterdam, meanwhile, were frustrated by a decade-long delay in their own expansion plan.[28]

A new set of multinational port operators also became vocal advocates for mainport restructuring. In 2006, just four businesses—Hutchison Port Holdings of Hong Kong, PSA of Singapore, APM of Denmark, and DP World based in the United Arab Emirates—operated privatized terminals that handled almost half of the world's container traffic. These firms are the children of reform. As a United Nations study noted in 2007, their growth has been made possible by policy decisions that provided "new market opportunities" for privatized port operators. But reform is now self-reinforcing: businesses fostered by it now advocate for its extension.[29]

The same is true in the airport industry, increasingly dominated by a few "global commercial enterprises." By 2005, BAA—the privatized operator of Heathrow and other British airports—had expanded operations to the

United States and four other countries. (In 2006, it was acquired by Grupo Ferrovial, a Spanish infrastructure firm.) AENA, the state-owned company that operates Spain's airports, had operations in eight other countries. The Schiphol Group, operator of Amsterdam's airport, expanded to Sweden, Italy, the United States, Australia, and Indonesia; its rival Fraport, meanwhile, operator of the Frankfurt airport, expanded to Bulgaria, Greece, India, Egypt, Peru, and Senegal.[30]

The Limits of Autonomy

Thirty years of liberalization produced an environment in which policy makers, egged on by a powerful combination of commercial interests, came to believe three things: first, that the key to economic growth lies in the expansion of mainport capacity; second, that the failure to improve mainports would have immediate and painful consequences because of competition from other mainports; and third, that the formula for improving capacity was decentralization and autonomization of mainports and perhaps privatization as well. But this prescription for reform was not easy to execute.

Some of the reasons are familiar. Some autonomous mainports struggled to purge corruption, just as autonomous revenue authorities did. This task was sometimes complicated by the fact that mainports were not allowed to screen staff before they were transferred to a new autonomous organization. Mainports also faced backlashes over their attempts to shed "social functions," such as the provision of worker housing or employment.

Mumbai International Airport Pvt. Ltd. (MIAL), a private consortium, wrestled with these problems in 2006 as it took over operation of Chhatrapati Shivaji International Airport (CSIA) at Mumbai. MIAL estimated in 2007 that it was involved in almost three hundred court cases involving airport operations. It was compelled to deal with protests by powerful local politicians, allied with labor unions, over job losses. At the same time, it struggled to dismantle networks of corruption that had long penetrated airport operations and confronted the extraordinarily difficult task of relocating more than four hundred thousand slum dwellers who lived on airport property. "In India," MIAL's director concluded in 2008, "infrastructure development is about taking care of vested interests without compromising your objectives."[31]

In fact, protests over job losses proved to be a pervasive difficulty. In 1999, Brazilian president Fernando Henrique Cardoso threatened to use military force to reopen ports that were shut down by dockworkers still protesting the 1993 law that reorganized that country's ports. In 2005, employees of the Airports Authority of India launched a nationwide strike against the restructuring of major airports. In 2008, French port workers shut down the nation's major ports in a protest against reform proposals that government officials said were essential to reversing losses to other countries' ports.[32]

However, there were also broader considerations that also complicated the process of autonomization. One issue was raised inadvertently by advocates of reform. If mainports really are the engine of regional economic development, as advocates routinely claim, then the idea of detaching them from political processes became in some respects more problematic. Governments might find that their own ability to plan for development would be compromised by the need to negotiate with an organization that had formal independence. Coherent planning seemed to require integration, not segmentation.

At the same time, governments in most countries confronted rising public sensitivity about damage to the environment. Mainports impose substantial costs on neighboring communities—in the form of noise and air and water pollution as well as congestion on connecting highways and railroads. Environmental activism is one of the most important ways in which the democratic impulse has been manifested over the past four decades. Voters are more alert to environmental issues, and stakeholder groups are more numerous and powerful.

Attempts at autonomization often were frustrated because of governments' concern about potential harm to planning capacity and environmental protection. In New Zealand, for example, the national government attempted to reform the country's fourteen ports by transforming them into separate corporations in 1988. Initially, local and regional governments held shares in these enterprises, but they were encouraged to sell them to private investors. Few did, despite evidence that divestment would have improved the ports' financial performance.

In fact, local leaders in Auckland—home to the country's busiest port—took exactly the opposite tack. The regional government bought shares until it had complete ownership of the new enterprise. The port controls a large part of Auckland's crowded waterfront, and poorly planned expansion would have threatened other priorities, such as tourism and urban renewal. Complete ownership, the Auckland regional government announced in 2005, would reduce the port's sensitivity to the expectations of private shareholders and "assist in the integrated development of the total waterfront area."[33]

Similar concerns led to a watering down of plans for reform of the Port of Rotterdam. Previously a department of municipal government, the port became a formally independent corporation in 2004, "no longer controlled directly by the municipality," in the words of two Dutch transport specialists. The aim was to give the port a "business-driven structure." Still, city leaders had good reason for wanting to maintain close oversight of the port, which was about to embark on a massive expansion of its facilities. The project, known as Maasvlakte 2, had been the subject of ten years of tortuous negotiations involving many local governments, a half dozen national ministries, and a swath of nongovernmental groups.[34]

The stakes were too high to tolerate a policy of true autonomization. Even after reorganization, the port was still wholly owned by the municipality of Rotterdam. And municipal officials continued to exercise substantial influence over the port. An observer of the end stages of the Maasvlakte 2 negotiations observed that representations from the port and municipality of Rotterdam were "often considered interchangeable in spite of the fact that the Port Company was technically an autonomous private entity." When the Dutch central government agreed to endorse the project, it also demanded a stake in the port corporation, eventually acquiring one-third ownership.[35]

The following year, and for similar reasons, Amsterdam's city leaders scuttled Schiphol airport's attempt at further autonomization. Schiphol was already structured as a corporation jointly owned by the Dutch central government and the municipality of Amsterdam. In the 1990s, however, Schiphol's administrators pressed the two governments to sell their interests in the corporation, arguing that this would give it a freer hand in global expansion. ("Our state-owned enterprise image . . . hurts us when we bid for stakes in privatized airports," said its chief executive.) However, the corporation was entangled in a debate over its plan for expansion of Amsterdam's own airport, which detractors said would generate too much noise over city suburbs. As with Maasvlakte 2, debate over the proposed expansion was unprecedented in breadth and intensity. The city of Amsterdam vetoed any sale of shares in the airport in 2006. "Privatization is off the table," a municipal spokesman said. "Schiphol is too important."[36]

Even when mainports appeared to win significant independence, they had no assurance that development plans would proceed. BAA, the operator of London's Heathrow Airport, was established as an independent authority in 1966 and privatized in 1986. Both moves were justified as a way of encouraging "efficient operation" of Britain's major airports. A legislative committee reviewing the case for creating BAA conceded that it would limit parliamentary control but declared that the new organization "would be autonomous, would be able to take decisions more quickly...and would be able to react in a commercial manner to what was essentially a commercial situation."[37]

But formal autonomy did not help Heathrow deal quickly with a major impediment to improvement, the lack of runway capacity. BAA first made the case for an additional runway in 1969, but the British government gave a hedged endorsement of the improvement only in 2009—four decades later. BAA's attempt to build a fifth terminal at Heathrow was only slightly less difficult. Its 1993 proposal triggered the longest planning inquiry in British history, with more than fifty thousand Britons registering opinions on the merits of the proposal. The terminal opened fifteen years later.[38]

BAA's troubles suggest a broader difficulty with the way in which advocates of reform thought about autonomy. It can be defined in two ways. The concept could be construed narrowly, as operational autonomy—that is, the freedom to run a mainport largely as it stands. The other, broader definition could be called strategic autonomy—the freedom to craft and execute a plan for expansion of the mainport's capacities. This is a crude distinction, but it helps our thinking. Operational autonomy is easier to establish and can lead to short-term improvements in mainport efficiency. However, lasting solutions to problems of congestion come through the expansion of capacity, and to do this a mainport requires strategic autonomy. But this is much more difficult to attain.

The Heathrow runway debate speaks to the essence of the problem. Urbanization means that, as a result of expansion, the costs borne by Heathrow's neighbors are higher than they used to be. At the same time, the public's willingness to tolerate those costs—its perception of the reasonableness of noise and air pollution and traffic congestion—has declined. One consequence of this decline in tolerance is that the system of laws and bureaucratic procedures that affect expansion—including the processes for expropriation, regulation of land use, and control of environmental and health impacts—has become more complex. All of this has vastly complicated the task of obtaining approvals for significant additions to capacity.

BAA never had the authority to make unilateral decisions about expansion, but over time the number of other players with the ability to veto its expansion plans has increased. Perversely, battles over expansion also helped to strengthen its opponents, by providing them with experience in mobilizing citizens and constructing alliances among diverse interests (fig. 5.2). "The extraordinary logic of expansion in the aviation industry," Steven Grigg and David Howarth observed in 2006, "has been accompanied by a

Figure 5.2   Heathrow Airport protests, February 2008.

In 2008, protesters from the action group Plane Stupid climbed to the roof of the
Houses of Parliament and unfurled banners reading "BAA HQ" and "NO
THIRD RUNWAY."

Source: Getty Images.

dialectic of protest and resistance.... The linking together [of opposition
groups has] politicized airport expansion in a new way."[39]

The Port Authority of New York and New Jersey served as a model for
BAA, but in reality this Progressive Era organization also never had true
strategic autonomy. Much of the authority's early work—such as the recon-
figuration of marine, rail, and road transportation and the construction of
new bridges and tunnels—simply could not be undertaken unilaterally.
Cooperation among state and local government agencies was often needed.
The authority got that cooperation because it was backed by a powerful
coalition of commercial interests favoring expansion. The authority also
became adept at exploiting the power of that coalition in its negotiations
with other agencies. In other words, the authority's influence came not
because it was detached from politics, but because it was deeply embedded
in it.[40]

The New York–New Jersey port authority soon learned how its own ability to pursue a strategy of expansion hinged on favorable political conditions. Only a decade after acquiring its three airports, the authority's staff

calculated that growth in air traffic would soon exceed their combined capacity. The United States was entering the jet age, and over the next decade passenger volume would increase at annual rates comparable to those of India and China today. In 1959, the authority proposed its solution: a massive fourth airport, to be built in Morris County, New Jersey, thirty miles west of Manhattan.[41]

The port authority won the endorsement of prominent business and political leaders, as it had in the past. But it failed to recognize the rising power of new constituencies—environmentalists concerned about the destruction of wetlands, suburbanites concerned about noise and congestion—that were deeply hostile to its proposal. The authority aggravated its troubles by attempting to stonewall these critics, refusing to acknowledge the legitimacy of their complaints. This was a fatal error. By 1966, the Morris County plan was dead. A subsequent attempt to expand Kennedy Airport also was defeated, by neighborhood groups and environmental activists.[42]

The port authority's attempt to execute a expansion strategy was undone because the plan proved to be politically untenable. Perhaps the authority was unaware of the extent to which its apparent freedom in pursuing expansion had been an artifact of favorable but transient political conditions. If so, it was not alone in making such mistakes. MassPort, the independent authority that operated Boston's Logan Airport—at the time, one of the busiest in the world—ran into similar difficulties in the 1960s. As a matter of law, MassPort appeared to have substantial autonomy: the statute creating it made clear that it could not be controlled by any part of state government. MassPort also had the support of business leaders, construction unions, and many legislators. And so it launched an aggressive program to expand the airport's capacity.[43]

The program quickly sparked opposition. Logan Airport is located close to the center of Boston—largely constructed on a reclaimed part of Boston Harbor, hard against the old neighborhoods of East Boston and Winthrop. Residents there protested the expropriation of land and the inevitable traffic congestion and the noise that would be emitted by the new generation of jet aircraft. In September 1968, mothers and children of East Boston even waged a "baby-carriage blockade" against trucks entering the airport.[44]

MassPort believed it could ignore the protests. One MassPort report conceded that Logan's neighbors might have valid complaints about the disruption of their lives—"But whatever the merits their case may have in human terms, similar arguments have never counted for much in the past when progress was at stake." MassPort's executive director, Edward King, dismissed the protesters as "rabble-rousers" whose demands would "set the airport back twenty years." "Not everyone in the world lives in East Boston or Winthrop," King said in 1974. "We're serving the greatest good of the greatest number." The authority's dismissive attitude was encouraged by MassPort's success in some early battles over expansion.[45]

But MassPort underestimated its opponents. In fact, its prolonged war with neighborhood groups enabled them to refine their mobilization skills while its bullheadedness stimulated public sympathy for their cause. New federal and state policies on environmental protection, noise, and congestion also legitimized complaints and provided new tools for pursuing remedies. By the early 1970s, MassPort had lost the support of Massachusetts' governor, Boston's mayor, and many legislators. By 1974, Massachusetts governor Francis Sargent had made enough appointments to gain control of MassPort's governing board, and Edward King was forced to resign as its director. Meanwhile, Boston mayor Kevin White obtained an injunction blocking MassPort's proposal to add a fifth runway to Logan Airport. MassPort's expansion slowed substantially. A fifth runway eventually went into operation thirty-two years later.[46]

Similar conflicts arose at ports along the West Coast of the United States as trade shifted from the northeast. In the early 1960s, the busiest West Coast gateway was San Francisco Bay, not San Pedro Bay. Within San Francisco Bay, the largest share of commerce was handled by the Port of San Francisco rather than by its cross-bay rival, the Port of Oakland. But canny business decisions by the independent authority that runs the Port of Oakland soon gave it the advantage. In 1961, it built capacity to serve the new fleet of containerships that it expected would be launched over the next decades. This was a gamble on containerization, an innovation only five years old. By 1970, Oakland was the dominant port in San Francisco Bay and the busiest container port on the West Coast. In the next three years, it handled more container traffic than Los Angeles and Long Beach combined.[47]

However, Oakland confronted a limit to growth. It knew that future generations of containerships would have drafts too deep for its harbor. In 1972, the port asked the federal government for approval to dredge the harbor—as it had twice before, in 1927 and 1962—to accommodate larger ships. Like the airport authorities, the Port of Oakland did not realize how much the legal and political climate had shifted. There were now more approval requirements and, therefore, more opportunities for environmentalists and fishermen to block the plan. This was aggravated by the port's own lack of sensitivity to the shift. To some environmentalists, the port was "a very powerful force that operated without sufficient outside control." The dredging was not completed for almost a quarter-century.[48]

The Port of Oakland lost, and never recovered, its lead in containerized shipping. But a change in bureaucratic attitudes and capabilities helped it avoid a repeat of the controversy sparked by the 1972 plan. The port acquired environmental specialists, became more adept at anticipating opposition, and spent more money on mitigation of environmental damage. It also learned how to negotiate agreements with potential opponents so that its proposals were not caught in prolonged litigation. When the port unveiled another expansion plan in 1997, it included extensive measures to reduce environmental harms. When poor minority residents of neighboring West Oakland complained about increased noise and smog, the port avoided lawsuits by promising further mitigation efforts. The port's sharpest critics conceded that it had greatly improved its community relations. This expansion project was completed in just six years.[49]

Over a quarter century, the Port of Oakland had learned that its freedom to execute expansion plans was actually very limited; it depended on the support (or at least forbearance) of a broadening range of constituencies, many of whom could exploit new planning and environmental laws to protect their interests. The only way in which the port could advance its own plans was through bargaining with those key constituencies. To do this, it had to overhaul its own operations. The port acquired new staff with skills in environmental protection, community relations, and lobbying. It also changed the ways it talked about growth and produced expansion plans. In a sense, this renovation was antithetical to the idea of autonomization. The formal–legal reforms that gave independence to mainports was mainly concerned with *buffering* them from external constituencies. But Oakland had learned that it was necessary to build the capacity to *bridge* to those constituencies.[50]

At the height of the trade boom, the twin ports of San Pedro Bay were learning the same lesson. The two ports spent almost four billion dollars on infrastructure improvements in the 1990s. At the same time, however, popular resistance to expansion mounted. Adjacent communities complained about increased noise, freeway congestion, and the increasing number of respiratory illnesses that were tied to ship and truck exhaust. (A 2000 study estimated that the San Pedro port complex was the largest single source of diesel emissions in southern California.) Residents of the adjacent communities of Wilmington and San Pedro launched movements to secede from the City of Los Angeles and take control of its port.[51]

In 2003, a "rebellion" by residents of Wilmington and San Pedro forced the Port of Los Angeles to delay the opening of a new 174-acre terminal. It lay idle until the port settled a lawsuit brought by the National Resources Defense Council (NRDC), an environmental advocacy group, on behalf of residents. The settlement committed the port to spending $60 million on pollution-reduction measures. The Los Angeles port director, criticized by community leaders for insensitivity and by the shipping industry for bending too quickly to political pressure, resigned in 2004. An NRDC spokesman warned: "Our next stop is the Port of Long Beach."[52]

It was now obvious that the political environment of the two ports had become more treacherous. The number of groups resisting port expansion was growing, and single-issue groups were more adept at building alliances. One of the most prominent was the Coalition for Clean and Safe Ports, which mounted a sophisticated media campaign on behalf of thirty-six community, environmental, public health, religious, and labor organizations. Political leaders in local and state government responded to this advocacy. A promise to clean the ports was included in the platforms of Los Angeles mayor Antonio Villaraigosa, elected in 2005, and Long Beach mayor Bob Foster, elected in 2006.

The two ports quickly adapted to the more hostile climate. The Port of Long Beach rebranded itself as an "environmentally friendly port" and announced an internal restructuring to give "top-level" status to its environmental planning division. There was "a complete shift in attitude," a senior port official later said. The two ports also collaborated on their Clean Air Action Plan, released in 2006, that committed $2 billion over five years to mitigate environmental and health impacts. Shipping lines were given incentives to reduce emissions while port tenants were warned that lease renewals would hinge on new measures to lower emissions.[53]

At the same time, the ports began to court key stakeholders more aggressively. The Port of Los Angeles established a community advisory committee that included neighborhood groups and local legislators. The Port of Long Beach launched several new outreach programs—including community meetings about port activities, port tours, jobs programs for local youth, and scholarships for local schools. Studies were commissioned to show the economic importance of the ports. The Port of Long Beach's expenditure on lobbying of state government officials more than doubled between 1997 and 2007 while its federal lobbying expenditure almost doubled in a comparable span.[54]

These actions represented a substantial shift in the way the ports conducted business—in terms of actual policy on development, organizational capabilities, and the breadth and character of external relations. Port officials said the policies were built on the premise that there need not be conflict between growth and the interests of neighboring communities and environmental groups. ("We can grow and still clean the air," new LA port director Geraldine Knatz said in 2007.) The underlying political reality was that rapid growth would be impossible if the political opposition to its consequences could not be contained. "Unless we can clean the air, we aren't going to move forward with any of these [expansion] projects," the Port of Long Beach's top environmental official conceded in 2007. "The community won't allow it."[55]

In early 2008, it was difficult to say whether these adjustments would work. Polarization over growth appeared to intensify throughout the spring of that year. The NRDC threatened the Port of Long Beach with further litigation, claiming it had failed to comply with its environmental commitments. The NRDC withdrew that threat after the two ports took promised steps to reduce truck emissions, but these actions were quickly challenged by a trucking industry group. Meanwhile, a coalition of community and environmental groups again challenged a proposed terminal modernization at the Port of Los Angeles. The port negotiated another settlement, promising to impose a levy on container traffic that would fund a nonprofit organization to monitor the health effects of expansion.[56]

Crisis and After

The financial crisis of 2007–2009 provided a substantial and unwelcomed reprieve from problems of mainport congestion. International trade collapsed in fall 2008. The World Trade Organization forecast that global trade would decline by almost 10 percent in 2009—the sharpest drop in eighty years.[57]

Data on marine shipping suggested a more severe downturn. In early 2009, the largest container shipping line, A. P. Moeller-Maersk, reported that its global business had declined by 20 percent in one year. The company said that the entire industry had sunk into a "crisis of historic proportions." According to a survey of U.S. ports, a similar drop in container traffic occurred between January 2008 and June 2009. At some ports, the decline was even steeper. The San Pedro Bay ports reported in April 2009 that container movements were almost 40 percent lower than a year earlier. Air traffic suffered similarly: the International Air Transport Association reported in early 2009 that air freight volumes had dropped more than 20 percent in one year. Passenger traffic declined by more than 10 percent in the same period.[58]

In fact, by mid-2009, shippers and airlines were dealing with a different kind of congestion. Roughly two thousand airliners—about one-tenth of the global fleet—were decommissioned in 2008–2009. Unused airliners soon filled desert "boneyards," such as southern California's Victorville airport. Hundreds of idle freighters were anchored in the Singapore Straits and near Rotterdam and Gilbratar, and hundreds more were scrapped in the middle of construction.[59]

The reprieve from battles over mainport growth is likely temporary. As the global economy revives, so will marine and air traffic—although it may be several years before they return to pre-boom levels. And mainport operators might be disadvantaged in future debates over mainport expansion by public perceptions that trade flows—the pretext for the sacrifices they are being asked to make—are unpredictable. Trade in San Pedro Bay boomed and busted once; maybe it will do so again.

Skeptics about mainport reform can also question the logic that underpins calls for autonomization. The rhetoric of mainport reform drew more directly from Progressive Era thinking than from the work of late-twentieth-century economists, but it nonetheless comprised another instance in which the logic of discipline was applied to governmental reform. The idea was to extract mainports from governmental bureaucracies so that they could be freed from the influence of political processes that caused them to be inefficient and unresponsive to industry demands. The primary mechanism for transforming mainport capability was the adoption of laws that confirmed each mainport's status as an independent entity.

However, the logic of discipline proved either indefensible or unworkable when applied to mainports. If it implied that mainports should be given significant freedom in defining a strategy for expansion, then the formula was indefensible because expansion clearly raised broader questions about the distribution of benefits and costs from expansion, and about the path of regional economic development, that were properly the subject of political debate. If, conversely, autonomization was primarily about an increase in operational flexibility, then it had nothing to say about the key question: how to organize public decision making so that communities could make choices about mainport expansion that were broadly regarded as legitimate.

In any case, autonomy never proved to be a workable goal. Again, the distinction between operational and strategic freedom is key. Some mainports attained operational freedom and used it to improve short-term efficiency. But the capacity of any mainport to pursue longer term goals has always been constrained by the balance of forces in everyday politics. When mainports felt the freedom to expand, it usually was because a powerful "growth coalition" backed the mainport and enabled it to avoid roadblocks that might have been imposed by legislatures or other agencies. When the relative power of those coalitions declined, as it did in many developed countries after the 1960s, the capacity of mainports to pursue expansion strategies was narrowed.[60]

Successful mainports are those that do not take the political balance of forces for granted. As James Doig has observed, they "thrive because they are deeply involved in alliances which are a mix of politics and economics." Successful mainports are constantly engaged in monitoring for the rise of new interests and in assessing their potential to promote or hinder development. When old coalitions are no longer effective, they negotiate among competing stakeholders to craft a new coalition that is durable enough to support continued growth. To do this, mainports must adjust their internal capacities. They must have organizational capabilities that allow them to anticipate threats, negotiate settlements, and deliver on promises.[61]

This is not primarily technical work; it is, on the contrary, political. And this is the sense in which the logic of discipline is most clearly misguided. To say that mainports must be extracted or buffered from politics is wrong, or at least too imprecise to be useful. In important respects the important thing is not that mainports are detached from politics, but that they have developed the capacity to participate constructively in the processes by which communities make decisions about economic growth.

Protecting Capital
Independent Regulators and Super Courts

Our ambassador, U.S. trade representatives, our embassy in Quito,
our consulate general in Gualaceo, the State Department here, the
National Security Council—we have all told various Ecuadorian
government officials that the investment climate is very
important, that anything that would abrogate the bilateral
investment treaty would sour that climate even more, and rather
than attract investment, which Ecuador needs so desperately,
would scare away that investment.

—*U.S. State Department spokesperson, 2004*

In the early 1990s, CMS Energy was a long-established Midwestern U.S.
energy company with new ambitions. For over a century, CMS had sold
electricity and natural gas to consumers and industries in the state of
Michigan. But the prospects for growth in the state were limited. The company's competitors were expanding into newly liberalized markets in the
developing world and realizing rates of return from their investments of 20
to 30 percent per year. "The growth opportunities in these areas are phe-
nomenal," CMS chairman William McCormick Jr. said in 1994. Telling
investors that CMS would no longer be "a plain vanilla utility," McCormick
raised U.S.-dollar loans to finance an overseas expansion. Argentina was one
of his targets: a large and growing market that was in the process of privatizing its electricity and gas sectors.[1]

Foreign investors in countries like Argentina usually worry about "political risk"—that is, the danger that governments will take actions that reduce

the value of their investments. Many governments in Latin America have a history of treating foreign investors roughly. The most serious risk is a governmental takeover of the business, usually with inadequate compensation. Another risk is regulatory action that limits the scope of the business or the prices it can charge. Utilities like CMS are particularly vulnerable because they must make large up-front investments in infrastructure. Politicians may be tempted to impose politically popular price controls on utilities, knowing that their owners can do little to escape.[2]

But CMS had two reasons for believing that the political risks associated with its planned investment in one of Argentina's newly privatized natural gas distribution companies would be manageable. Argentina's 1992 gas law—lauded by the World Bank for "its transparency and procompetitive stance"—transferred responsibility for oversight of the gas industry from a ministry of Argentina's national government to a new independent body, Ente Nacional Regulador del Gas, or ENARGAS. Tariff adjustments for CMS's utilities would be approved by ENARGAS and not by government ministers directly.[3]

CMS also had the reassurance of a bilateral investment treaty, or BIT, signed by Argentina and the United States in 1991. The BIT provided guarantees of fair treatment for American investors in Argentina. It also said that firms with complaints about unfair treatment were not required to pursue those complaints in Argentinian courts. Instead, they could ask for arbitration by the International Centre for the Settlement of Investment Disputes (ICSID), a small body housed within World Bank headquarters in Washington, D.C. Argentina agreed that ICSID's decisions would be final and binding and promised to pay damages promptly if ICSID found that they had behaved improperly.[4]

Argentina was not alone in undertaking such reforms. During the era of liberalization, hundreds of independent regulatory agencies were created and well over two thousand bilateral investment treaties signed. This was another massive experiment with the logic of discipline. But the experiment did not always produce the expected results, as CMS would shortly discover. Governments sometimes escaped the constraints they had promised to honor. And where constraints continued to bind, troubling questions about the corrosion of democratic governance were raised.

Independent Regulators

Of the two mechanisms used to reassure investors, the independent regulatory agency (or IRA) was the most prominent. The substance of this reform was straightforward. Traditionally, government ministries that are directly accountable to ministers and legislatures have undertaken a host of regulatory functions—setting rules on prices, treatment of workers and consumers, competition with other businesses, environmental protection, and food and medicine safety. The premise was that these tasks should be transferred to new organizations that are "deliberately insulated from political control." Laws would be adjusted to assure this insulation. New IRAs would be structurally separated from ministries and given a formal grant of powers. The independence of the agency would be affirmed, and its heads would be appointed for fixed terms. Ideally, IRAs would be given complete control over their finances and internal organization.[5]

Several now-familiar arguments were advanced for IRAs. A minor theme is the value of the operational flexibility, such as the ability to hire specialized workers more easily and pay them better than in government ministries. Agencies that were able to collect fees directly from regulated industries avoided the strains felt by ministries that were still operating under tight budget constraints. Politicians and senior bureaucrats were conscious also of the danger of meddling in increasingly complicated regulatory decisions. They lacked the technical capacity to do it well and were more likely to be challenged by regulated industries or advocacy groups when they did it badly.

However, the most important argument for regulatory autonomy centered on the importance of commitment. IRAs were valued because they seemed to provide hard evidence to important constituencies that political influence over regulatory decision making had been permanently restricted.

Sometimes the aim was to demonstrate commitment to voters and consumers. In France, for example, politicians used the IRA model as a device for restoring public confidence after a serious of scandals triggered by their failure to act swiftly against threats to public health. In the most notorious case, top government officials authorized the distribution of blood products which they knew were contaminated with the AIDS virus, causing the death of more than three hundred people. Power to make decisions about the safety of blood products was shifted from the French health ministry to a new regulatory body that would make expert decisions "independent of political, social or economic pressures."[6]

The crisis over BSE (Bovine spongiform encephalopathy, popularly known as mad cow disease) in the United Kingdom prompted a similar reform. Before 1999, the British system of food safety regulation gave broad discretion to the agriculture minister, who acted on the advice of specialists in his ministry. But the ministry was criticized for slowness in responding to evidence that contaminated beef could cause a fatal brain infection in humans. Senior officials, an independent inquiry concluded, were unskilled in risk assessment and preoccupied with the possibility of economic harm to British farmers. The slowness of their response led to the deaths of almost one hundred people and a collapse in confidence in British agricultural products throughout Europe. In 1999, the U.K. government shifted regulatory powers to the independent Food Standards Agency.[7]

However, the IRA model was used also to signal commitment in a second and far more important way: to entice foreign investors by reassuring them that the value of their investment would not be undermined by regulatory actions limiting their ability to do business. The major force behind the adoption of the IRA model, according to Fabrizio Gilardi, who has studied its diffusion throughout Europe, "is the state's dependency on capital and its consequent need to appease capital by committing itself to providing an attractive market environment and a stable regime for investment. The more privatized the economy is, the greater its dependency on private capital and consequently the greater is the need to establish a stable institutional design that is technocratic rather than political in its orientation." Giandomenico Majone agrees: without the "credible regulatory commitment" provided by independent agencies, "companies will refuse to invest, or will not invest enough to satisfy demand and to maintain existing infrastructure."[8]

Thus the IRA model has been applied most vigorously in circumstances where the need to demonstrate commitment to capital is felt most intensely. For example, the growth in IRAs was fastest in the electricity and telecommunications sectors, where the fear of exploitation arises with greatest force. In addition, governments have taken more extreme measures to affirm the formal autonomy of utilities regulators than they have for social regulators. Efforts to demonstrate the formal independence of electricity and gas regulators were also more pronounced in states with a tradition of state ownership. And left-of-center governments, whose reliability is more suspect, proved more likely to adopt measures affirming the autonomy of regulators. IRAs, Stephen Wilks observed, seemed to provide a "quasi-constitutional" guarantee about commitment to the market system.[9]

The connection between arguments for IRAs and those for central bank independence is not accidental: this was yet another field in which Blinder's "nasty little thought" was vigorously applied. Arguments about the virtues of IRAs as commitment technologies drew an explicit parallel with problems in the formulation of monetary policy. The critical issue was perceived to be politicians' tendency "to behave in a shortsighted and populist manner that reduces welfare summed over a medium to long-term period." And

advocates and scholars interested in regulatory reform again focused on easily observed markers of de jure independence, citing the early research which
appeared to show that central banks with de jure autonomy were more effective in controlling inflation.[10]

The IRA model—defined in such formal–legal terms—diffused widely
throughout the era of liberalization. For example, there were only fifteen
autonomous regulatory agencies in Europe in 1980; by 2002, there were
more than ninety (fig. 6.1). A survey of telecommunications and electricity
regulation in seventy-one countries between 1977 and 1999 found that "separation" and "depoliticization" of regulators was a widespread phenomenon.
In 1977, there were only two telecom and electricity regulators in these
countries that had been separated and depoliticized; by 1999, there were
seventy-nine. A broader survey by David Levi-Faur found that the number
of separate telecom regulators increased from 6 in 1979 to 113 in 2001 while
the number of separate electricity regulators grew from 3 in 1985 to 57 in
2001.[11]

Another survey of forty-nine OECD and Latin American countries, looking at a much broader range of economic and social regulation, found that
the number of autonomous regulatory agencies had grown from 49 in 1980

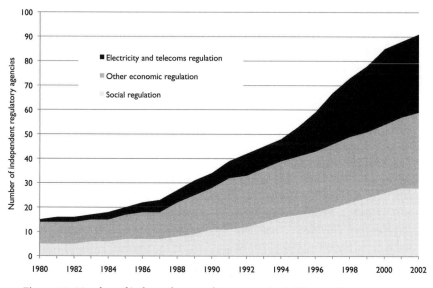

Figure 6.1 Number of independent regulatory agencies in Western Europe,
1980–2002.

Source: Fabrizio Gilardi, *Delegation in the regulatory state*. (Cheltenham, UK: Edward Elgar,
2008), appendix 4.

to 466 in 2002. Indeed, there was "explosive growth" in the number of IRAs in Latin America during this period. A survey of twelve areas of regulation in nineteen Latin American countries found that the number of autonomous regulators grew from just 2 in 1979 to 101 in 2002.[12]

At the start of the era of liberalization, IRAs were institutional anomalies—but three decades later, the IRA model was regarded as a "hegemonic institution grounded in a new convention in economic governance." The growing importance of foreign investment obviously played an important part in this transformation. So, too, did international organizations. The OECD actively promoted independent regulation, asserting that it was clearly superior to "regulatory functions embedded in line ministries." In Europe, the creation of autonomous regulators was sometimes mandated by directives issued by the EU. Emerging economies that received assistance from international financial institutions such as the World Bank were sometimes told that aid was contingent on the promise to establish autonomous regulators.[13]

Super Courts

Less often noted, but equally impressive, was the rapid growth of a second mechanism designed to reassure foreign investors. This second mechanism was not concerned with reorganizing any major national institution. On the contrary, it was aimed mainly at supplanting national institutions that were not trusted by foreign investors. This was done by negotiating BITs that detailed new procedures for dealing with complaints about unfair treatment. The result was the diversion of those complaints away from national courts to international arbitration bodies, such as the ICSID.

Concern about the mistreatment of investors was not new. Expropriation was a common phenomenon in the quarter century following World War II. Countries that had once been colonies were often deeply distrustful of multinational corporations based in the capitals of their former imperial masters. Foreign investment was often regarded as a form of economic exploitation. Businesses that had invested in the resource sector or heavy industry—regarded as the core of a well-planned national economy—were most likely to see their assets seized by the state.[14]

Remedies for the owners of expropriated businesses were limited. Lawyers in the advanced economies argued that international norms required expropriating states to pay compensation. But these norms were difficult to define with precision and could be enforced only if investors persuaded their own governments to challenge the offending state before the International Court of Justice in The Hague. And many poorer countries denied that the court had the right to make any decisions about expropriation cases. Latin American governments subscribed to the Calvo Doctrine, under which foreign investors could seek remedies only in the courts of the country in which they had invested. Investors countered that these courts were often politically influenced, corrupt, or simply prejudiced against foreigners. They wanted "access to a tribunal outside the sway of the host state."[15]

In the postwar decades, many attempts were made to negotiate a multilateral treaty that would set standards for the treatment of foreign investment. But these efforts always failed because of the inability to reach consensus among the governments of advanced and developing economies. In 1959, however, West Germany took an alternate route. It negotiated a bilateral treaty with Pakistan that contained promises about fair treatment and a provision that disputes would be settled by a special arbitration panel appointed by the two countries. This was an adaptation of the arbitration methods already widely used to settle commercial disputes within the private sector. In the next seven years, West Germany struck similar agreements with a dozen other developing countries. The model was gradually adopted by other countries as well.

The Convention on the Settlement of Investment Disputes between States and Nationals of Other States, a multilateral agreement adopted in 1966, complemented these bilateral agreements by providing a new forum for arbitration of investment disputes. The Washington Convention, as it was called, created ICSID as an office within the World Bank and gave it a mandate to provide support for arbitration panels. BITs signed after the 1966 convention usually specified ICSID as the preferred forum for undertaking arbitration cases. At the time, U.S. Treasury Secretary Henry Fowler predicted that ICSID would "promote an atmosphere of mutual confidence between private foreign investors and countries which wish to attract a larger flow of private international capital."[16]

Few contemporary observers shared his optimism. Most regarded the Washington Convention as a poor substitute for the true prize, a well-drafted multilateral agreement on the protection of foreign investment. "There are probably no more than a handful of people…who believe it represented a major step," one commentator wrote about the convention in 1968. "It will have extremely limited utility or effect." This prognosis initially seemed to be right. ICSID had no casework at all in its first five years and scarcely more than a case a year over the next quarter century. Similarly, there was no great increase in the number of bilateral investment treaties that might have created a workload for ICSID: by 1978, there were only about one hundred in force.[17]

However, the number of BITs exploded in the era of liberalization. In 1988, there were 261 signed BITs; by 1997, there were 1,611; and by 2005, 2,454 (fig 6.2). This was largely a consequence of the equally dramatic growth in global capital flows in the same period. "Stated simply," says one attorney working in the field, investment guarantees "developed and expanded because of money." Investors in home countries put more pressure on their own governments to negotiate safeguards for their overseas investments while host countries recognized that BITs might be a useful means of gaining advantage over other nations competing for the same pool of capital.[18]

The content of BITs also changed in three important ways. Promises about the limits on state action were laid out in more detail, creating an "economic bill of rights" for foreign investors. Also, arbitration rules were amended so that cases could be started by the wronged investor without the support of its home government. (This adjustment—allowing nongovernmental actors to demand accountability of a sovereign state in an international forum—has been described as a "revolutionary innovation" in

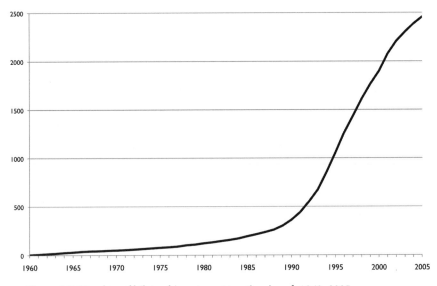

Figure 6.2 Number of bilateral investment treaties signed, 1960–2005.
Source: United Nations Conference on Trade and Development (UNCTAD).

international law.) Finally, BITs increasingly waived any requirement that investors pursue remedies in national courts before turning to arbitration. Investors had long complained that the obligation to use national courts was a "time-consuming obstacle" to relief. Now they were able to circumvent the national legal system entirely.[19]

ICSID began to function as a sort of super court in the sense that it was layered over and superseded national judicial systems. And as BITs proliferated, ICSID's workload increased. Between 2002 and 2007, ICSID began more arbitrations than it had in the preceding thirty-five years of its existence. ICSID-supervised arbitration became the "dominant vehicle" for resolving claims of maltreatment lodged by investors against states. The prospects for a system for investor protection based on bilateral agreements and ICSID arbitration had been dismissed in 1966, but by 2007 the system was exponentially larger and deeply entrenched. "The legal architecture for protection of foreign investment," two specialists observed in 2005, "has changed dramatically." This architecture was built on the logic of discipline. As Jason Webb Yackee says, it was intended to serve as a method of "law-based credible commitment" designed to reassure investors who do not believe that political leaders or national courts will exercise discretion properly.[20]

Like all of the other reforms canvassed in this book, the BIT architecture also had the effect of placing power in the hands of a new class of technocrat-guardians, in this case an elite cadre of individuals who serve as arbitrators or specialize in the representation of investors and states before arbitration panels. (Each party to a dispute typically nominates one member of the three-person arbitration panel; the two nominees then agree on the third arbitrator.) This is a small and closed group, predominantly male and drawn disproportionately from the advanced economies, whose claim to authority is based on the mastery of specialized knowledge. "This is a mafia," in the view of one experienced arbitrator. "It's a mafia because people appoint one another. You always appoint your friends—people you know. It's a mafia because policymaking is done at these gatherings."[21]

Form and Substance

The question, again, is whether these formal–legal reforms had the intended effect—that is, whether they actually succeeded in constraining governmental behavior. The results were varied, both for independent regulators and the BIT architecture.

In Europe, experiments with the IRA model appear to have produced the expected result. In general, according to Mark Thatcher, European regulators "have tended to gain power and importance. They have become key actors in decisions, acquiring expertise, reputations and political weight." And they have largely succeeded in maintaining "relational distance" from ministers and legislators. Political leaders rarely attempt to remove unfriendly regulators or reverse regulatory decisions.[22]

Given, as we shall see in a moment, that the IRA model has failed elsewhere, it is important to ask why it is so well ensconced in Europe. Explanations must reach beyond the language of the law itself. One simple reason may be that Western European countries are not prone to economic or political crises as are many developing economies. A long period of relative stability may give IRAs the opportunity to consolidate their position. Or it might be that European governments and regulators have developed informal methods of dialogue and accommodation that avoid open conflicts and the need for direct challenges to an IRA's autonomy. "If a regulator expects to be politically independent," a British regulator said in 2001, "then he had better adopt some of the habits of politicians."[23]

In Europe, the creation of IRAs is also part of a much larger project of continental integration that is valued not simply because of economic gains, but also as a grand strategy for maintaining peace in the wake of two devastating wars. This fact discourages backsliding as well. Overt challenges to the role of IRAs might be construed as equivocation about the larger project itself. In some sectors—such as telecommunications and electricity— attempts to limit the autonomy of regulators would also contravene directives issued by the EU.

In many sectors, national regulators have formed pan-European networks, often with the encouragement of EU institutions. In this respect they have behaved much like major central banks. For example, energy regulators have their own club, the Council of European of Energy Regulators, a nonprofit organization established in 2000. Similarly, national competition agencies are now connected through the European Competition Network, established in 2002. The explicit function of these networks is to share information and coordinate policy, but the practical effect is to reinforce the autonomy of each regulator from national political leaders. Attempts at political influence can be interpreted as an assault on norms about regulation that have been legitimized by the network.[24]

By contrast, the IRA model has not fared nearly so well outside the advanced economies. Here, the distinction between form and substance has proved to be critically important. An emphasis on the legal attributes of regulators, say Jon Stern and John Cubbin, often causes outside observers to "overstate the quality of regulatory governance, usually by substantial amounts...regulatory *practice* is typically significantly different from what legal provisions would lead one to expect." A 2005 survey by the World Bank reached a similar conclusion. "Formal requirements for integrity, independence, transparency, and accountability...are far from sufficient," the study concluded. "The experience so far raises doubts that governments will observe the spirit of the law and implement proper, consistent regulatory procedures—especially when their choices are influenced (and constrained) by external pressures and loan conditions." In China, Margaret Pearson has observed, "Regulatory independence is constrained by the broader political–institutional context...while impressive changes during the past decade have given the agencies that regulate China's strategic industries the initial *appearance* of independent regulators, the actual *function* of an independent regulatory structure is far from established."[25]

There are many reasons for the fading of early optimism about the feasibility of creating IRAs in developing and transitional economies. In many countries, political executives unaccustomed to checks on their power have continued to interfere with regulatory decision making and to override politically unpopular rulings. In Mexico, for example, Mauricio Dussauge-Laguna has found that formally independent regulators have struggled unsuccessfully to overcome an "administrative tradition" of politicized central control.[26]

Bureaucratic politics also undermined regulatory independence in developing countries. In India and China, ministries with regulatory powers and businesses still under state control resisted the loss of authority to autonomous bodies. Central planners who were still committed to government-guided industrial development were similarly ambivalent about the delegation of authority. Regulatory agencies often had limited resources with which to defend against these assaults. South Africa's telecom regulators, for example, have had "a constant problem to retain vitally needed staff." Latin America's regulators also struggled to cope with the "surge of regulatory problems" in the 1990s. Colombia's telecom regulator had a staff only one-quarter the size of Norway's in 2000, even though the country's population is ten times larger and its telecom system twice as large. ("No one with any sense," concludes Stern, "would expect economic regulation in developing countries to be anything other than very limited in scope and skills.")[27]

The weaknesses of the IRA model became apparent to CMS Energy, the Michigan-based utility, soon after its entry into the Argentinian natural gas industry in the early 1990s. CMS began business in Argentina on the understanding that its gas transmission company could charge customers in U.S. dollars and regularly adjust those fees to keep pace with a U.S.-based inflation index. However, Argentina's economy slumped in the late 1990s, and its new regulatory systems were strained. Throughout 1999 and 2000, ENARGAS refused requests for tariff increases to accommodate changes in the inflation index.

CMS's attempts to negotiate or appeal ENARGAS decisions proved fruit-less. Meanwhile, Argentina slid into a full-blown economic crisis that led to riots and deadly protests over government policies, which President Fernando de la Rúa sought to quell by declaring a state of siege in December 2001. The next month, the Argentinian government adopted an emergency law that reversed the promise that prices charged by companies like CMS could be calculated in U.S. dollars. Tariffs were now fixed in pesos, whose value against U.S. currency decreased by 75 percent over the next eight months. At the end of 2002, CMS reported to its shareholders that the net value of its Argentine investments had dropped by $400 million.[28]

The first commitment device—the independent regulator ENERGAS—had failed, and so CMS turned to the second, making a demand for arbitration by ICSID under the bilateral investment treaty signed by Argentina and the United States in 1991. CMS was not alone. Argentina had been an enthusiastic adopter of BITs, signing similar treaties with fifty-six other countries between 1990 and 2001. By 2004, ICSID was backlogged with investor protests seeking compensation for more than $20 billion from the Argentinian government.[29]

Argentina responded with a broad assault on the BIT regime. It attempted to revive a version of the Calvo Doctrine by asserting that investors could not go to ICSID before they had pursued remedies in Argentinian courts. Next it argued that ICSID had no jurisdiction to review the effect of its 2002 emergency law, which it said was an expression of "general economic policy" rather than a targeted attack on foreign investors. Then it said that Argentina's BIT obligations were trumped by a constitutional duty to protect human rights. And finally it claimed a defense of necessity—that the national emergency was so grave that the government was justified in ignoring its treaty commitments.[30]

In most cases—but not all—the arbitration panels appointed by ICSID rejected these arguments. In 2005, for example, the panel that heard the CMS complaint—a Canadian lawyer, a Brazilian judge, and a Chilean professor—rejected all of these challenges and decided that Argentina should compensate CMS for losses of $133 million. But Argentina refused to pay

CMS or other successful complainants, alleging that ICSID had a "pro-business bias" and insisting that it had no right to judge Argentina's overall economic policy. Argentina's legislature, meanwhile, was pressing for a renunciation of the bilateral investment treaty with the United States as well as the 1966 Washington Convention, which established ICSID's authority to arbitrate disputes.[31]

Other Latin American states also turned against the BIT architecture. In Bolivia, popular anger about perceived exploitation by multinationals resulted in a 2005 law that unilaterally increased the government's share of revenues from energy projects from 18 to 50 percent. In 2006, President Evo Morales deployed the military to seize oil and gas fields and gave multinationals six months to negotiate new contracts on terms even more favorable to the government. Many of these multinationals were from countries that had signed investment treaties with Bolivia, but none demanded arbitration, preferring instead to accept more onerous terms. Still, Bolivia announced plans to renegotiate the twenty BITs it had signed since 1987, and in 2007 it became the first country ever to withdraw from the Washington Convention.[32]

Nicaragua and Venezuela threatened to withdraw from the convention as well, although by 2009 neither had done so. Venezuela also resisted overtures from the United States to negotiate a BIT that would protect the investments of U.S. oil and gas producers. In 2007, the government of President Hugo Chavez issued a decree that unilaterally redefined the terms of its contracts with foreign oil producers and insisted that disputes over compensation could be resolved only by Venezuelan courts. Officials warned that companies that sought arbitration would be excluded from future contracts. As in Bolivia, most investors accepted the new terms.[33]

Ecuador, too, recoiled against the BIT architecture. In 2006, its government seized the assets of Occidental Petroleum, the country's largest U.S. investor. It then launched an unsuccessful effort to deny ICSID's jurisdiction to arbitrate Occidental's complaint under the Ecuador–U.S. BIT. Ecuador's socialist prime minister, Rafael Correa, elected in 2006 on a promise to end "multinational petroleum company abuses," also threatened to repudiate investment treaties with the United States and other countries. In 2008, Ecuador renounced nine BITs and said it would review sixteen others, including its agreement with the United States.[34]

The usefulness of the BIT architecture as a commitment mechanism is obviously undermined when nations rebel against the structure in this way. However, there are less spectacular ways in which the BIT architecture fails as a commitment mechanism. From an investor's point of view, an effective mechanism is one that reduces uncertainty: it defines clear rules for government behavior and provides timely and effective remedies for rule violations. By this standard, the BIT architecture often falls short. The guarantees contained in bilateral investment treaties are sometimes called "clear and well-defined obligations." This might be true compared to the international norms that were relied upon before the invention of BITs, but the commitments contained in these treaties—for example, the promise of "fair and equitable treatment"—are still vaguely worded. This is unavoidable. Even meticulous drafting cannot anticipate all of the contingencies that affect government–investor relationships.[35]

Given the vagueness of the promises themselves, the enforcement procedure becomes critically important as a device for clarifying what the language actually means. "The remedy trumps in practical effectiveness the definition of the right," concludes Thomas Wälde. "The effectiveness of substantive rights [provided in investment treaties] is…linked to the availability of an effective (i.e., independent) enforcement procedure." But arbitration, although preferable from an investor's viewpoint to the host country's courts, is still an imperfect remedy. It is costly and often slow.[36]

A larger difficulty for investors is inconsistency in arbitration decisions. Because arbitration panels do not consider themselves to be bound by previous rulings, as courts are, and because appeal mechanisms are weak, it is not unusual for tribunals to reach different conclusions about the level of protection investors should expect. For example, the arbitration panel that considered the CMS case rejected the Argentinian government's claim that its actions were justified as emergency measures, but another arbitration panel hearing a complaint filed by another investor, LG&E Energy, accepted the same claim. An appeals panel acknowledged the inconsistency but said it lacked authority to reconcile the decisions.[37]

Another vivid example of inconsistency arose in 1999 when American businessman Ronald Lauder sought arbitration under the U.S.–Czech BIT over the alleged misbehavior of the government of the Czech Republic. Lauder argued that Czech officials had manipulated media regulations in ways that reduced the value of his investment in the republic's first privately owned television station. (In its early days, the station thrived on an "attention-grabbing schedule of nude weather forecasts and Baywatch re-runs.") At the same time, Lauder's investment vehicle—a Dutch corporation— sought arbitration of the dispute under the Netherlands–Czech BIT. In 2001, the two arbitration panels reached conclusions that were diametrically opposed on most key issues—one deciding that the Czech Republic was obliged to pay damages, the other absolving it of responsibility. An appeals body again said it lacked authority to reconcile the two decisions.[38]

Czech authorities were frustrated. The conflict between the two decisions "brings the law into disrepute, it brings arbitration into disrepute," a Czech official complained. "The whole thing is highly regrettable." But the inconsistency is equally troubling for those in business because the BIT architecture failed to accomplish its primary aim of reducing uncertainty about the treatment of foreign investment. And the Lauder cases were not anomalous: inconsistency plagued the interpretation of other key provisions in bilateral investment treaties. Better appeal procedures might improve uniformity in arbitration decisions but at the price of added delay. The advantage of arbitration was supposed to be that it provided quick and clear answers about investor–state disputes.[39]

Problems of Legitimacy

Inconsistency in decisionmaking also contributed to public discontent with the BIT architecture, because it required governments to compensate investors even when the legal basis of their claim was disputed by another ICSID arbitration panel. This was an awkwardness faced by the Argentinian government in the CMS case and Czech government in the Lauder case.

This was only one of the ways the legitimacy of the BIT architecture was strained. These mechanisms for resolving investment disputes have been described as a system of "offshore justice." ICSID tribunals, it is said, "essentially act as international investment courts." But this arbitration system is not modeled on the judicial system of any established democracy. Instead, it is based on older systems for the resolution of commercial, and sometimes diplomatic, disputes. In critical respects the procedures for resolving investment disputes do not conform to popular understandings about the ways in which justice should be dispensed.[40]

Consider, for example, the principle of transparency. In most democracies, it is well established that the pleadings of parties, oral arguments, and judicial decisions should be publicly accessible except in rare circumstances. The credibility of judicial system is understood to depend on openness. As a U.S. federal court said in 2001: "While we deliberate in private, we recognize the fundamental importance of issuing public decisions after public arguments based on public records. The political branches of government claim legitimacy by election, judges by reason. Any step that withdraws an element of the judicial process from public view makes the ensuing decision look more like fiat, which requires compelling justification."[41]

By contrast, commercial and diplomatic arbitration has traditionally operated on the presumption of confidentiality. For decades the Washington Convention was interpreted to require closed hearings, and a ban on publication of tribunal decisions without the consent of both parties, "as a matter of principle." In 2006 ICSID edged toward greater transparency, giving tribunals the discretion to open hearings unless one of the parties objects. It also promised to release excerpts of the legal reasoning of a tribunal if either party blocks publication of the whole decision. (However, the pleadings of parties remain confidential.) ICSID's revised rules constitute progress toward transparency, but still fall short of the standards imposed on national courts in established democracies. In addition, citizens and non-governmental groups face practical barriers to accessibility for hearings that are often held thousands of miles from the capital of the country in which the investment was made.[42]

The method of selecting arbitrators also creates problems of legitimacy. The advanced-economy slant of the arbitration community, although not so pronounced as it once was, fuels perceptions in developing countries that the arbitration process is biased in favor of investors. Checks against conflict of interest are also relatively weak. To assure independence, judges in national courts are usually given long tenure and fixed salary, and barred from pursuing other work that might create real or perceived conflicts of interest. Arbitrators, by contrast, have neither tenure nor fixed salary: they compete for the right to work on a case-by-case basis. And precisely because they are not permanent appointees, arbitrators usually have other professional commitments—as advisors to governments or investors, or as appointees to corporate boards—that can create real or perceived conflicts. Rules to assure impartiality, although stronger than they once were, are still relatively weak.[43]

If the rules contained in investment treaties were relatively narrow, these procedural defects might not matter so much. But in many cases the impact of investment treaties can be very broad. This was illustrated in the Tecmed case, the subject of an ICSID arbitration concluded in 2003. Tecmed was a Spanish company that acquired a hazardous waste landfill from the municipality of Hermosillo, Mexico in 1996. The following year a new mayor was elected, and a citizens' movement began to protest the environmental impact of the landfill. In 1998, authorities refused to renew Tecmed's permit, shutting the landfill down. Tecmed alleged unfair treatment, in violation of the

Spanish-Mexican BIT. An ICSID arbitration panel agreed and awarded Tecmed five million dollars in damages.

The Tecmed dispute was problematic because it was not a conventional case about seizure of assets. This was regulatory action that was justified by elected officials as a measure necessary to protect public health. But in the view of the arbitrators, this was outweighed by the fact that municipal authorities had behaved erratically, making a permitting decision that was inconsistent with the policies that prevailed when Tecmed made its investment. Foreign investors, the arbitrators ruled, had a right to expect that municipal authorities would "act in a consistent manner, free from ambiguity and totally transparently."

Put aside the irony of a complaint by an arbitration panel about inconsistency and opacity in decisionmaking. The predicament is that this demand for consistency collides with the right of a community to make choices about policy. What if the aroused citizenry of Hermosillo had simply decided that the operation of Tecmed's landfill was no longer tolerable? The arbitration panel doubted that this was the case, challenging evidence that there was broad concern about the landfill. (The protests included a six-month sit-in at Hermosillo's city hall.) The opposition, it said, was "intense, aggressive and sustained" but not "massive": despite "an active and continuous and public campaign in the mass media," there were never more than a few hundred protesters at the landfill's gates. There was no "genuine social crisis," the panel decided, and in the absence of this, Tecmed was entitled to compensation.[44]

The implications of the Tecmed decision are substantial, because it implies that governments will be constrained from changing policies that harm foreign investors unless they can make a compelling case about the need of change. The case illustrates the extent to which investment treaties can become mechanisms for "clipping the sovereignty" of popularly elected governments. But if arbitration panels assume such a substantial role in determining the content of public policy, then complaints about the defects in their own procedures take on more weight. As Barnali Choudhury observes, "A system that curtails democratic principles ... by removing issues that directly affect citizens to a system that is inaccessible and structurally isolated from public input, creates a democratic deficit."[45]

The same argument is made against independent regulatory agencies. Many specialists who have charted the rise of IRAs have recognized that they pose a challenge to traditional understandings about the way in which public authority should be organized. "We could now be experiencing a transformation from representative democracy to indirect representative democracy," says David Levi-Faur. "Democratic governance is no longer about the delegation of authority to elected representatives but a form of second-level representative democracy—citizens elect representatives who control and supervise 'experts' who formulate and administer policies in an autonomous fashion from their regulatory bastions." This is a hopeful view because it implies that experts within these "regulatory bastions" are still supervised by elected officials. Skeptics question the ability to exercise oversight and claim that the transfer of power to IRAs contributes to a democratic deficit as well.[46]

This is not a new issue. The United States was a forerunner in creating independent regulatory agencies during the Progressive and New Deal eras, and engaged in the same debate about the threat to democratic values. By the 1940s it was commonplace for critics of the new regulatory authorities to rail against the emergence of a "headless fourth branch" within US government that "[does] violence to the basic theory of the American Constitution." The independent agencies, critics complained, enjoyed power without responsibility. But over the next quarter-century, legislators developed sophisticated mechanisms for taming regulators. This consisted largely of new rules that dictated how their power could be exercised—for example, by requiring disclosure of proposed policies; opportunities for public comment before decisions were taken; and clearly-stated reasons for actions. Courts also became more aggressive in policing regulatory agencies to ensure that they stayed within their statutory mandates and obeyed these procedural requirements.[47]

Europe's more recently established regulatory agencies have gone through a similar adaptation. Newly established regulators were often criticized for closed decisionmaking but eventually adopted many of the techniques used by their US counterparts. European regulators have learned to disclose more information about their decisionmaking processes and allow more opportunities for regulated industries and civic organizations to comment on proposed actions. Some took measures to bolster the capacity of consumer groups to participate in regulatory deliberations. European courts have also become more willing to overturn regulatory decisions that are poorly reasoned or inconsistent with an agency's mandate.[48]

In Europe there is guarded optimism that such reforms will provide an adequate check on regulatory power and cloak IRAs with a form of "procedural legitimacy." For example, a British parliamentary committee concluded in 2004 that there was no inevitable conflict between autonomy and legitimacy so long as regulators establish "effective processes for achieving accountability... [a] duty to explain; exposure to scrutiny; and the possibility of independent review." In a sense, these procedural reforms can be regarded as accommodation of two impulses—one toward discipline, the other toward popular sovereignty. And in a significant sense they constitute a compromise of the idea of regulatory autonomy. These procedural reforms allow other actors—consumers, advocacy groups, rival industries—to "enter the 'regulatory space'", as Mark Thatcher puts it. They effectively limit an agency's freedom of movement. Regulators gain legitimacy by ceding influence within their domain.[49]

In other regions, such checks on regulatory power are less developed. Many poorer countries lack administrative procedure laws that impose requirements for disclosure, public comment, or reason-giving. Norms of fairness or transparency in administrative decisionmaking may also be poorly established. The possibility of obtaining judicial remedies against regulatory misconduct is also diminished if the court system itself is understaffed or politicized. Procedural legitimacy for regulators thus remains more elusive. Of course the same is true for arbitration panels established under bilateral investment treaties. The complaints made about defects in arbitration processes mirror those made against independent regulators.[50]

The Limits of Law-Based Commitment

These two reform movements—one dedicated to the construction of independent regulators, the other to the construction of the BIT architecture—were largely disconnected from one another. But the ideas which they advanced were closely related. Both deployed the logic of discipline. Constraints were to be imposed on errant politicians whose decisionmaking was unpredictable, short-sighted, and self-serving. Discipline would be imposed because foreign investors required stability and evenhandedness. The means by which discipline would be imposed was through legal transformation—either through *de jure* independence for regulators, or by treaties establishing new super-courts. These were mechanisms for "law-based commitment," to borrow Jason Webb-Yackee's phrase.

By the end of the era of liberalization there were clear signs of exhaustion within both of these reform movements. Some skeptics began to complain about IRA fetishism—that is, an irrational enthusiasm for the creation of independent regulators even in the most unfriendly conditions, such as those in developing countries. Perhaps, they suggested, there were better ways of providing the substantive assurances about clarity and stability demanded by foreign investors. There was a similar reaction against "invest-ment treaty mania." The evidence that BITs played an important role in attracting foreign investment was still equivocal. And it also seemed possible to imagine other ways of allaying investor concerns about mistreatment—"a world without BITs."[51]

These hesitations were signs of a growing recognition of the limits of the logic of discipline. As a practical matter, there were clearly circumstances in which these techniques of law-based commitment was infeasible: that is, they could not be made to work. Some more complicated story about the pre-conditions for effective legal reform was clearly necessary—some account of "the broader political-institutional context," as Margaret Pearson calls it. At the same time, some kind of story had to be told about why these legal forms should be regarded as defensible in a democratic system. This second problem was closely tied to the first. The inability to defend the legit-imacy of a reform also jeopardized its viability.

The logic of discipline had little to say about either of these questions. The naive-institutionalist view of reform did not know how to anticipate the many factors that affected the durability of formal-legal changes, and did not offer techniques for legitimating those innovations. If the logic of disci-pline worked, it was because something else—a favorable set of conditions, or modifications to assure legitimacy—had been added to it. In short, there was more to the attainment of discipline in practice than was accounted for within the logic of discipline itself.

Devils in the Details

Long-Term Infrastructure Contracts

7

We have an infrastructure crisis. . . . In politics, winning elections
and protecting a party majority is more important than solving
problems. So short-term pork invariably wins over long-term
investing. . . . That's the disconnect that gets so many elected
officials unwilling to make commitments for long-term projects,
and most infrastructure is long-term.

—*New York City mayor Michael Bloomberg, 2008*

The infrastructure crisis that was said to confront many countries throughout the era of liberalization included worries about the adequacy of mainports and utilities that we discussed in chapters 5 and 6. It also reached
further—to the supply and condition of every hard asset traditionally used
by government: schools, hospitals, prisons, government offices, computer
systems, roads, bridges, and tunnels. Before the era of liberalization, such
assets were usually financed and built by government itself. During the era of
liberalization, however, many governments experimented with a new method
of infrastructure development: the long-term infrastructure contract. A powerful commercial lobby pushed for its use, but this innovation proved just as
problematic as many of the others promoted under the logic of discipline.

To be precise, there were two distinct infrastructure crises. The predicament of the advanced economies was less severe. These countries went
through a period of rapid economic growth and urbanization in the quarter
century that followed the Second World War. This transformation created
an enormous need for new infrastructure. The United States, for example,

built one million miles of paved roads between 1950 and 1970. Annual investment in sewer and water systems increased fourfold to keep pace with residential and business construction. The capacity of elementary and secondary schools doubled while that of universities and colleges tripled. Office buildings were constructed to house the seven million civilian workers added to the public sector payroll in these two decades.[1]

As a result of this boom, most advanced economies had a substantial endowment of high-quality infrastructure by the early 1970s. But at this point, public spending on infrastructure began a steady decline. Expenditure on welfare-state programs (pensions, health care, education, and aid to the poor) began to claim a larger share of government budgets. Deficits grew, and so did popular resistance to tax increases. Reduced infrastructure spending became a relatively easy way to ease budget pressures because the consequences were not immediately evident. In the United States, capital investment by the public sector declined from 5 percent in the mid-1960s to about 3 percent by the 1990s. European governments made similar cuts (fig. 7.1.).

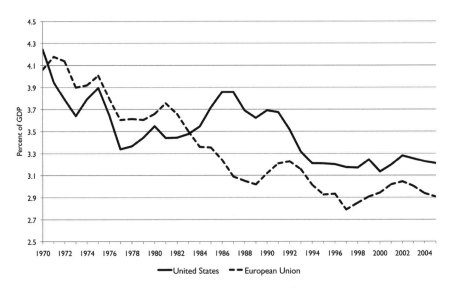

Figure 7.1 Public investment in major EU countries and the United States, 1970–2005.

Public investment is computed as government fixed capital formation as a percentage of GDP. Data for EU is an unweighted average for Austria, Belgium, Greece, Finland, France, Germany, Ireland, Italy, Luxembourg (from 1977), Netherlands, Portugal (from 1990), and Spain.

Source: Roland Straub and Ivan Tchakarov, *Assessing the impact of a change in the composition of public spending*, IMF Working Paper No. 07/168, July (Washington, DC: IMF, 2007), 37.

The result was a steady fall in the total value of publicly owned infrastructure relative to GDP in most advanced economies.[2]

By the turn of the millennium, the consequences of this decline were becoming more obvious. It was widely accepted, as a bipartisan task force reported in 2008, that the United States faced an infrastructure crisis manifested in overloaded roads, water and power systems, schools, and hospitals. "Aging and overburdened infrastructure," concluded another report by the American Society of Civil Engineers, "threatens the economy and quality of life in every state, city and town in the nation." The danger was illustrated by the collapse of an aging interstate highway bridge in Minnesota in 2007. Comparable concerns about the decline of infrastructure were voiced in the major economies of Western Europe.[3]

The second infrastructure crisis—faced by developing countries—is more serious. In a sense it reprises the advanced economies' challenge of 1950–1970, only on a vastly larger scale. It is estimated that between 2000 and 2030 the urban population of less developed countries will increase by two billion people. This is seven times the increase in urban population in the developed world in the postwar period. Per capita GDP in the advanced economies grew at an annual rate of 3.8 percent between 1950 and 1973. But the two largest developing economies—India and China—grew at twice this rate in the last years of the era of liberalization. In 2007, the Indian government estimated that it would need to double its annual spending on infrastructure to roughly one-tenth of GDP to maintain this level of economic growth.[4]

For many developing countries, such an increase in public infrastructure spending seems impossible to attain. On the contrary, the drive to demonstrate fiscal discipline throughout the era of liberalization usually caused a reduction in capital spending, just as it did in the advanced economies. Public investment "bore the brunt of fiscal adjustment" in many poorer countries, a World Bank study has observed. "Politically, these [investments] were much easier to cut than current expenditures." In Latin America, for example, public investment declined by fifty percent between 1988 and 1998.[5]

The most popular solution to these crises has been the enlistment of private capital to finance the development of infrastructure. According to the consulting firm Deloitte Touche Tohmatsu, there has been "a paradigm shift…[a] revolution…in how governments provide infrastructure." Deloitte is not impartial; one of its own ambitions is to mediate the relationship between governments and private investors. But Deloitte is not alone in thinking that there has been "a sea-change in the infrastructure paradigm."

The infrastructure boom of 1950–1970 was largely a public venture. By contrast, private capital was expected to solve infrastructure crises in the era of liberalization.[6]

This "sea-change" was not driven just by financially distressed governments. The transformation of capital markets played a part as well. The elimination of restrictions on foreign investment made it possible for advanced-economy investors to contemplate financing infrastructure projects abroad. Also, rules for large institutional investors in the advanced economies were loosened to allow investment in infrastructure projects. A resulting irony is that government employees of advanced economies—through their pension funds—became major stakeholders in privately provided public services abroad, even while their unions protested privatization at home. For example, public sector teachers in the province of Ontario, Canada, had about one-tenth of their retirement savings invested in privately financed infrastructure projects in 2007.[7]

Investor enthusiasm for infrastructure projects varied throughout the era of liberalization, but shortly before the financial crisis of 2007–2009 the mood was bullish. "Banks and private investment firms have fallen in love with public infrastructure," Business Week reported in 2007. "They're smitten by rich cash flows...and the monopolistic advantages that keep those cash flows as steady as a beating heart." More than seventy new funds were established in 2006–2007 to invest in the infrastructure industry. By 2007, the world's twenty largest infrastructure funds had $130 billion under management, mostly raised in the preceding two years. The stock prices of major firms directly engaged in infrastructure projects more than doubled between 2003 and 2007 (fig. 7.2).[8]

The era of liberalization also witnessed the emergence of a new class of global corporations focused exclusively on infrastructure provision. Most of these enterprises grew rapidly through mergers and acquisitions of other firms. The global water industry, for example, is dominated by two French firms—Suez Environnement and Veolia Environnement. The Spanish company Cintra is now a major investor in toll highways throughout Europe and North America while the Anglo–Dutch firm G4S emerged as a global operator of detention facilities and prisons. American health care firms now compete to operate facilities in the United Kingdom, and British utilities have become major operators of electricity infrastructure in the United States.[9]

Together, investors and operators formed the core of a powerful lobby for private provision of infrastructure. They were joined by financiers and lawyers who negotiated infrastructure deals. The Washington-based National Council for Public–Private Partnerships, established in 1985 to advocate

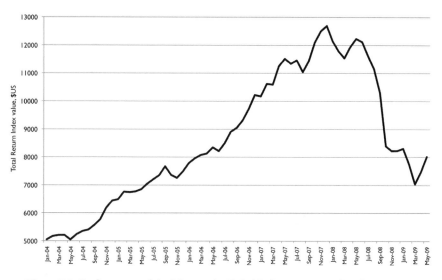

Figure 7.2 Performance of the Macquarie Global Infrastructure Index, from inception at December 2003 to May 2009.

The index "is designed to reflect the stock performance of companies within the infrastructure industry, principally those engaged in the management, ownership and or operation of infrastructure and utility assets."

Data Source: FTSE Group: http://www.ftse.com/Indices/Macquarie_Global_Infrastructure_Index_Series

for privately operated infrastructure, was supported by firms such as Bechtel Infrastructure and Veolia Environnement, the investment bank Lehman Brothers (until its failure in 2008), and the libertarian Reason Foundation. In 1993, Canada acquired a similar industry-supported advocacy group, the Canadian Council for Public–Private Partnerships. In the United Kingdom, the promotional role was assumed by Partnerships UK, a company established in 2000 to counsel public agencies on infrastructure privatization.[10]

In the developing world, advocates of private financing found powerful allies within the World Bank and International Monetary Fund. Both institutions began actively promoting the virtues of private financing in the 1980s and 1990s. In 1999, the World Bank collaborated with the British and Japanese governments to establish the Public–Private Infrastructure Advisory Facility to help developing countries "tap the full potential of private involvement in infrastructure."[11]

There was, therefore, a powerful combination of interests that favored the expansion of private provision of infrastructure: financially stressed governments, liberated investors, a new set of globalized operators, and lobby and advisory groups ready to mediate among them.

Long-Term Infrastructure Contracts

One of the main devices for enlisting private capital was the long-term infrastructure contract or LTIC. These contracts were negotiated between governments and private operators of infrastructure. LTICs varied widely in structure, but they usually obligated the private operator to find its own financing for construction of an asset and to maintain the asset in good condition for the whole its life. Sometimes governments would make periodic payments to the private operator for use of the asset, and sometimes the private operator would be allowed to recoup costs by levying charges for services (highway tolls, for example) directly on users. These latter projects were sometimes said to be financially freestanding. LTICs differed from conventional government contracts in several ways. The deals often ran for several decades, were highly complex, and put private operators in charge of activities that were once thought to be at the core of the public sector.

Among the advanced economies, the United Kingdom was the most systematic in applying the LTIC model. Like other countries, the United Kingdom experienced a sharp fall in public investment after 1973. In 1992, the Conservative government of Prime Minister John Major announced the launch of its Private Finance Initiative, or PFI, a program which the government said would use LTICs to "unlock new resources and...increasingly replace old style public sector capital spending." PFI signaled "a dramatic shift from the general presumption against the use of private finance" in infrastructure. In the last five years of Conservative rule (until 1997), public spending on infrastructure declined further as the U.K. government experimented with privately operated prisons, hospitals, schools, roads, bridges, and information technology systems.[12]

The Labour government of Prime Minister Tony Blair applied PFI even more aggressively. Determined to increase infrastructure investment, but equally determined not to frighten international financial markets, the Labour government promised to "reinvigorate" PFI by removing obstacles to the execution of new contracts. Over the next decade, the British government negotiated more than six hundred PFI contracts that were expected to result in private investment exceeding £50 billion. In some policy sectors, such as health, PFI contracts accounted for most new capital expenditure.[13]

Governments in other countries emulated the United Kingdom's program of using LTICs to attract private finance. They often set up special offices—as the United Kingdom had—to recruit investors and remove bureaucratic roadblocks. But even where the initiative was not centrally guided, as it was in the United Kingdom, the use of LTICs to rehabilitate or build public infrastructure grew steadily throughout the era of liberalization.[14]

The Logic of Discipline at Work

The enthusiasm for long-term infrastructure contracts provided more evidence of the logic of discipline at work. As with other efforts at autonomization, the LTIC model was premised on the assumption that political leaders too often used public services as tools for rewarding supporters—by padding payrolls, for example, or giving subcontracts to unqualified allies—at the cost of operational effectiveness. In theory, the transfer of infrastructure responsibilities to a contractor would help to "remove undue political interference in service provision." The contract would "drive a wedge between politicians and managers."[15]

A more specific claim was made about the inability of civil servants to execute infrastructure projects properly. Partly this was an argument about the advantages enjoyed by highly specialized infrastructure operators over bureaucrats for whom the execution of a large infrastructure project may be a unusual event. But an argument was also advanced about the difference in incentives confronting infrastructure managers in the public and private sectors. Bureaucrats, it was argued, rarely pay a high price for failing to meet promises on project performance; similarly they rarely receive substantial rewards when promises are kept. Contractors, by contrast, have "high-powered incentives" to meet their promises because of the penalties and rewards that are laid out in the contract.[16]

LTICs are also viewed as devices for dealing with the shortsightedness of conventional budget decision making. Experience suggests that politicians and bureaucrats who are under fiscal pressure will squeeze spending on maintenance of assets to protect other programs whose benefits are more immediately obvious to constituents. But this tactic causes assets to deteriorate more quickly than they should. An LTIC serves as a kind of commitment mechanism: it requires government to pay the operator for maintenance expenses that it knows ought to be incurred but which it would otherwise be tempted to avoid. Long-term maintenance appears to be "locked-in." As a study of the United Kingdom's PFI project observes: "We would expect to walk into a PFI hospital or school in twenty years' time and find a well maintained asset still performing to the original specification. We would not have the same level of confidence if the asset had been conventionally procured."[17]

LTICs also seem to correct a second kind of shortsightedness. Sometimes governments may want to pay for infrastructure with new charges levied on the users of that infrastructure. If a project is government-run, elected officials may face continual pressure to reduce or eliminate those charges, in which case the overall fiscal position of the government is compromised: it ends up with greater costs but not greater revenue. A financially freestanding LTIC—one that allows the private operator to collect and spend tolls—seems to fix this problem by binding political leaders to a revenue scheme they could not sustain on their own. Voters might protest the signing of the LTIC itself, but this is a one-off battle rather than an ongoing struggle over charges. Once the contract is signed, government's hands again appear to be tied.[18]

All of these arguments about the virtues of LTICs hinge on an assumption about the power of contracts to constrain the behavior of governments and private operators. For example, private operators may not face high-powered incentives if the performance requirements contained in contracts are not enforced. Similarly, governments are not locked-in to long-term commitments on maintenance spending or user charges if they can find ways of abrogating their contractual obligations. Early advocates of LTICs tended to minimize these difficulties. In this sense they reflected the naive institutionalist's faith in the efficacy of legal instruments in shaping governmental behavior.

Fiscal Illusions

With experience, many observers came to realize that the LTIC model suffered from several weaknesses. One immediate problem had to do with the claim that LTICs serve as commitment devices that constrain shortsighted governments.

Consider, for example, a situation in which a government already operates infrastructure—a highway, perhaps—and collects tolls for its use. Suppose that the government signs a contract that simply transfers the highway and the right to collect tolls to a private operator and that in return the government receives a substantial one-time payment. Imagine that elected officials use that payment to cover the cost of immediate benefits to their constituents. This arrangement is not really concerned with countering the tendency of elected officials to neglect long-term infrastructure development. On the contrary, it is doing something very shortsighted: it is selling a physical asset and an existing revenue stream to finance current consumption.

We can imagine a more severe variation of this example, in which the up-front payment is inflated, with the expectation that the private operator will recoup the increased cost by charging higher tolls later on. In this case, the LTIC becomes a device for financing increased current consumption by creating heavier liabilities for future generations.

A financially freestanding LTIC works as a commitment mechanism only when it binds the government to a path it would not pursue otherwise—that is, the collection of new revenues that are used for the development of infrastructure. Determining whether LTICs actually work in this way sometimes requires detailed scrutiny of their terms. But there is evidence that recent infrastructure contracts have not been rigorously structured to serve this purpose. For example, the State of Illinois received an up-front $1.8 billion from the sale in 2004 of the Chicago Skyway to a partnership of Spain's Abertis Infrastructure and the U.S. Citi financial group while Indiana received $3.8 billion for the 2006 sale of the Indiana Toll Road to a consortium of the Spanish firm Cintra and Australia's Macquarie Infrastructure. In both cases, elected officials used some of the proceeds to fund immediate financial needs. A 2008 review by the Government Accountability Office questioned whether the two deals had been strictly designed to "provide long-term benefits to future generations."[19]

There is another sense in which LTICs might be a tool for escaping rather than achieving discipline. One of the main features of these contracts is that the money borrowed for infrastructure is generally regarded as a liability of the private operator rather than the government. Public debt does not increase; consequently, governments do not worry about falling out of compliance with fiscal rules or about market judgments of its overall creditworthiness. However, this is an illusion because the government is contractually bound to make a decades-long series of payments. It is just that the present value of these obligations is not recognized in the government's accounts. If these long-term obligations *were* recognized, governments might be compelled to make harder choices between current expenditure and long-term investment to keep in compliance with fiscal rules.[20]

Complaints about the manipulation of public accounts dogged the United Kingdom's Private Finance Initiative. Critics alleged that PFI was mainly a device for avoiding the government's self-imposed budget constraints and that the Labour government was building a "fiscal time bomb" by signing contracts whose total consequences were never properly tallied. The U.K. government eventually responded by providing more information about its cumulative long-term commitments under PFI contracts. In 2008, it finally agreed to abide by new accounting standards that require PFI debt to be shown on the government's accounts. As one commentator said shortly before advent of the credit crisis in late 2008, this change alone would have caused a breach of the Labour government's fiscal rules and eliminated "one of the main advantages of the PFI from the point of view of the Treasury."[21]

In several countries, the desire to keep infrastructure debt off government accounts created incentives to misrepresent the benefits of the LTICs. Accounting standards usually stipulated that the private operators' debt could only be excluded from government accounts if it could be shown that significant project risks were being transferred to the operators. The aim of these standards was precisely to avoid the use of contractors as a channel for covert accumulation of government debt. But the effect was to create strong incentives for governments to overstate the amount of risk that is actually transferred to contractors. In the United Kingdom, for example, government officials were sometimes embarrassed by private operators who refinanced their projects on more favorable terms soon after contracts had been concluded—a signal that lenders found the projects to be much less risky than government officials had claimed.[22]

By obscuring total indebtedness, LTICs helped to maintain an illusion of fiscal discipline. That illusion was kept up also when governments set up privately financed projects that rely on user charges rather than a stream of payments from government itself. It was sometimes claimed that these financially freestanding projects provided infrastructure "at little or no cost to taxpayers." But this was another bookkeeping trick: obviously some taxpayers pay the charges that are levied by the private operator. That payments are not going into the government's coffers does not diminish the extent to which citizens are out of pocket. There might be virtue in concentrating the cost of projects on users, but society as a whole does not get something for nothing.[23]

Disrupting Accountability

Widespread adoption of the LTIC model also led to a second problem: the weakening of processes for popular oversight of public services. As Paul Maltby and Tim Gosling have observed about the British experiment with

LTICs, the shift of responsibility for infrastructure to the private sector "clearly disrupt[ed] the traditional model of accountability" for public services. A chronic complaint was the secrecy that often surrounded LTICs, undermining the capacity of legislators and other watchdogs to monitor the government-contractor relationship.[24]

This is another instance in which two broad trends in governmental reform collided. For advocates of democratization, one of the most important developments of the past three decades has been the strengthening of policies designed to improve transparency in government. "Open government," according to a 2005 OECD report, "is increasingly recognized to be an essential ingredient for democratic governance." Over seventy governments adopted laws modeled on the U.S. Freedom of Information Act during the era of liberalization. The United Kingdom's own version of the U.S. law was adopted in 2000. The Blair government said it was intended to counter the "excessive secrecy [that] has become a corrosive influence in the decline of public confidence."[25]

However, the demand for openness was not easily reconciled with the shift to private financing of infrastructure. Governments often refused to release contracts for the operation of prisons, highways, hospitals, and other services, claiming they were bound by promises to protect the commercial interests of private operators. In Scotland, an investigator responsible for examining complaints about a privately financed toll bridge was "stunned" to learn that he could not see the document that allowed the bridge operators to levy tolls "because [these] things were allegedly commercially confidential." Critics complained that the private agencies responsible for rating the private operators' debt were given more information about contracts than were legislators. Governments often acquiesced to private operators' demands for secrecy because disclosure would heighten their own accountability for the terms of an LTIC or its enforcement.[26]

Excessive secrecy undermined the ability of legislators, auditors, and advocacy groups to challenge the terms of contracts or monitor the performance of private operators. "Few Members of Parliament understand the deals being done," an Australian critic lamented in 2006. "Our MPs apparently support these deals on blind trust." Secretiveness also weakened the legitimacy of private financing as a device for infrastructure development, fueling public suspicion that the real concern was "the welfare of the private sector...[and establishment of] a new and inescapable form of corporate control." Lack of transparency is cited as a primary reason for the collapse of public support for privatized service delivery in Latin America.[27]

The threat to accountability did not come from secrecy alone. Legislators and nongovernmental groups also lacked the resources or skills needed to inspect contracts or monitor operators. LTICs can easily incorporate hundreds of pages of "mind-numbing detail." In 2002, it was estimated that contractual documentation for the PFI arrangement to overhaul London's underground extended to about three thousand pages or two million words—"and growing all the time as further complexities and issues of potential contention emerge." This was four times the length of the King James Bible.[28]

Limits of Contract

A third problem with LTICs was an overestimation of the capacity of contracts to bind governments and private operators. In fact, contracts proved to be highly malleable. Contractual terms could be neglected or renegotiated and often were. In such cases, governments were not locked-in to long-term commitments, and contractors did not face "high-powered incentives" to perform well.

The Skye Bridge project, one of the first undertaken under the U.K. Private Finance Initiative, illustrated the limitations of LTICs as a commitment mechanism. Opened in 1995, this toll bridge is the only road connection between the Scottish mainland and the Isle of Skye. The project initially became controversial when an audit showed that the decision to rely on private borrowing from the Bank of America, rather than government borrowing, added £4 million in financing charges to a project with a total cost of only £28 million. But more trouble was caused by the tolls themselves. Political opposition to the charges grew quickly, and in 1997 the U.K. government agreed to subsidize a reduction in tolls. In 1999, responsibility for the bridge shifted to the newly formed Scottish Parliament, whose leaders quickly agreed on the need for more drastic action. The bridge was purchased by the Scottish government in 2004, and tolls were immediately eliminated.[29]

At first, the U.K. government's 1991 contract for construction of the Skye bridge seemed to lock in a new revenue stream that would finance a badly needed piece of infrastructure. But the binding effect of contract was overestimated. As political costs mounted, elected leaders could not hold to the 1991 commitment. In the end, the bridge became a governmental liability—larger than it would have been without the experiment of private financing and no longer accompanied by a new revenue stream to pay for it.

A more famous case of governmental reversal occurred in Cochabamba, a city of one-half million in central Bolivia. Cochabamba's publicly run water utility was poorly maintained and unequal to the demands of the growing city. In 1999, the Bolivian government negotiated an agreement that gave a multinational consortium led by the American firm Bechtel a forty-year contract to repair and expand the water system with the cost of improvements to be recouped by new user charges. The privatization, which had been encouraged by the World Bank, was ratified in a law passed by the Bolivian government.

Residents of Cochabamba rebelled against a 35 percent increase in water charges and attempts by the consortium to stop service to nonpayers. By January 2000, the city's central plaza was the center of massive demonstrations. The city became a flashpoint for protests by workers and students angered by the economic shock that they claimed had been forced on Colombia by the International Monetary Fund and World Bank. Protestor and police violence spread beyond Cochabamba, and in April 2000 Colombian president Hugo Banzer declared a state of siege.

The Water War, as it became known, attracted international attention. Meanwhile, Bolivia's political leadership began to retreat from their commitments to the consortium. Project managers fled Cochabamba after police said their safety could not be guaranteed. The Bolivian government then announced that the concession had been abandoned and that, as a consequence, the contract would be revoked. Control over Cochabamba's water supply was returned to a state agency, fees were reversed, and a new law was adopted that affirmed the priority of "social needs" in water supply.[30]

The example of Cochabamba was only one of many instances of governments attempting to unwind their agreements with private investors. The mayor of Limeira, Brazil, revolted against a multinational consortium that had negotiated a contract with his predecessor, refusing to approve fee increases stipulated in the contract. The regional government of Pernambuco, Brazil, unilaterally cut fees for a toll road concession shortly before elections. In Tucuman, Argentina, a newly elected government also reneged on water charges that had been agreed by its predecessor. In 2008, the Indian government pressed the operators of the newly opened Hyderabad and Bangalore airports to reduce user fees that were authorized by contracts it had signed just three years earlier.[31]

It is possible that private operators were sometimes caught off guard by the unanticipated consequences of pressures for democratization that also operated throughout the era of liberalization. For example, the public campaign against the Skye bridge was ultimately successful because the U.K.

Labour government devolved power to a new Scottish Parliament— a move that it promoted as a way of extending "democratic control" over public services. Similar contradictions were evident in developing countries. "[T]he number of informal stakeholders activated and mobilized in opposition to privatization and private participation in infrastructure has skyrocketed," one analyst observed in 2005. "[W]ith the spread of democratic values and a steady growth in disposable income, these people came to feel more empowered than before, to express interests and opposition in socially and politically sensitive areas." At the same time, and as the Cochabamba dispute clearly showed, technological change enabled the emergence of globalized civil society networks that could transform local conflicts between private operators and their customers into international phenomena.[32]

LTICs also proved to have limitations as mechanisms for controlling the behavior of private operators. The assumption had been that operators would face strong incentives to manage projects well because of the penalties and rewards laid out in the contract. But this assumed that governments would enforce contractual terms rigorously when performance targets were not met.

In fact, there was substantial evidence from both developed and developing countries that governments balked at enforcing contracts rigorously. In the United Kingdom, contractors acquired a "very powerful position" because government officials were reluctant to bear the political and administrative costs associated with litigation or termination of contracts. Government agencies, a British parliamentary committee asserted in 2003, were "too willing to bail out PFI contractors who get into trouble." An independent commission established to review the British experience with private financing agreed, noting "an apparent asymmetry in risk allocation between the public and private sectors. When things go right the private sector appears able to make significant financial gains. When things go wrong it sometimes appears to be difficult for the public purchaser to impose very significant penalties on the private contractors." Reviews of North American projects also found that contractors could exploit the "political imperative to prevent projects from terminating."[33]

Privately financed infrastructure projects in the developing world were similarly marred by a "troubling pattern of failure and renegotiation." In Latin America and the Caribbean, roughly forty percent of contracts made between 1985 and 2000 for services in the water, transport, and electricity sectors were renegotiated. A separate study of privately financed highway projects in Latin America found that "the promised benefits of highway privatization failed to materialize" largely because of "the continuous renegotiation of franchise contracts." Similarly, a study of privately financed power projects in developing countries determined that most agreements were renegotiated.[34]

Contract renegotiations often favored the private operator rather than government by allowing delays in proposed investment, decreases in payments directly to government, or increases in tariffs. Sometimes renegotiations were provoked by economic shocks that undermined the viability of projects. But contractors also exploited the fact that governments were reluctant to risk the interruption of essential services or bear political costs associated with contract failure, just as in the advanced economies. In some countries there was also evidence that private operators had "captured" government officials through bribery or other forms of political influence. As in developed countries, legislators and nongovernmental groups were often frustrated by the secrecy that surrounded negotiations and enabled the capture of officials by contractors.[35]

The effect of many renegotiations was again to "privatize profits but socialize losses" from the operation of privately financed infrastructure. A vivid illustration is the bailout of Mexican toll roads. In the late 1980s, the Mexican government began an expansion of its interstate highway system comparable to the U.S. highway construction program undertaken in the 1950s. The crucial distinction—emblematic of the shift in policy over three decades—was that the U.S. program had been publicly financed, whereas the Mexican effort was undertaken by private capital. Billions of dollars were privately borrowed to finance the construction of fifty toll highways and toll bridges.[36]

By the early 1990s, many of these projects were in deep trouble. Private operators overestimated demand and could not generate revenues to cover their financing costs. The Mexican government renegotiated many of its contracts to help the highway operators. Under pressure to refinance their debts on more manageable terms, the private operators also negotiated new dollar-denominated loans from major U.S. investment banks. But Mexico devalued its currency in 1994, plunging operators who had borrowed in U.S. dollars into even deeper trouble. In 1997, the Mexican government conceded that the program had largely failed. The government nationalized most of the toll operations and assumed almost $8 billion in debt, equal to roughly 1.5 percent of GDP.[37]

Boom and Bust

A fourth problem with privately financed infrastructure had to do with the ambivalence of capital itself. Private investment in infrastructure followed a boom–bust cycle over the past twenty years. The first boom came between

1990 and 1997. Private investment in the infrastructure of developing countries grew at a rate of 30 percent a year, multiplying from a flow of $18 billion in 1990 to $128 billion in 1997. "There was almost a 'gold rush' mentality toward certain sectors and regions" that was driven in part, according to a 2003 World Bank review, by "wildly optimistic" forecasts about the profits to be earned from those investments.[38]

But investment collapsed after 1997. The financial crisis that began in East Asia in 1997 was the primary cause of this reversal. Broad concerns about the economic instability of developing economies triggered a flight to safety among investors. By 2001, annual infrastructure investment flows to poorer countries were more than fifty percent below their high-water mark in 1997. The water multinationals Suez and Veolia announced plans to withdraw from risky emerging markets in order to shore up their financial position. A 2002 World Bank assessment of private investment in power projects described medium-term prospects as "discouraging." Most prospective investors reported being "less interested or retreating" from poorer countries.[39]

But another infrastructure boom began in 2003, as fears about the instability of emerging markets receded. Investors remained wary of Latin America, the chief target of the first boom: in this second wave, a larger proportion of investment went to Eurasia. As the boom progressed, fears about risk diminished. The consulting group McKinsey and Company reported that there was an "astonishing flood of money" into the infrastructure sector between 2006 and 2008. Infrastructure fund managers were "exploring the fringes of the investment world in search of fresh opportunities," according to *Business Week.* "The money is here," a McKinsey study claimed in February 2008, "What about the deals?"[40]

Six months later, the second boom collapsed. Many infrastructure funds relied heavily on leverage to increase profitability: that is, they borrowed money at low rates to buy more infrastructure assets. As the financial crisis of 2008 deepened, cheap loans could no longer be found. Desperate to maintain profitability, funds reduced their borrowing needs by unloading their interests in infrastructure projects. As the credit crunch intensified, divestment of assets by infrastructure funds seemed "in danger of turning into a stampede." New projects were also delayed or canceled as sources of private financing dried up. The reversal was not limited to developing countries. Several major highway and airport privatization plans in the United States collapsed for lack of investors. In the United Kingdom, the amount of private money committed to new PFI projects declined by 90 percent between the first and second halves of 2008.[41]

By early 2009, many executives in the infrastructure sector were appealing for government intervention to protect projects jeopardized by the financial crisis. Governments responded to the call. In March 2009, the U.K. government announced that it would provide private operators with all of the debt needed for planned PFI projects to proceed. Treasury officials said the aid was necessary to assure that "crucial and valuable public investment will not be disrupted," but critics pointed out that the PFI scheme could no longer be properly described as a *private* financing initiative. In India and Brazil, government-owned banks also replaced private investors as the major source of funding for planned infrastructure projects. The World Bank announced that it would channel money from the advanced countries' government-owned development banks to infrastructure projects in poor countries that had been left "high and dry" by the retreat of private investment.[42]

At the start of the era of liberalization, private financing was justified as a way of correcting the myopia and fickleness of governments in matters relating to infrastructure. But the durability of the private-financing solution was clearly compromised by the fickleness of capital itself as well as the increased instability of globalized financial markets. At the end of the era of liberalization governments once again found themselves playing the dominant role in infrastructure investment. This reversal was given more momentum as governments adopted stimulus programs to counter the economic downturn in 2008–2009. A significant part of this spending was allocated to publicly funded infrastructure projects. In the United States, federal outlays on physical capital investment jumped by 40 percent between 2007 and 2009.

Second Thoughts

By the end of the era of liberalization, the LTIC model had lost much of its luster. Clear evidence about the superiority of privately operated infrastructure was surprisingly thin. Changes in rules about the treatment of private operators' debt in government accounts also diminished the appeal of private provision as a device for maintaining the appearance of fiscal discipline. The LTIC lobby itself had been knocked back by the financial crisis. And in some regions, public opinion had turned firmly against further experimentation with the model. In Latin America, for example, public perceptions were judged in 2003 to be "so overwhelmingly negative...as to be a serious constraint" on further private investment in infrastructure. Pollsters concluded in 2009 that the persistence of statist attitudes in the region was bound to undercut the legitimacy of further efforts at private service provision.[43]

Experience also revealed the weaknesses of what came to be known as the "legal paradigm" of infrastructure provision. Investors from the advanced economies, Erik Woodhouse suggested in 2005, had suffered from "an irrational exuberance…that project risks in developing countries could be managed through detailed contracting." This was a misguided enterprise for two reasons: because it was impossible for any contract to anticipate all of the contingencies that might upset a decades-long project and because it simply assumed that a succession of governments would honor the contract language. Meanwhile, Ryan Orr has suggested, insufficient attention was paid to the "robustness of the deal"—that is, the extent to which political and economic conditions would affect the survival of the arrangement over time.[44]

A 2003 World Bank study reached a similar conclusion about the limitations of the legal paradigm. "The expectations of investors and governments were simply out of step with reality," it concluded. Investors underestimated the political risks associated with their projects while governments overestimated their own ability to contain public hostility. As a consequence, many deals proved to be unsustainable. A 2005 Bank report concurred: "Infrastructure reforms are political processes, prone to backlash. Reform 'losers' may aim to recover the benefits they enjoyed in the past, while reform 'winners' may not feel like they have really benefited.…If those who stand to lose have veto power, the reforms will not consolidate."[45]

This was yet another example of the failure of naive institutionalism. Governments and investors learned that their faith in the power of contract had been misplaced. Investors would have to appraise political risks more carefully and develop other techniques for discouraging governmental reversals on contract terms. (Partnering with prominent local businesses was one of these techniques.) And governments, for their part, would have to be more careful in devising governance structures for privately provided services so that they would be regarded as legitimate by powerful constituencies. The hope had been that LTICs would take the politics out of infrastructure provision. Once again, this proved to be an impossible task.[46]

Beyond Discipline

The era of economic theocracy, in which unelected
experts ran the global economy, is over.

—Financial Times, *August 2009*

The logic of discipline is a reform philosophy built on the criticism that standard democratic processes for producing policies are myopic, unstable, and skewed toward special interests and not the public good. It attempts to make improvements in governance through changes in law that impose constraints on elected officials and citizens, often by shifting power to technocrat-guardians who are shielded from political influence.

We have had three decades of experience with the logic of discipline and can now clearly see that it suffers from several limitations. The first is a lack of candour about motivation. Reforms advanced during this period under the banner of discipline were often promoted as a means of promoting the general welfare. This view, though, is too simplistic. As a strategy for governmental reform, the logic of discipline has been closely tied to the advance of global capitalism. And its most vigorous advocates have been financial and commercial concerns that stand to benefit from globalization: investors and lenders, manufacturers relying on transnational production systems and the retailers that sell their products, shippers, infrastructure operators, and the array of professionals (lawyers, bankers, consultants, and lobbyists) who serve these groups. Beneath the claim that discipline has served the general welfare is the reality that these reforms have also advanced the immediate material interests of these constituencies.

This is not the only respect in which the logic of discipline is simplistic. As a political philosophy—a doctrine about the right way to organize authority in society—the logic of discipline is woefully underdeveloped. Citizens and legislators who take the rhetoric of democratization seriously understandably have questioned the legitimacy of reforms aimed at binding their discretion and putting authority in the hands of technocrat-guardians. The response to these challenges by the advocates of discipline has been at times clumsy and delayed.

Another substantial defect of the logic lay in its conception of how governmental processes are reformed. Advocates of discipline have a naive faith in the capacity of legal instruments—laws, treaties, and contracts—to shape behavior and cause enduring shifts in the distribution of political power. Where formal–legal changes appear to have had the intended effect—in the case of central banking, for example—it is probably because a range of other factors were working in their favor. More often, the broader context was not favorable, and as a consequence, reform efforts failed.

Reforms that survived sometimes proved to have unexpected flaws. The single innovation that seemed most clearly to demonstrate the virtues of the logic of discipline—and which served as an archetype for reform in several other areas—was the renovation of central banks. Formal bank independence was one aspect of a robust anti-inflation regime built over the course of thirty years, and until 2007 it seemed highly effective in assuring price stability. After 2007, however, we learned that one of the defects of this regime was insensitivity to other dangers, such as the rising threat to systemic stability. The "pressure of social conformity," as Barry Eichengreen has called it, blinded the guardian class.

Why did advocates of discipline not anticipate the problems they encountered in attempting to implement reforms? A generous interpretation would be that they were inexperienced and thus failed to anticipate the practical impediments to, and undesirable side effects of, reform. Or perhaps they were caught off guard by the democratic surge that went along with liberalization and that complicated many attempts to impose or sustain discipline.

We should be careful about accepting these explanations too quickly. As we have seen, some of these reforms were not wholly new. Earlier experiments with the autonomization of regulatory agencies and mainports provided warnings about the dangers of taking the concept of independence too seriously. And as we noted in chapter 1, there was already a significant literature on policy implementation that warned about the ways in which formal–legal innovations could, in practice, be subverted. Indeed, a substantial body of research in many fields—public and business administration, organizational psychology, sociology, and cultural anthropology—could have been tapped to develop more sophisticated plans for institutional renovation. There was an equally substantial literature about the risks associated with the accretion of guardian power. (Irving Janus's influential book *Groupthink* was published in 1972.) Advocates of discipline seemed either unaware of this body of experience and research or disinclined to take it seriously.[1]

In fact, there were incentives for many actors to promote simple solutions to complex problems. It was convenient for development specialists to promote formal–legal reforms because they were easy to explain and easy to adopt. Custom-made reforms, tailored to fit the circumstances of a particular country, would have taken longer to design and implement. Also, tailored reforms are more easily challenged by citizens and legislators who can reasonably claim to know their countries better than foreign analysts do. For governments, formal–legal reforms have the added advantage of being easy to see. If the point is to signal to investors, or to international institutions like the IMF and World Bank, or to other countries, then observability is a key consideration. The difficulty, of course, is that the signal can be misleading.

Formal–legal reforms also had allure for academics. The era of liberalization was one in which cross-national analysis of politics and economics became very popular. Scholars wanted to find patterns in economic development and governmental performance based on the experience of a large number of countries. To do this, they needed some convenient way of summarizing the key features of each country's political and economic system. Once again, formal–legal features had the advantage of being easily observed and counted. Scholars often saw the dangers inherent in this method. But the temptation to continue formulating indices for comparative analysis that were based on easily observed features was strong.[2]

A sharper criticism can be made about the work of scholarly economists who formulated some of the key reforms advanced under the banner of discipline. Simplistic assumptions about the way in which the world works were often transformed into dogma before research could confirm their accuracy.

An example will help to illustrate the process by which this occurred. Consider the first two sentences of an influential 1985 paper on central bank independence:

> This paper addresses a narrow and well-defined aspect of the broader question: Why do inflation rates vary across countries? Specifically, it investigates the cross-country relationships between monetary

policies and the laws which establish and delimit the powers of central banks.

Observe how the general question in the first sentence (Why inflation rates vary across countries) is immediately reduced to a question of formal–legal differences (the laws that establish and delimit the powers of central banks) in the second. The authors acknowledge that they have taken a vastly simplified view of the larger issue. Indeed, they eventually concede that:

> We have completely omitted any discussion of the effect of what might be called informal rules and arrangements which may in important ways modify the written law of the central bank and influence its *de facto* relationship with the government.... [and] we have completely ignored the potential influence of intellectual ideas and painful "collective" memories of such phenomena as mass unemployment or hyperinflation. These omissions constitute potentially important limitation of the results that have been discovered and reported here.

These are tremendously important caveats. But the fact remains that the paper examines only the de jure independence of central banks. No reason is given for emphasizing this explanatory variable rather than the others. This paper was not unusual in taking this approach. Other contemporaneous research adopted the same methodological two-step: posing the large question and then immediately reducing it to a study of formal–legal differences.[3]

Eventually, research would be produced that questioned the centrality of formal bank independence as a determinant of inflation rates. But by this point, policy elites had already rendered judgment: de jure independence was the orthodoxy, and the revolution in central banking was under way. Furthermore, the orthodoxy affected reform in other areas. As we have seen, proponents of enhanced treasury power, autonomous revenue agencies, and independent regulators all invoked the example ostensibly set by the formal liberation of central banks. An assumption about the importance of formal–legal rules shaped the research agenda in one area, quickly became settled wisdom, and served as a model for reform in other areas.

But why did this assumption gain traction in the first place? It is difficult to say. Perhaps it was just the fact that formal–legal rules are easily observed. It might also reflect a crude theory of politics hidden beneath a superstructure of complex mathematical modeling, that is, the presumption that the behavior of political systems is driven largely by their formal–legal arrangements. This way of thinking about politics was largely abandoned in political science seventy years ago. Political scientists discarded the viewpoint because it was clearly inadequate as a framework for explaining the dynamics of everyday politics.

There were other ways in which the reasoning of some scholarly economists was flawed. Suppose, for the moment, that it could be firmly established that formal bank independence is an important determinant of a country's success in fighting inflation—or to take another example, that enhanced treasury power really does improve budget control. Does it necessarily follow that central banks *should* be made independent or that treasury power *should* be enhanced? Economists sometimes took the view that these conclusions followed naturally. As Kenneth Rogoff posited in 1985, "society can make itself better off" by shifting power to a conservative central banker. Or as a World Bank study reported in 2005, the "prevailing economic orthodoxy...favors the insulation of economic policymaking in the executive."[4]

But these conclusions do not follow naturally from the empirical findings. Consider an analogous case. Suppose that it could be shown that countries have lower crime rates if they have stronger police forces and weaker due process guarantees for criminal defendants. Or suppose that countries are proven to be less vulnerable to terrorist attacks if they bolster domestic surveillance and hold suspects in indefinite detention. Less crime and terrorism is unambiguously desirable. But is it therefore clearly settled that we should want stronger police and intelligence agencies and fewer guarantees for civil liberties? Certainly not. We would want to think carefully about the trade-off between contending values—in this example, security versus privacy and other civil liberties.

The same holds true in the economic sphere. Delegation of power to technocrat-guardians implies a weakening of the public's ability to participate in decisions that affect the welfare of the country. We could be troubled by this—even if we know that the public, left to its own devices, tends to make bad decisions. Similarly, the transfer of power to technocrat-guardians might undermine the legitimacy of government. People might become alienated from, and eventually rebel against, a system in which power is closely held, even if technocrat-guardians tend to make decisions that are manifestly better for the public in the long run.

Any reform prescription about the reallocation of governmental power has to make a judgment about whether concerns such as these should be taken seriously. This question cannot be determined by empirical research. It is a question of political philosophy. Scholarly economists who jumped immediately from description to prescription were either unaware that they had shifted into a field in which they had no special competence or were content to make judgments about political philosophy under the cloak of the economic sciences.

Slipping from description to prescription also raised a second kind of problem. The statement that countries *should* adopt a particular reform implies the judgment that they *can* adopt the reform. After all, it takes a certain perversity to recommend a policy that cannot be implemented or sustained. But scholarly economics had little to say about the viability of their reform prescriptions or about the process by which formal–legal reforms could be implemented and made robust. The favored method of economic reasoning—with its preference for highly abstracted models and "stylized facts"—was not suited to answering questions about the process of governmental reform, which is so heavily shaped by details about political context, history, and culture.[5]

Three Ill-Chosen Words

The reforms canvassed in this book were closely connected with the larger project of advancing global capitalism, and the extent to which someone favors aspects of this reform program hinges substantially on his or her opinion of the wisdom of that larger project. But a citizen can be skeptical about globalization and nonetheless concede the seriousness of some of the problems canvassed in this book, such as fiscal drift, uncontrolled inflation, or declining tax ratios. The question is how to best address these problems. How do we craft reforms that are effective and durable?

An important preliminary step is to develop a more sophisticated way of thinking about the goals and process of reform. We can begin by abandoning three words that featured prominently in reform debates in the era of liberalization: depoliticization, autonomization, and discipline. In some contexts, these three concepts might serve a useful purpose. But in the cases we have described, this vocabulary does more harm than good. It obscures precisely what reform is intended to do as well as the key issues that must be addressed to make reforms work.

Depoliticization?

Much of this book has described efforts to depoliticize various aspects of governmental work. Some advocates of discipline might not have used the word "depoliticization," but all understood the concept. It is the process of making something—a particular subject or organization—nonpolitical or putting it beyond the range of political debate and contestation. Certain subjects were to be "removed from the political thicket" or taken "out of politics."

There is an assumption buried here that ought to be considered more closely. It is the notion that depoliticization is feasible—that is, that some topics or organizations really can be made nonpolitical. The assumption is never directly challenged, although it could be. What evidence is there that it is actually possible to place certain subjects above politics? What examples can be given of subjects that really have been depoliticized? To put it another way, why should we prefer this assumption to the alternative—that depoliticization is not feasible at all?

From a philosophical point of view, it is easier to make a strong case for the alternative proposition—that depoliticization is simply infeasible. Harold Lasswell once argued that politics is essentially about the distribution of benefits and burdens within society: "who gets what, when, and how." This is roughly the same definition adopted by a 2007 World Bank report. "Politics," one contributor wrote, "is about winners and losers." By this definition, though, all the subjects canvassed in this book are indisputably political. There are clear winners and losers in every chapter. Maybe the distribution of gains and losses can be justified, but there can be no doubt that distributive choices are being made.[6]

There are other ways to define politics, but none makes it possible to defend the discipline agenda as an exercise in depoliticization. One alternative definition says that politics is concerned with the allocation and use of power within society. But it is difficult to see how this viewpoint can regard reforms that are explicitly aimed at the transfer of power from elected officials to technocrat-guardians as nonpolitical. Yet another definition regards politics as a process for deciding between competing values. But no one would argue that the choices made by technocrat-guardians are devoid of value conflicts. And at a fundamental level all of the reforms we have canvassed are premised on a very big value trade-off: the deliberate suppression of political participation rights so that society as a whole is better off in the long run.[7]

There is another, practical sense in which we might say that a subject has been depoliticized: if we can show that there is broad and enduring agreement among powerful stakeholders that they will not attempt to influence the content of policy in that area. A certain topic (or an organization with authority over a certain topic) becomes a generally recognized "no-go" zone. This is probably how most people think about depoliticization. Because it is a practical test, we can ask a practical question: is there any evidence that such broad and enduring agreement is ever attained—in other words, that "no-go" zones can really be constructed?

Thirty years of experience ought to make us skeptical. Few of the decision makers empowered by the reforms we have canvassed—central bankers, treasury officials, regulators, arbitrators, operators of mainports and privatized infrastructure—would characterize their positions as noncontentious. Even at the zenith of the era of liberalization, it was common for decision makers to confront questions about the legitimacy of their authority as well as challenges to their exercise of power. Some of these technocrat-guardians succeeded in holding on to their authority while others did not. Success in holding on to authority sometimes hinged on the capacity of technocrat-guardians to call on like-minded stakeholders to help defend their position. Guardians who did this were not above politics; rather, they were actively engaged in it.

In a sense, these refined discussions about the various ways of defining depoliticization are unnecessarily subtle. We have seen how this reform program was linked to the larger project of economic globalization. No one would deny the ineluctably political character of that larger project. But it would be odd to concede that the larger project was politically charged while at the same time insisting that the institutional reforms made necessary by the larger project were politically neutral.

Autonomy?

These reforms often tried to give autonomy to organizations that performed various tasks. Autonomy was not a precisely defined concept. The Oxford English Dictionary describes it as the freedom to act independently. Advocates of reform sometimes characterize autonomy as a state in which technocrat-guardians are "distanced from governments," "isolated from external influences," or "free from state policy constraints." The concept of autonomy is also premised on an assumption about feasibility: that it is actually possible to endow technocrat-guardians with the freedom to act independently.

This was a proposition that technocrat-guardians themselves came to regard skeptically. In practice, leaders of formally autonomous organizations often recognized the tacit limitations on their power. As former Federal Reserve chairman Paul Volcker reflected in 2005: "The Federal Reserve is meant to be independent of parochial political interests. But it's got to operate—I think of it as a kind of band, sometimes wide, sometimes narrow—within the range of understanding of the public and the political system. You can't just go do something that is just outside the bounds of what people can understand, because you won't be independent for very long if you do that." The United Kingdom's first water regulator, Ian Byatt, had the same notion in mind when he told an interviewer in 2001: "If a regulator expects to be politically independent, then he had better adopt some of the habits of politicians." The operator of Mumbai's recently autonomized airport was more direct. Infrastructure development, he said, "is about taking care of vested interests without compromising your objectives."[8]

The extent to which autonomous organizations enjoy freedom of movement is likely to hinge on the balance of forces in society at large. Indeed, it might not be an exaggeration to say that autonomy in the broad sense is illusory—simply an artifact of this broader alignment of interests. Progressive Era mainports could expand easily in their early years because they were backed by powerful "growth coalitions." As the power of these coalitions declined in the postwar years, mainports saw their own freedom of action constrained. Similarly, central bank independence gained favor partly because the traditional enemies of bank autonomy—such as organized labor—saw their power wane while the influence of allies such as financial institutions rose.

Organizations that were theoretically freed from external influences also made substantial investments in capabilities necessary to manage relationships with key stakeholders. Sometimes the aim was to negotiate new coalitions that would permit an organization to continue pursuing its objectives. And sometimes organizations had to make internal adaptations to deal with legitimacy problems—for example, by developing consultative mechanisms and transparency rules to counter complaints about insensitivity and secretiveness. These adaptations enhanced the prospects for organizational survival and growth but also tied these organizations more closely to the expectations of influential stakeholders.

As we have seen, technocrat-guardians were constrained in other ways as well. Central bankers were tightly integrated into scholarly networks and to some degree were accountable to other actors within those networks. They were sensitive to critical reviews of their work by academic economists. In addition, bankers and regulators were connected through transgovernmental professional networks that made them susceptible to judgment by peers in other countries. They were also sensitive to the judgment of financial markets. Similarly, mainports worried that shippers and air carriers would take business elsewhere if performance was unsatisfactory.

In sum, all of these organizations were embedded in a complex web of relationships that determined what they could or could not do. The influence of politicians might have been reduced, relative to many of these other stakeholders; but autonomy was hardly the word to describe the circumstances in which organizations found themselves after reform. It would be better to say that each of these organizations was regulated by a performance regime that included a complex combination of formal and informal accountabilities. The ambition of reformers was to modify the web of accountabilities so that certain policy outcomes would be preferred.[9]

Discipline?

As we have argued, the biggest idea underlying these reforms was that of discipline. The pervading idea was that liberal democracies lacked the capacity to make hard choices and that mechanisms were necessary to force those choices or empower technocrat-guardians who would make them on society's behalf. Here, again, was another assumption: that democratic systems *could* be disciplined—that a polity could be forced to do things which, left to its own devices, it would not be prepared to do.

We should acknowledge, but discount, two situations in which discipline might be attainable. The first is the extreme case in which democratic institutions are completely extinguished and an authoritarian regime is put in its place, perhaps through a coup d'état. Sometimes coups have broad public support, and once power is seized a military-backed dictator could impose distasteful policies for a very long time. But it is not clear that we should consider this as an example of discipline *within* a democratic system. Rather, it is the supplanting of a democratic system with something else. By contrast, we are looking for examples of discipline within political systems in which the basic requirements of democracy—the selection of leaders through competitive elections based on near-universal suffrage—continue to be respected.[10]

For similar reasons we should discount cases in which discipline is imposed in the context of a severe national crisis. Many countries that confront economic emergencies go through something like a "treasury coup," during which technocrats impose unpopular policies that would not otherwise be adopted. But this is not an example of democratic systems accepting enduring restrictions on popular sovereignty. It is, rather, the momentary suspension of democratic processes to deal with a major threat—analogous to the use of emergency powers during a national security crisis. If treasury power persists and becomes normalized after an emergency has passed, then we might say that discipline has been attained. But as we saw in chapter 3, this does not appear to be the usual outcome.[11]

An advocate of discipline might argue that durable checks on sovereignty are clearly feasible; after all, this is the essential function of constitutions. Transient majorities are blocked from acting on their preferences by a nation's fundamental law. But even here we might disagree. As a practical matter, constitutions are more malleable than we might think. For example, the United States is the only G7 nation that did not undergo significant constitutional changes in the postwar period. Furthermore, constitutions are not self-enforcing. They work because judges, legislators, and bureaucrats are prepared to enforce their terms and because citizens are prepared to accept the results, even if as individuals they might have preferred a different outcome. In other words, there is broad support for the idea of constitutional government even if there is little support for the result in a particular case.

This broad support is sometimes called regime legitimacy. Its significance is often overlooked by advocates of discipline, who are tempted to regard constitutional limitations as examples of externally imposed restraints on sovereignty. But these restraints are not external to the system. In large part they work because there is a broadly shared belief within the system that the rules should be respected. Of course, the same argument can be made about any formal–legal rule and not just constitutional provisions. The willingness of a polity to honor commitments contained in laws, treaties, or contracts is ultimately contingent on the strength of public support for the general proposition that such commitments ought to be honored.[12]

Evidence about the importance of regime legitimacy has been presented throughout this book. In Latin America, for example, the "robustness" of independent regulation, long-term infrastructure contracts, and the BIT architecture is clearly affected by the persistence of statist attitudes and skepticism about global economic integration. There is a significant disconnect between the new formal–legal order and popular attitudes about the proper organization of government and the economy. In Europe, by contrast, the survival of independent regulators and the European Central Bank might be encouraged because of broadly shared support for the project of continental integration, a decades-old exercise driven by the memory of two devastating wars as well as the desire for economic growth.

The process of building regime legitimacy is slow and complex. It relies on mechanisms whose workings are largely unexplored by advocates of discipline. In most countries, respect for governing institutions is the product of a vast enterprise of cultural reproduction that includes methods of public education, elaborate civil rituals, and long-established traditions of political rhetoric.[13]

Nonetheless, it can be important for advocates of institutional change to understand how the process of building regime legitimacy works, as the following illustration may show. Germany is widely regarded as a distinctive case among the advanced economies because of the depth of public support that prevails for an autonomous central bank with a firm anti-inflation focus. It is sometimes argued that the German public's support for bank autonomy reflects a public aversion to inflation triggered by the memory of hyperinflation during the Weimar Republic.[14]

But the years of hyperinflation were 1921–1923. Only one in a thousand Germans is old enough to have lived through it. How could it be, ninety years later, that the recollection still strongly influences policy? The answer is that there are complicated processes for distilling and retelling historical experience such that "memories" are disseminated to individuals who are far too young to recall them directly. Anyone who has an interest in influencing popular attitudes about the organization of institutions for economic policy making, or in adjusting institutions to suit popular attitudes, would want to know how these processes work.

We would also expect that processes of ideological reproduction would vary from one country to another. For example, it is far from certain that the United States—which has distinct educational practices, media structures, and immigration patterns—would replicate ideas about regime legitimacy over generations in exactly the way that Germany would. Again, this general observation might have immediate practical significance. During the era of liberalization, respect for the idea of central bank independence was directly affected in the United States by public recollections of the Great Inflation. But personal experience of that period also is fading: most Americans alive today were not yet teenagers when the U.S. economy began to unravel in the early 1970s. (Millions who might have been old enough to remember the Great Inflation were living someplace else.) Will the memory of the Great Inflation be carried forward, as the memory of German hyperinflation was, or will the demise of the cohort that lived through the Great Inflation result in a decline in respect for the idea of an autonomous, inflation-fighting central bank?

How to Think about Reform

As we have said throughout, enthusiasm for many of the reforms advanced under the banner of discipline will necessarily be colored by attitudes toward the larger project of global economic liberalization. And at the end of three decades, there is good reason to take a jaded view of the merits of this larger project. State reform had been justified on the claim that democratic processes were susceptible to three vices: myopia, fickleness, and capture by special interests. Reform was intended to promote the virtues of farsightedness, consistency, and public-spiritedness.

But these virtues proved illusive. It transpired that poorly regulated markets were prone to the same vices as unconstrained democratic states. The system of global capitalism, as it existed at the end of the era of liberalization, was crisis-prone, subject to wild swings in investment and trade, and driven largely by the short-term profit seeking of investors and businessmen. The volatility of the system as a whole compromised the ability of governments to engage in thoughtful long-term planning, and undermined governmental legitimacy because of the perceived need to concentrate power in the hands of technocrat-guardians in moments of crisis. The consolidation of reforms in the face of popular resistance was hindered by the inability of the economic system to deliver an important prerequisite for consolidation: long periods of stability and growth. And technocrat-guardians themselves proved to be susceptible to error on critical issues.

Experience also taught us something about the process of state reform more generally. Stated abstractly, the aim of reform is to redesign governmental systems so that they give higher priority to certain values or policy goals. This point cannot be evaded by invoking arguments about the virtues of depoliticization and neutral expertise. The case for a reorientation of priorities must be made explicitly.

The process of reform itself is complicated and contingent. It is complicated because any governmental system consists of much more than a formal set of legal rules directing the exercise of power. The behavior of the system is heavily influenced by various tacit understandings of the ways in which power is to be exercised as well as widely held beliefs about the proper structure of government and the economy. The behavior of the system hinges also on the distribution of de facto political power among a range of governmental and nongovernmental actors whose relationships are mediated through powerful but informal networks. The process of reforming any governmental system is contingent because so many of these other factors are the product of long historical processes. They are peculiar to a place.

It follows that the design of a reform program should begin with a consideration of the ways in which the system as a whole (and not simply its formal–legal rules) tends to generate policy goals. Next, it should consider how the system as a whole could be modified to produce different results. We might find that the most effective way of modifying the behavior of the system is not necessarily through the modification of formal–legal rules. On the contrary, modified formal–legal rules might prove to be an after-thought—a post hoc ratification of the new order. The survival of those new rules will be contingent on their compatibility with the other features of the political system.

This general approach can be applied to the bundle of reforms discussed in this book. Their aim was to reconfigure governmental systems so that certain goals—price stability, budgetary balance, consistency in tax enforcement, facilitation of trade, regulatory predictability, fair treatment of investors—would be preferred over others. Of course, the major failing was the fixation on formal–legal changes, and the major lesson was the need to reconcile formal–legal reforms with the range of factors just noted. Sometimes formal–legal innovations had to be modified to accommodate other factors; sometimes other factors (the power of various stakeholders, for example) could be adjusted so that they favored the survival of formal–legal innovations.

A common technique for privileging certain policy goals is to delegate power to technocrat-guardians who are selected because they are trusted to take those goals seriously. Delegation is usually contentious, but a host of other steps can be taken to discourage its reversal. The leaders of guardian organizations can learn how to use their powers judiciously. Guardian organizations can integrate themselves into buttressing networks. They can also develop the internal capacities needed to mediate relationships with important stakeholders and defuse challenges to their legitimacy. Of course, much of this assumes that guardian organizations are capable of acquiring the human and financial resources needed to make all of these adaptations.

We have just described a way of thinking about reform that is compatible with the project of economic liberalization but that avoids those three unhelpful words depoliticization, autonomy, and discipline. This approach improves the probability that reforms will be durable and, coincidentally, does much to allay concern that they will undermine the principle of democratic accountability. To some degree, the adaptations are a way of reconciling the two concurrent programs of globalization and democratization. However, one implication of this approach is that the potential for systemic reform should not be over-estimated. Governmental processes might be tilted so that they give preference to certain priorities, but it is impossible to assure that these priorities will dominate. Within democratic systems, policy preferences cannot be locked in.

We began with the claim that many proponents of reform deployed a way of thinking described here as naive institutionalism. They adopted the sensible proposition that "institutions matter" as determinants of a country's economic performance but then robbed this proposition of much of its value by taking a reduced view of precisely what institutions are. In part, we are recognizing the need for a return to the more nuanced view proposed by Douglass North and other scholars. But we then we must also remember North's caution about the prospects for quick overhaul of complex systems: "[T]he single most important point about institutional change, which must be grasped if we are to begin to get a handle on the subject, is that institutional change is overwhelmingly incremental....Although formal rules may change overnight as the result of political or judicial decisions, informal constraints embodied in customs, traditions and codes of conduct are much more impervious to deliberate policies."[15]

Notes

Chapter 1

1. Matthew V. Flinders, *Delegated governance and the British state: Walking without order* (New York: Oxford University Press, 2008), 235 and 239; Colin Hay, *Why we hate politics* (Malden, MA: Polity, 2007), 78–87 and 91–95.

2. Francis Fukuyama, "The end of history?" *National Interest* 16, no. 3 (1989): 3–16; Hans-Dieter Klingemann, "Mapping political support in the 1990s: A global analysis," in *Critical citizens: Global support for democratic governance*, ed. Pippa Norris (New York: Oxford University Press, 1999), 31–56, 42–46; U.S. Department of State, "From the editors," *Issues of Democracy* 5, no. 1 (2000): 2–3, 2.

3. See, for example, the work of the International Institute for Democracy and Electoral Assistance, which celebrated its tenth anniversary in 2005: http://www.idea.int. Also Antonio Octavio Cintra and Marcelo Barroso Lacombe, "Executive-legislative relations and democratic consolidation," in *The construction of democracy*, ed. Jorge Domínguez and Anthony Jones (Baltimore, MD: Johns Hopkins Press, 2007); Hans Peter Olsen, *Fra idé til institutioner: Ombudsmaninstiutioners globale udbredelse* (Copenhagen: Institut for Statskundskab, Københavns Universitet, 2005) and *Hybrid governance of standardized states: Causes and contours of the global regulation of government auditing* (Copenhagen: School in Economics and Business Administration, 2007), ch. 3.

4. Merilee S. Grindle, *Going local: Decentralization, democratization, and the promise of good governance* (Princeton, NJ: Princeton University Press, 2007), 4.

5. Ann Florini, *The right to know: Transparency for an open world* (New York: Columbia University Press, 2007), 348; David Banisar, *Freedom of information around the world 2006: A global survey of access to government information laws*, July 2006, atfreedominfo.org; M. Amir-Ul Islam, *Right to know is right to liberty* (Dhaka, BD: Legal Education and Training Institute, 1999); Richard Calland and

Guy Dehn, eds., *Whistleblowing around the world* (Capetown, SA: Open Democracy Advice Centre, 2004).

6. Organization for Economic Cooperation and Development (OECD), *Citizens as partners* (Paris: OECD, 2001), 8; Éric Montpetit, "Public consultations in policy network environments: The case of assisted reproductive technology policy in government," *Canadian Public Policy* 29, no. 1 (2003): 95–110, 96; Bruce A. Ackerman and James S. Fishkin, *Deliberation day* (New Haven, CT: Yale University Press, 2004); United Nations, *Auditing for social change: A strategy for citizen engagement in public sector accountability* (New York: UN Department of Economic and Social Affairs, 2007), 6.

7. Tony Blair, speech to the Labour Party Conference, September 28, 2004, and September 27, 2005; Andrei Cherny, *The next deal: The future of public life in the information Age* (New York: Basic Books, 2000), 37 and 50.

8. James Surowiecki, *The wisdom of crowds* (New York: Doubleday, 2004), xiii and 270. See also Thomas Frank, *One market under God* (New York: Anchor, 2001), 29; Fareed Zakaria, *The future of freedom: Illiberal democracy at home and abroad* (New York: Norton, 2003), ch. 9.

9. Andrew Keen, *The cult of the amateur: How today's Internet is killing our culture* (New York: Doubleday, 2007), 35–63; John Lukacs, *Democracy and populism: Fear and hatred* (New Haven, CT: Yale University Press, 2005), 11; Ramachandra Guha, *India after Gandhi: The history of the world's largest democracy* (New York: Ecco, 2007), 690–691; emphasis in original. See also Alan Wolfe, "The dangers of conservative populism," in *America at risk: Threats to liberal self-government in an age of uncertainty*, ed. Robert Faulkner and Susan Shell (Ann Arbor: University of Michigan Press, 2009), 96–116.

10. James Reston, "The crisis of democracy," *New York Times*, March 3, 1974, and June 29, 1975.

11. Michel Crozier, Samuel P. Huntington, and Joji Watanuki, *The crisis of democracy: Report on the governability of democracies to the Trilateral Commission* (New York: New York University Press, 1975), 8, 114–115, 161–164. For other expressions of the overload thesis see Anthony King, "Overload: Problems of governing in the 1970s," *Political Studies* 23 (1975): 284–296; Richard Rose, *Challenge to governance: Studies in overloaded polities* (Beverly Hills, CA: Sage, 1980); Samuel P. Huntington, *American politics: The promise of disharmony* (Cambridge: Harvard University Press, 1981); Anthony Birch, "Overload, ungovernability, and delegitimation," *British Journal of Political Science* 14, no. 2 (1984): 135–160.

12. Dennis Mueller, *Public Choice III* (New York: Cambridge University Press, 2003), 1–2. Public Choice also gained the distinction of becoming the only academic theory that spawned a situation comedy, Britain's *Yes Minister*.

13. James M. Buchanan and Gordon Tullock, *The calculus of consent: Logical foundations of constitutional democracy* (Ann Arbor: University of Michigan Press, 1962); Mancur Olson, *The logic of collective action: Public goods and the theory of groups* (Cambridge: Harvard University Press, 1971); William Niskanen,

"The peculiar economics of bureaucracy," *American Economic Review* 58, no. 2 (1968): 293–305; Gary S. Becker, "A theory of competition among pressure groups for political support," *Quarterly Journal of Economics* 98, no. 3 (1983): 371–400.

14. Crozier, Huntington, and Watanuki, *Crisis of Democracy*, 113–115; James M. Buchanan and Richard E. Wagner, *Democracy in deficit: The political legacy of Lord Keynes* (New York: Academic Press, 1977), 125–126; Herman Schwartz, "Public Choice Theory and public choices: Bureaucrats and state reorganization in Australia, Denmark, New Zealand and Sweden," *Administration and Society* 26, no. 1 (1994): 48–77, 56.

15. Daniel Yergin and Joseph Stanislaw, *The commanding heights* (New York: Simon & Schuster, 1998).

16. Flinders, *Delegated governance and the British state*, 264. Peter Burnham, "The politics of economic management in the 1990s," *New Political Economy* 4, no. 1 (1999): 37–54.

17. Theodore Draper, *A very thin line: The Iran-contra affairs* (New York: Hill and Wang, 1991), 580–598; Deborah Pearlstein, *Form and function in the national security constitution* (Princeton, NJ: Princeton University Program in Law and Public Affairs, 2008); Aaron B. Wildavsky, *The presidency* (Boston: Little Brown, 1969), 230–245; Aaron B. Wildavsky, *The beleaguered presidency* (New Brunswick, NJ: Transaction, 1991), 29; Eric Alterman, *Who speaks for America? Why democracy matters in foreign policy* (Ithaca, NY: Cornell University Press, 1998), 4.

18. Alasdair Roberts, "The rhetorical problems of the management expert" (PhD diss., Harvard University, 1994), 14.

19. On Progressivism see Robert H. Wiebe, *The search for order, 1877–1920* (Westport, CT: Greenwood, 1980). A survey of the role of autonomous bodies in monitoring elections and protecting basic rights is provided in Bruce A. Ackerman, "The new separation of powers," *Harvard Law Review* 113, no. 3 (2000): 633–729.

20. World Bank, *World development report 1997: The state in a changing world* (Summary), (Washington, DC: World Bank, 1997); Douglass C. North, *Institutions, institutional change, and economic performance: The political economy of institutions and decisions* (New York: Cambridge University Press, 1990).

21. North, *Institutions, institutional change, and economic performance*, 4, 6, and 36–37. For other broad definitions of "institution" and related statements about the difficulties of institutional change see Peter A. Hall, *Governing the economy: The politics of state intervention in Britain and France* (New York: Oxford University Press, 1986), 19; John L. Campbell, *Institutional change and globalization* (Princeton, NJ: Princeton University Press, 2004), 19; Ronald Jepperson, "Institutions, institutional effects, and institutionalism," in *The new institutionalism in organizational analysis*, ed. Walter Powell and Paul DiMaggio (Chicago: University of Chicago Press, 1991), 143–163, 145; Paul Pierson, *Politics in time: History, institutions, and social analysis* (Princeton, NJ: Princeton University Press, 2004), ch. 1.

22. Dani Rodrik, *One economics, many recipes: Globalization, institutions, and economic growth* (Princeton, NJ: Princeton University Press, 2007), 184.

23. James A. Bill and Robert L. Hardgrave, *Comparative politics: The quest for theory* (Washington, DC: University Press of America, 1981), 3; Harry Eckstein, "On the 'science' of the state," *Daedalus* 108, no. 4 (1979): 1–20, 2–3; Marian D. Irish, "Advance of the discipline?" *Journal of Politics* 30, no. 2 (1968): 291–310, 298.

24. Per Molander, "Budgeting procedures and democratic ideals," *Journal of Public Policy* 21, no. 1 (2001): 23–52, 23; Rodrik, *One Economics, Many Recipes*, 165 and 182.

25. "One of the main virtues of indicators of rules is their clarity.... This clarity has made such indicators very appealing to aid donors interested in linking aid with performance indicators in recipient countries, and in monitoring progress on such indicators." Daniel Kaufmann and Aart Kraay, *Governance indicators: Where are we, where should we be going?* World Bank Policy Research Working Paper No. 4370, October 1 (Washington, DC: World Bank, 2007), 8 and 10.

26. Eugene Bardach, *The implementation game: What happens after a bill becomes a law* (Cambridge: MIT Press, 1977); Jeffrey L. Pressman and Aaron B. Wildavsky, *Implementation: How great expectations in Washington are dashed in Oakland* (Berkeley: University of California Press, 1984); Francis Snyder, "The failure of law and development," *Wisconsin Law Review* 1982, no. 3 (1982): 373–396; Curtis J. Milhaupt and Katharina Pistor, *Law and capitalism: What corporate crises reveal about legal systems and economic development around the world* (Chicago: University of Chicago Press, 2008), 207–212; Daniel Berkowitz, Katharina Pistor, and Jean-Fran ois Richard, "The transplant effect," *American Journal of Comparative Law* 51, no. 2 (2003): 163–203.

27. World Bank, *Economic growth in the 1990s: Learning from a decade of reform* (Washington, DC: World Bank, 2005), xiii, 5, and *The political economy of reform: Issues and implications for policy dialogue and development operations*, Report No. 44288-GLB, November 10 (Washington, DC: World Bank, 2008), vii; Rodrik, *One economics, many recipes*, 163–166; Howard Stein, *Beyond the World Bank agenda: An institutional approach to development* (Chicago: University of Chicago Press, 2008), 105–106 and 125–128.

28. Brief summaries of the unfolding financial crisis are provided by Olivier Blanchard, *The crisis: Basic mechanisms and appropriate policies*, IMF Working Paper No. 09/80, April (Washington, DC: IMF, 2009); International Monetary Fund, *World economic outlook*, April 22 (Washington, DC: IMF, 2009); High-Level Group on Financial Supervision in the EU, Jacques de Larosière (chair), *Report*, February 25 (Brussels: European Commission, 2009), 1–12; Financial Services Authority, *The Turner review: A regulatory response to the global financial crisis*, March (London: Financial Services Authority, 2009), 11–28. The following paragraphs draw on these summaries.

29. John Maynard Keynes, *The general theory of employment, interest, and money* (New York: Harcourt, Brace, 1936); Arthur Bloomfield, "Postwar control of international capital movements," *American Economic Review* 36, no. 2 (1946): 687–709, 688.

Chapter 2

Sources for epigraphs: Theodore H. White, *America in search of itself: The making of the president, 1956–1980* (New York: Harper & Row, 1982), 148; Dean Baker, *Plunder and blunder: The rise and fall of the bubble economy* (Sausalito, CA: PoliPointPress, 2008), 144–145.

1. See chapter 2 of the 1992 Treaty on European Union as well as, annexed to the treaty, the Protocol on the statute of the European system of central banks and of the European central bank. For a review of concerns about the legitimacy of the ECB see Paivi Leino, *The European Central Bank and legitimacy*, Harvard Jean Monnet Working Paper No. 1/01 (Cambridge: Harvard Law School, 2000).

2. Edmund Andrews, "European banks, acting in unison, cut interest rate," *New York Times*, December 4, 1998; Gary Duncan and David Lister, "Defiant ECB rejects calls to cut rates," *Times* (London), April 12, 2001.

3. John Kenneth Galbraith, *The new industrial state* (Boston: Houghton Mifflin, 1967); Paul Keating, "The Reserve Bank: Let the Parliament rule," *Sydney Morning Herald*, September 22, 1989.

4. Alan S. Blinder, *The quiet revolution: Central banking goes modern* (New Haven, CT: Yale University Press, 2004); Sucheen Patel, "An independent Bank of England: The political process in historical perspective," *Public Policy and Administration* 23, no. 1 (2008): 27–41, 29; Paul Bowles and Gordon White, "Central Bank independence: A political economy approach," *Journal of Development Studies* 31, no. 2 (1994): 235–264.

5. Robert J. Samuelson, *The great inflation and its aftermath: The transformation of America's economy, politics, and society* (New York: Random House, 2008).

6. An excellent overview of American economic policy during this period is provided by Jeffry A. Frieden, *Global capitalism: Its fall and rise in the twentieth century* (New York: Norton, 2006).

7. On the relationship between Nixon and Burns see Donald F. Kettl, *Leadership at the Fed* (New Haven, CT: Yale University Press, 1986), 113.

8. Theodore H. White, *America in search of itself: The making of the president, 1956–1980* (New York: Harper & Row, 1982), 153–155; Edgar Fiedler, "Inflation and economic policy," *Proceedings of the Academy of Political Science* 33, no. 3 (1979): 113–131, 113.

9. Edward Gramlich, "Monetary and fiscal policies," *Proceedings of the Academy of Political Science* 33, no. 3 (1979), 141 and 144; White, *America in search of itself*, 138.

10. Kettl, *Leadership at the Fed*, 173–188; William Greider, *Secrets of the temple: How the Federal Reserve runs the country* (New York: Simon and Schuster, 1989), 351–534.

11. Robin Bade and Michael Parkin, *Central bank laws and monetary policy* (London: University of Western Ontario, 1985); Kenneth Rogoff, "The optimal degree of commitment to an intermediate monetary target," *Quarterly Journal of Economics* 100, no. 4 (1985): 1169–1189; Alberto Alesina and Lawrence Summers, "Central bank independence and macroeconomic performance," *Journal of Money, Credit, and Banking* 25, no. 2 (1993): 151–162; Stanley Fischer, "Maintaining price stability," *Finance and Development* 33, no. 4 (1996): 34–37.

12. See, for example, Donald E. Fair, *Relationships between central banks and governments in the determination of monetary policy* (Wien, AT: Societé Universitaire Européenne de Recherches Financières, 1978); Bade and Parkin, *Central bank laws and monetary policy*; Donato Masciandaro and Guido Tabellini, "Fiscal deficits and monetary institutions: A comparative analysis," in *Monetary policy in the Pacific Basin countries*, ed. Hang-sheng Cheng (Boston: Kluwer, 1988), 125–152; Alberto Alesina, "Macroeconomics and politics," *NBER Macroeconomics Annual* 3 (1988): 13–52; Vittorio Grilli, Donato Masciandaro, and Guido Tabellini, "Political and monetary institutions and public financial policies in the industrial countries," *Economic Policy* 6, no. 13 (1991): 342–392, 366–371. A summary of early research that emphasized de jure independence is provided by Marco Arnone, Bernard Laurens, and Jean-Francois Segalotto in *The measurement of central bank autonomy: Survey of models, indicators, and empirical evidence*, IMF Working Paper No. 06/227, October (Washington, DC: IMF, 2006), 8–20.

13. Bade and Parkin, *Central bank laws and monetary policy*; Alesina, "Macroeconomics and Politics"; Grilli, Masciandaro, and Tabellini, "Political and monetary institutions and public financial policies in the industrial countries"; Alex Cukierman, Steven B. Webb, and Bilin Neyapti, "Measuring the independence of central banks and its effect on policy outcomes," *World Bank Economic Review* 6, no. 3 (1992): 353–398; Alesina and Summers, "Central bank independence and macroeconomic performance."

14. B. W. Fraser, *Central bank independence: What does it mean?* (Sydney: Reserve Bank of Australia, 1994); Adam Posen, "Why central bank independence does not cause low inflation: There is no institutional fix for politics," in *Finance and the international economy 7*, ed. Richard O'Brien (Oxford: Oxford University Press, 1993), 40–65; Adam S. Posen, "Declarations are not enough: Financial sector sources of central bank independence," *NBER Macroeconomics Annual* 10 (1995): 253–274; Marta Campillo and Jeffrey Miron, *Why does inflation differ across countries?* (Cambridge, MA: National Bureau for Economic Research, 1997); Jakob de Haan and Willem J. Kooi, "Does central bank independence really matter? New evidence for developing countries using a new indicator," *Journal of Banking & Finance* 24, no. 4 (2000): 643–664; Jan-Egbert Sturm and

Jakob de Haan, *Inflation in developing countries: Does central bank independence matter?* CESifo Working Paper Series No. 511, June (Munich: Center for Economic Studies and Ifo Institute for Economic Research, 2001): papers.ssrn. com/sol3/papers.cfm?abstract_id=277288; Luis Jacome and Francisco Vázquez, *Any link between legal central bank independence and inflation? Evidence from Latin America and the Caribbean* (Washington, DC: IMF, 2005); Lavern McFarlane, Wayne Robinson, and Goohoon Kwon, *Public debt, money supply, and inflation: A cross-country study and its application to Jamaica*, IMF Working Paper No. 06/121, May 17 (Washington, DC: IMF, 2006).

15. Posen, "Why central bank independence does not cause low inflation," 41; Gavyn Davies, "The arguments for an independent old lady," *Independent*, November 22, 1993; "Narrow money," *Economist*, August 28, 1993.

16. Masciandaro and Tabellini, "Fiscal deficits and monetary institutions," 146; Thomas F. Cargill, Michael M. Hutchison, and Takatoshi Ito, *Financial policy and central banking in Japan* (Cambridge: MIT Press, 2000), 92 and 112; Anthony Seldon, *Blair* (London: Free Press, 2005), 280–281; Martin Marcussen, "Central banking reform around the world: Only by night are all cats grey," in *Transcending new public management*, ed. Tom Christensen and Per Laegreid (Aldershot, UK: Ashgate, 2007), 135–154, 136; Kathleen McNamara, "Rational fictions: Central bank independence and the social logic of delegation," *West European Politics* 25, no. 1 (2002): 47–76; Marco Arnone, Bernard J. Laurens, Jean-Fran ois Segalotto, and Martin Sommer, *Central bank autonomy: Lessons from global trends*, IMF Working Paper No. 07/88, April (Washington, DC: IMF, 2007).

17. Manuel Pastor and Sylvia Maxfield, "Central bank independence and private investment in developing countries," *Economics & Politics* 11, no. 3 (1999): 299–309, 300; Maxfield, *Gatekeepers of Growth*.

18. Kenneth Rogoff, *Globalization and global disinflation* (Washington, DC: IMF, 2003).

19. Rogoff, *Globalization and disinflation*. Among the other explanations: a "historic shift" in technology that improved productivity and lowered upward pressure on prices; weakening of the power of organized labor, allowing improvements in productivity and reducing the likelihood that upward price pressures might be reflected in higher wages; and increased competition from low-wage nations, which discouraged domestic firms and workers from raising prices and wages. Alan Greenspan, *The age of turbulence: Adventures in a new world* (New York: Penguin, 2007), 166; David Harvey, *A brief history of neoliberalism* (New York: Oxford University Press, 2005); Andrew Glyn, *Capitalism unleashed* (New York: Oxford University Press, 2006).

20. Arthur Burns, *The anguish of central banking* (Belgrade: Per Jacobsson Foundation, 1979), 15 and 22. One adjustment in the legal regime governing the Federal Reserve was made by the Humphrey–Hawkins Act of 1978, which added price stability as a goal of national economic policy. The significance of this change has been debated. On presidential support for Volcker see Kettl,

Leadership at the Fed, 176–179 and 185; Greider, *Secrets of the Temple*, 121 and 449; Sean Wilentz, *The age of Reagan: A history, 1974–2008* (New York: Harper, 2008), 147–148 and 275; Samuelson, *The great inflation and its aftermath*, ch. 4.

21. Samuelson, *The great inflation and its aftermath*, 112–113; Joseph Schneider, "Social problems theory: The constructionist view," *Annual Review of Sociology* 11 (1985): 209–229.

22. James V. Higgins, "UAW calls for elected Fed chairman," United Press International, October 12, 1981; Ken Thomas, "UAW membership falls below 500,000; lowest level since WWII," Associated Press, March 28, 2008. On the importance of "societal coalitions" in preserving central bank independence see John B. Goodman, "The politics of central bank independence," *Comparative Politics* 23, no. 3 (1991): 329–349, and *Monetary sovereignty: The politics of central banking in Western Europe*, Cornell Studies in Political Economy (Ithaca, NY: Cornell University Press, 1992). Goodman draws on Peter Gourevitch, "The second image reversed: The international sources of domestic politics," *International Organization* 32, no. 4 (1978): 881–912.

23. Jelle Visser, "Union membership statistics in 24 countries," *Monthly Labor Review* 129, no. 1 (2006): 38–49, table 3; Glyn, *Capitalism unleashed*, 121–126; John McIlroy, "The enduring alliance? Trade unions and the making of New Labour, 1994–1997," *British Journal of Industrial Relations* 36, no. 4 (1998): 537–564.

24. John Boyd and Bruce Champ, *Inflation and financial market performance: What have we learned in the last ten years?* Working Paper No. 03–17 (Cleveland, OH: Federal Reserve Bank of Cleveland, 2003); John Boyd, Ross Levine, and Bruce Smith, "The impact of inflation on financial sector performance," *Journal of Monetary Economics* 47, no. 2 (2001): 221–248; Jonathan Temple, "Inflation and growth: Stories short and tall," *Journal of Economic Surveys* 14, no. 4 (2000): 395–432, 403; Posen, "Declarations are not enough" 257; Frieden, *Global capitalism*; Greider, *Secrets of the temple*, 491–493 and 570–574; Michael King, "Epistemic communities and the diffusion of ideas: Central bank reform in the United Kingdom," *West European Politics* 28, no. 1 (2005): 94–123, 106.

25. For discussion of the contingencies that affect the power of the financial sector see Posen, "Why central bank independence does not cause low inflation" and "Declarations are not enough"; Lucia Quaglia, "An integrative approach to the politics of central bank independence: Lessons from Britain, Germany, and Italy," *West European Politics* 28, no. 3 (2005): 549–568, 553. On the growth of the financial sector see Greta R. Krippner, "The financialization of the American economy," *Socioeconomic Review* 3, no. 2 (2005): 173–208; Jane Hardy, "The changing structure of the British economy," *International Socialism*, no. 106 (2005); Arjun Jayadev and Gerald Epstein, *The correlates of rentier returns in OECD countries*, January 24 (Amherst: Political Economy Research Institute, University of Massachusetts Amherst, 2007). On the phenomenon of financialization see Thomas I. Palley, *Financialization: What it is and why it matters* (Washington, DC: Levy Economics Institute, 2007); Kevin Phillips, *American theocracy: The*

peril and politics of radical religion, oil, and borrowed money in the 21st century (New York: Viking, 2006), 268.

26. Silja Göhlmann and Roland Vaubel, *The educational and professional background of central bankers and its effect on inflation—An empirical analysis* (Essen, DE: Rhine–Westphalia Institute for Economic Research, 2005); Christopher Adolph, "The dilemma of discretion: Career ambitions and the politics of central banking" (PhD diss., Harvard University, 2005).

27. Blinder, *Quiet Revolution*, xiii, 34–62; Ethan S. Harris, *Ben Bernanke's Fed: The Federal Reserve after Greenspan* (Boston: Harvard Business Press, 2008), 127–137.

28. Pierre St-Amant, Greg Tkacz, Annie Guérard-Langlois, and Louis Morel, *Quantity, quality, and relevance: Central bank research, 1990–2003*, Bank of Canada Working Paper No. 05–37 (Ottawa: Bank of Canada, 2005), table 1A; Sylvester Eijffinger, Jakob de Haan, and K. Koedijk, "Small is beautiful: Measuring the research input and output of European central banks," *European Journal of Political Economy* 18, no. 2 (2002): 365–374.

29. Vitor Gaspar and Juan Luis Vega, "Research at a policy making institution: Launching research at the ECB," *Swiss Journal of Economics and Statistics* 138, no. 4 (2002): 359–376, 361; Marvin Goodfriend, Reiner König, and Rafael Repullo, *External evaluation of the economic research activities of the European Central Bank* (Frankfurt: European Central Bank, 2004), 2 and 27; Laurence Meyer (chair), Martin Eichenbaum, Douglas Gale, Andrew Levin, and James McAndrews, *External review of economic research activities at the Bank of Canada*, External Review Committee report, February 1 (Ottawa: Bank of Canada, 2008), 2,4, and 23; Eijffinger, de Haan, and Koedijk, "Small is beautiful"; Eric Jondeau and Henri Pagés, *Benchmarking research in European central banks*, Sveriges Riksbank Working Paper Series, May (Paris: Banque de France, 2003).

30. Martin Marcussen, "The transnational governance network of central bankers," in *Transnational governance*, ed. Marie-Laure Djelic and Kerstin Sahlin-Andersson (New York: Cambridge University Press, 2006), 180–204.

31. Liaquat Ahamed, *Lords of finance: The bankers who broke the world* (New York: Penguin, 2009); Gianni Toniolo, *Central bank cooperation at the Bank for International Settlements, 1930–1973*, Studies in Macroeconomic History (New York: Cambridge University Press, 2005); Martin Marcussen, "Central banks on the move," paper presented at the European Union Studies Association's 8th biennial international conference, March 27–29, 2003, Nashville, TN; Beth Simmons, "Why innovate? Founding the Bank for International Settlements," *World Politics* 45, no. 3 (1993): 361–405, 390; Claudio Borio and Gianni Toniolo, *One hundred and thirty years of central bank cooperation: A BIS perspective*, BIS Working Paper No. 197, February (Basel, CH: Bank for International Settlements, 2006); Marcussen, "Transnational governance network of central bankers," 181, 201, and table 189.184; Anne-Marie Slaughter, *A new world order* (Princeton, NJ: Princeton University Press, 2004), 54.

32. Marcussen, "Transnational governance network of central bankers," 191.

33. See Blinder, *Quiet Revolution*, 1. Blinder counted the number of articles in the EconLit database that include the phrase "central banking" and found that it quintupled between the 1970s and 1990s. An even sharper increase was found in a count of articles published between 1970 and 2008 that reference the phrase "central banks."

34. Christopher Adolph develops an argument about the importance of "career incentives" for senior officials in "Dilemma of discretion," 78. For a discussion about the mobility of bank researchers and the implications for compensation see Meyer et al., *External review of economic research activities at the Bank of Canada*, 12.

35. Menzie Chinn and Hiro Ito, *Capital account liberalization, institutions, and financial development: Cross country evidence* (Cambridge, MA: National Bureau of Economic Research, 2002); Barry J. Eichengreen, "Capital account liberalization: What do cross-country studies tell us?" *World Bank Economic Review* 15, no. 3 (2001): 341–365; Michael P. Dooley, "Capital flight: A response to differences in financial risks," *Staff Papers—International Monetary Fund* 35, no. 3 (1988): 422–436; Maxfield, *Gatekeepers of Growth*; Stephen Bell, "Open-economy central banking: Explaining Australia's recommitment to central bank independence," *Australian Journal of Political Science* 36, no. 3 (2001): 459–480; Stephen R. Gill, *Power and resistance in the new world order* (New York: Palgrave Macmillan, 2008), 107–116; Joseph Stiglitz, "Capital market liberalization, economic growth, and instability," *World Development* 28, no. 6 (2000): 1075–1086; Alan Greenspan, "The world must repel calls to contain competitive markets," *Financial Times*, August 5, 2008, 9.

36. Karl Polanyi, *The great transformation* (Boston: Beacon, 1957).

37. A concise indictment of the Federal Reserve is provided by Henry Kaufman, "How libertarian dogma led the Fed astray," *Financial Times*, April 28, 2009, 11.

38. Dean Baker, *Plunder and blunder: The rise and fall of the bubble economy* (Sausalito, CA: PoliPointPress, 2008), 140. In May 2009, Congress authorized the establishment of a Financial Crisis Inquiry Commission to explore the origins of the crisis; it held its first hearings in September 2009.

39. National Commission on Terrorist Attacks upon the United States, *Final Report* (New York, NY: Barnes and Noble Books, 2004), xvi; Commission on Intelligence Capabilities of the United States regarding Weapons of Mass Destruction, *Report to the president*, March 31 (Washington, DC: U.S. Government Printing Office, 2005), 766; Columbia Accident Investigation Board, *Report, volume one* (Washington, DC: U.S. Government Printing Office, 2003), 9; Senate Committee on Homeland Security and Governmental Affairs, *Hurricane Katrina: A nation still unprepared*, 109th Cong., 2d sess., 2006, S. Rept. 109–322, 211.

40. Stephen Wright and Andrew Smithers, *Stock markets and central bankers: The economic consequences of Alan Greenspan* (London: Birkbeck College, University of London, 2002), 20; Financial Services Authority, *The Turner Review: A regulatory response to the global financial crisis*, March (London: Financial Services Authority, 2009), 39–42.

41. Financial Services Authority, *Turner Review*, 84.

42. Barry J. Eichengreen, "The last temptation of risk," *National Interest*, May–June 2009: http://nationalinterest.org/Article.aspx?id=21274; Robert Shiller, "Challenging the crowd in whispers, not shouts," *New York Times*, November 2, 2008; Raghuram G. Rajan, *Has financial development made the world riskier?* NBER Working Paper No. W11728, November (Cambridge, MA: National Bureau of Economic Research, 2005); Federal Reserve Bank of Kansas City, *The Greenspan era: Lessons for the future* (Kansas City, MO: Federal Reserve Bank of Kansas City, 2005), 374, 387–389, and 394; William R. White, *Is price stability enough?* (Basel, CH: Bank for International Settlements, 2006) and "Past financial crises, the current financial turmoil, and the need for a new macrofinancial stability framework," *Journal of Financial Stability* 4, no. 4 (2008): 307–312, 310–311; Transcript of interview with William R. White, *Spectator* (London), 2009 (accessed May 3, 2009): http://spectatorinquiry.pbworks.com/William-White-transcript.

43. White, "Past financial crises, the current financial turmoil, and the need for a new macrofinancial stability framework," 311; Richard W. Stevenson, "Policymakers hone debate: When to hold, when to fold," *New York Times*, September 3, 2002. The financial journalist Martin Wolf observed in 2009: "Monetary policy would have to have been very much tighter to prevent the asset price bubble.... I simply don't see how the Fed Chairman could have done that and expected to survive." "The worst possible world," *American Interest* 4, no. 3 (2009): 46–51, 47.

44. Boyd and Champ, *Inflation and financial market performance*; Gillian Tett, *Fool's gold* (New York: Free Press, 2009); Lawrence Jacobs and Desmond King, "America's political crisis: The unsustainable state in a time of unraveling," *PS: Political Science and Politics* 42, no. 2 (2009): 277–285, 281; Robert O'Harrow and Jeff Gerth, "As crisis loomed, Geithner pressed but fell short," *Washington Post*, April 3, 2009; Roger T. Cole, "Risk management in the banking industry," Statement before the Senate Subcommittee on Securities, Insurance, and Investment, Committee on Banking, Housing, and Urban Affairs, U.S. Senate, Washington, DC, March 18, 2009.

45. Willem Buiter, "The unfortunate uselessness of most 'state of the art' academic monetary economics," *Financial Times.com*, March 3, 2009 (accessed May 5, 2009): http://blogs.ft.com/maverecon/2009/03/the-unfortunate-uselessness-of-most-state-of-the-art-academic-monetary-economics/.

46. James Grant, "Paying the price for the Fed's success," *New York Times*, January 27, 2008; André Meier, *Panacea, curse, or nonevent? Unconventional monetary policy in the United Kingdom*, IMF Working Paper No. 09/163, August 1 (Washington, DC: IMF, 2009), 20.

47. Allan Meltzer, "Inflation nation," *New York Times*, May 4, 2009; Krishna Guha, "Toxic assets 'bridge too far,'" *Financial Times*, June 1, 2009. Close cooperation between the Federal Reserve and the U.S. Treasury is also described by David Wessel, *In Fed we trust* (New York: Crown Business, 2009). Another theme of Wessel's work is the extent to which federal policy makers had the option of acting through either the Federal Reserve or the Treasury.

48. Mervyn King, "The institutions of monetary policy," *American Economic Review* 94, no. 2 (2004): 1–13, 11; Sam Fleming, "Strong-willed: Mervyn King took on Gordon Brown over fiscal discipline," *Daily Mail*, April 19, 2009.

49. Wessel, *In Fed we trust*, 4.

50. Meltzer, "Inflation nation"; Ralph Atkins and Krishna Guha, "Odd optics: Why two top central banks take so different a stance," *Financial Times*, April 9, 2008; Carter Dougherty, "In Europe, central banking is different," *New York Times*, March 6, 2008; Ralph Atkins, "ECB policymaker urges caution," *Financial Times*, April 29, 2009.

Chapter 3

Source for epigraph: Les Metcalfe and Sue Richards, *Improving public management* (Newbury Park, CA: Sage, 1987), 200.

1. Alan Blinder, "Is government too political?" *Foreign Affairs* 76, no. 6 (1997): 115–126.

2. Nicholas Gruen, "Greater independence for fiscal institutions," *OECD Journal on Budgeting* 1, no. 1 (2001): 80–106, 89 and 103; "43 billion reasons to avoid the next recession," news release, March 7 (Canberra, AU: Business Council of Australia, 2000).

3. Charles Wyplosz, "Fiscal policy: Institutions versus rules," *National Institute Economic Review*, no. 191 (2005): 64–79, 73–73 and 77; "Fiscal flexibility," *Economist*, November 27, 1999. See also Laurence Ball, *A proposal for the next macroeconomic reform* (Wellington: Reserve Bank of New Zealand, 1996); Barry J. Eichengreen, Ricardo Hausmann, and Jürgen von Hagen, "Reforming budget institutions in Latin America: The case for a national fiscal council," *Open Economies Review* 10 (1999): 415–442; Lars Calmfors, "Fiscal policy to stabilise the domestic economy in the EMU: What can we learn from monetary policy?" *CESifo Economic Studies* 49, no. 3 (2003): 319–352.

4. Vito Tanzi and Ludger Schuknecht, *Public spending in the 20th century: A global perspective* (Cambridge: Cambridge University Press, 2000), table 1.1. The phrase "fiscal drift" is used by Gruen, "Greater independence for fiscal institutions."

5. For an illustration of explanations in the latter camp see Lori L. Leachman, Guillermo Rosas, Peter Lange, and Alan Bester, "The political economy of budget deficits," *Economics & Politics* 19, no. 3 (2007): 369–420, 372–375; Gabriel

Filc and Carlos Scartascini, *Budget institutions and fiscal outcomes* (Washington, DC: Inter-American Development Bank, 2004), 4; W. Nordhaus, "The political business cycle," *Review of Economic Studies* 42 (1975): 169–190, 187.

6. Aaron B. Wildavsky, *The politics of the budgetary process* (Boston: Little, Brown, 1964) and *Budgeting: A comparative theory of budgetary processes* (Boston: Little, Brown, 1975), 7–8, 142. See also Donald Savoie, *The politics of public spending in Canada* (Toronto: University of Toronto Press, 1990).

7. Daniel Tarschys, "Curbing public expenditure: Current trends," *Journal of Public Policy* 5, no. 1 (1985): 23–67, 63.

8. Nordhaus, "Political Business Cycle," 188–189.

9. Alberto Alesina and Roberto Perotti, "Fiscal discipline and the budget process," *American Economic Review* 86, no. 2 (1996): 401–407, 401 and 405–406.

10. Jürgen von Hagen and Ian Harden, "Budget processes and commitment to fiscal discipline," *European Economic Review* 39, no. 3–4 (1995): 771–779, 776 and 779; Leachman et al., "Political economy of budget deficits," 396; Carlos Santiso, *Budget institutions and fiscal responsibility: Parliaments and the political economy of the budget process in Latin America* (Washington, DC: World Bank Institute, 2005), 1.

11. James Poterba and Jürgen von Hagen, eds., *Fiscal institutions and fiscal performance* (Chicago: University of Chicago Press, 1999), 10.

12. Alesina and Perotti, "Fiscal discipline and the budget process," 401; Jürgen von Hagen, *Budgeting procedures and fiscal performance in the European community* (Brussels: European Commission, 1992); von Hagen and Harden, "Budget processes and commitment to fiscal discipline"; Poterba and von Hagen, *Fiscal institutions and fiscal performance*, 6–12; Alberto F. Alesina, Ricardo Hausmann, Rudolf Hommes, and Ernesto Stein, "Budget institutions and fiscal performance in Latin America," *Journal of Development Economics* 59 (1999): 253–273; Filc and Scartascini, *Budget institutions and fiscal outcomes*; Holger Gleich, *Budget institutions and fiscal performance in Central and Eastern European countries* (Frankfurt: European Central Bank, 2003).

13. Lotte Jensen and John Wanna, "Better guardians?" in *Controlling public expenditure: The changing roles of central budget agencies*, ed. John Wanna, Lotte Jensen, and Jouke de Vries (Northampton, MA: Edward Elgar, 2003), 251–270, 259. See also Joanne Kelly and John Wanna, *Are Wildavsky's guardians and spenders still relevant? New public management and the politics of government budgeting* (Brisbane: Centre for Australian Public Sector Management, Griffith University, 2000).

14. Martin Wolf, *Fixing global finance: Forum on constructive capitalism* (Baltimore, MD: Johns Hopkins University Press, 2008), 31–34; Gérard Duménil and Dominique Lévy, *Capital resurgent: Roots of the neoliberal revolution* (Cambridge: Harvard University Press, 2004), 86; Luc Laeven and Fabian Valencia, *Systemic banking crises: A new database*, IMF Working Paper No.

08/224, October (Washington, DC: IMF, 2008), table 3; Carmen M. Reinhart and Kenneth S. Rogoff, *This time is different: A panoramic view of eight centuries of financial crises*, NBER Working Paper No. 13882, March (Cambridge, MA: National Bureau of Economic Research, 2008), 7.

15. John Cassidy, "Anatomy of a meltdown," *New Yorker*, 2008.

16. George Soros, *The new paradigm for financial markets: The credit crisis of 2008 and what it means* (New York: PublicAffairs, 2008), 237; "Taking stock of Henry Paulson," *Newsweek*, November 24, 2008. The Emergency Economic Stabilization Act of 2008 (Public Law 110–343) was signed by President Bush on October 3, 2008.

17. Simon Jenkins, *Thatcher & sons* (London: Allen Lane, 2006), 191–201.

18. Roy Hattersley, *Borrowed time: The story of Britain between the wars* (London: Little, Brown, 2007).

19. Dennis Kavanagh, "The Blair premiership," in *Blair's Britain, 1997–2007*, ed. Anthony Seldon (New York: Cambridge University Press, 2007), 3–15, 7; Jenkins, *Thatcher & sons*, 253; David Lipsey, *The secret treasury* (London: Viking, 2000), 165; Christopher D. Foster, *British government in crisis* (Oxford: Hart, 2005), 164; Richard Heffernan, "Prime ministerial predominance? Core executive politics in the UK," *British Journal of Politics and International Relations* 5, no. 3 (2003): 347–372, 361 and 365.

20. Ivor Jennings, *Cabinet government* (Cambridge: Cambridge University Press, 1965), 1; Nicholas Timmins, "UK chancellor accused of 'Stalinist' style," *Financial Times*, March 20, 2007, 2.

21. House of Commons Treasury Committee, *Third report, Session 2000–2001*, January 30 (London: House of Commons, 2001).

22. In a YouGov/*Sunday Times* poll conducted on March 15–16, 2007, 55 percent of respondents agreed that Brown "has shown by his actions that he does not really care about hardworking families." In a May 15–16, 2007, poll, 51 percent responded affirmatively to the statement that Brown "does not understand the concerns of people like you." See also William Rees-Mogg, "Mr. Brown's decisive first hundred days," *Times* (London), April 30, 2007; Allegra Stratton, "Former communities secretary Hazel Blears leaves Downing Street," *Guardian*, June 3, 2009.

23. Edward Greenspon and Anthony Wilson-Smith, *Double vision* (Toronto: Doubleday Canada, 1996), 53–59 and 243; Donald Savoie, *Governing from the centre* (Toronto: University of Toronto Press, 1999), 156–192.

24. Joanne Kelly and Evert Lindquist, "Metamorphosis in Kafka's castle: The changing balance of power among the central budget agencies of Canada," in Wanna, Jensen, and de Vries, *Controlling public expenditure*, 85–105, 86; Bruce Wallace, "For the love of power: Is Jean Chretien a closet autocrat?" *Maclean's*, October 19, 1998; Donald Savoie, *Court government and the collapse of accountability in Canada and the United Kingdom* (Toronto: University of Toronto Press, 2008), 273–274 and 329–330.

25. Jeffrey Simpson, *The friendly dictatorship* (Toronto: McClelland & Stewart, 2001).

26. Lotte Jensen, "Aiming for centrality: The politico-administrative strategies of the Danish ministry of finance," in Wanna, Jensen, and de Vries, *Controlling public expenditure*, 166–193; Niels Ejersbo and Carsten Greve, "Public management policymaking in Denmark, 1983–2005," paper prepared for the IIM/LSE workshop on "Theory and methods for studying organizational processes: Institutional, narrative, and related approaches," February 17–18, 2005, London School of Economics, London; Marian Döhler, Julia Fleischer, and Thurid Hustedt, *Government reform as institutional politics: Varieties and policy patterns from a comparative perspective* (Potsdam, DE: Universität Potsdam, 2007), 39; Carsten Greve, "Public management reform in Denmark," *Public Management Review* 8, no. 1 (2006): 161–169; Jón Blöndal and Michael Ruffner, "Budgeting in Denmark," *OECD Journal on Budgeting* 4, no. 1 (2004): 49–79; Lise Togeby, Jørgen Goul Andersen, Peter Munk Christiansen, Torben Beck Jørgensen, and Signild Vallgårda, *Power and democracy in Denmark: Conclusions* (Aarhus, DK: Aarhus University Press, 2003), 31; Jørgen Andersen, "Political power and democracy in Denmark: Decline of democracy or change in democracy?" *Journal of European Public Policy* 13, no. 4 (2006): 569–586, 571 and 577.

27. Herman Schwartz, "Small states in big trouble: State reorganization in Australia, Denmark, New Zealand, and Sweden in the 1980s," *World Politics* 46, no. 4 (1994): 527–555; Robert Gregory and Jorgen Gronnegaard Christensen, "Similar ends, differing means: Contractualism and civil service reform in Denmark and New Zealand," *Governance* 17, no. 1 (2004): 59–82; Malcolm McKinnon, *Treasury: The New Zealand Treasury, 1840–2000* (Auckland, NZ: Auckland University Press, 2003), 319–320 and 324.

28. Allan Schick, *The spirit of reform: Managing the New Zealand state sector in a time of change*, report prepared for the State Services Commission and the Treasury, August (Wellington: New Zealand State Services Commission, 1996), 14; Jane Kelsey, *The New Zealand experiment: A world model for structural adjustment?* (Auckland, NZ: Auckland University Press/Bridget Williams Books, 1995), 69.

29. Jack Vowles and Peter Aimer, *Voters' vengeance: The 1990 election in New Zealand* (Auckland, NZ: Auckland University Press, 1993), 45; Geoffrey Palmer, *New Zealand's constitution in crisis* (Dunedin, NZ: John McIndoe Ltd., 1992); Jack Nagel, "What political scientists can learn from the 1993 electoral reform in New Zealand," *PS: Political Science and Politics* 27, no. 3 (1994): 525–529; McKinnon, *Treasury*, 425–427; Gwenda Jensen, "Zen and the art of budget management: The New Zealand Treasury," in Wanna, Jensen, and de Vries, *Controlling Public Expenditure*, 30–56, 46–49.

30. Carlos Santiso, *Legislative budget oversight in presidential systems: Governance of the budget in Peru* (Lima, PE: Department for International Development, 2004), 3; Ernesto Stein, Ernesto Talvi, and Alejandro Grisanti,

Institutional arrangements and fiscal performance: The Latin American experience (Washington, DC: Inter-American Development Bank, 1998), 12; Santiso, *Budget institutions and fiscal responsibility*, 11.

31. Jeffrey Rinne, "The politics of administrative reform in Menem's Argentina," in *Reinventing leviathan: The politics of administrative reform in developing countries*, ed. Blanca Heredia and Ben Ross Schneider (Boulder, CO: Lynne Rienner, 2003), 33–58; Nathaniel Nash, "Argentina deregulates its economy," *New York Times*, November 2, 1991.

32. The IMF's concerns are raised in IMF Country Report Nos. 03/72 (March 14, 2003), 03/104 (April 21, 2003), 04/226 (July 28, 2004), and 07/99 (March 7, 2007).

33. Marion Wrobel, *Fiscal rules for the control of government*, Background Paper No. 358E, November (Ottawa: Research Branch, Library of Parliament, 1993); George Kopits and Steven Symansky, *Fiscal policy rules* (Washington, DC: IMF, 1998), 2; Manmohan Kumar and Teresa Ter-Minassian, *Promoting fiscal discipline* (Washington, DC: IMF, 2007), vi.

34. George Kopits, *Fiscal rules: Useful policy framework or unnecessary ornament?* IMF Working Paper No. 01/145, September (Washington, DC: IMF, 2001), 8; George Kopits, "Overview of fiscal policy rules in emerging markets," in *Rules-based fiscal policy in emerging markets*, ed. George Kopits (Houndmills, UK: Palgrave Macmillan, 2004), 1–12, 2.

35. European Commission, *Public finances in EMU, 2006* (Brussels: European Commission, Directorate General for Economic and Financial Affairs, 2006), 370; Ana Corbacho and Gerd Schwartz, "Fiscal responsibility laws," in Kumar and Minassian, *Promoting fiscal discipline*, 58–105, 58.

36. Arthur Okun, David Fand, and William Brainard, "Fiscal–monetary activism: Some analytic issues," *Brookings Papers on Economic Activity* 1972, no. 1 (1972): 123–172, 155.

37. Suzanne Kennedy and Janine Robbins, *The role of fiscal rules in determining fiscal performance*, Department of Finance Working Paper 2001–16 (Ottawa, CA: Department of Finance, 2001); George Kopits, *How can fiscal policy help avert currency crises?* (Washington, DC: IMF, 2000); Kopits, "Overview of fiscal policy rules in emerging markets," 6.

38. James M. Buchanan and Richard E. Wagner, *Democracy in deficit: The political legacy of Lord Keynes* (New York: Academic Press, 1977), ch. 12; Allen Schick, *The federal budget: Politics, policy, process* (Washington, DC: Brookings Institution, 1995), 274–276; Aaron Wildavsky, *The new politics of the budgetary process* (Glenview, IL: Scott, Foresman and Co., 1997), 274–276.

39. Richard Peach, "The evolution of the federal budget and fiscal rules," in *Fiscal rules*, ed. Fabrizio Balassone (Rome: Banca d'Italia, 2004), 217–236, 229–231; Meir Sokoler, *The interaction between fiscal and monetary policy in Israel* (Basel, CH: Bank for International Settlements, 2003); Selim Elekdag, Natan Epstein, and Marialuz Moreno-Badia, *Fiscal consolidation in Israel: A global fiscal*

model perspective (Washington, DC: IMF, 2006); Miguel Braun and Nicolás Gadano, "What are fiscal rules for? A critical analysis of the Argentine experience," *CEPAL Review*, no. 91 (2007): 53–65; Willem H. Buiter and Urjit R. Patel, *Excessive budget deficits, a government-abused financial system, and fiscal rules* (London: London School of Economics, 2005), 3.

40. Marco Buti and Gabriele Giudice, "Maastricht's fiscal rules at ten: An assessment," *Journal of Common Market Studies* 40, no. 5 (2002): 823–848; Maria Gabriella Briotti, *Fiscal adjustment between 1991 and 2002: Stylised facts and policy implications* (Frankfurt: European Central Bank, 2004); Adam Posen, *German experience with fiscal rules: Lessons for the US budget process* (Washington, DC: Institution for International Economics, 2005); Wyplosz, "Fiscal policy," 69–70; José González-Páramo, "The reform of the Stability and Growth Pact: An assessment," speech presented at the European Central Bank Conference "New Perspectives on Fiscal Sustainability," Frankfurt, October 13, 2005: http://www. ecb.int/press/key/date/2005/html/sp051013.en.html; Barry Anderson and Joseph J. Minarik, "Design choices for fiscal policy rules," GOV/PGC/SBO(2006)4, May 16 (Paris: OECD, 2006), 3.

41. Kennedy and Robbins, *Role of fiscal rules in determining fiscal performance*, 8; Jürgen von Hagen, *Fiscal rules and fiscal performance in the EU and Japan* (Bonn, DE: University of Bonn, 2005), 7 and table 2; "IMF concludes Article IV consultation with Japan," Press Information Number (PIN) 97/19, August 13 (Washington, DC: IMF1997); Paul Blustein, *The chastening* (New York: PublicAffairs, 2001), 169–170.

42. The New Zealand requirements are now contained in Part 2 of the Public Finance Act. The United Kingdom rules are contained in Part 6 of the Finance Act, 1998.

43. Michael Kell, *An assessment of fiscal rules in the United Kingdom* (Washington, DC: IMF, 2001), 12; Keiko Honjo, *The Golden Rule and the economic cycles*, IMF Working Paper No. 07/199, August (Washington, DC: IMF, 2007), 5; Chancellor of the Exchequer, "Exploiting the British genius: The key to long-term economic success," speech given in London. May 20, 1997; Carl Emmerson, "Bending the rules?" *Public Finance*, August 2005; Willem Buiter, "Welcome to a world of diminished expectations," *Financial Times*, August 6, 2008; International Monetary Fund, *United Kingdom: 2006 Article IV consultation—Staff Report*, IMF Country Report No. 07/91, March 2 (Washington, DC: IMF, 2007), 21.

44. Guillermo Perry, *Can fiscal rules help reduce macroeconomic volatility in the Latin American and Caribbean region?* (Washington, DC: World Bank, 2002), 8; Ludger Schuknecht, *EU fiscal rules: Issues and lessons from political economy* (Frankfurt: European Central Bank, 2004), 14–16.

45. Kennedy and Robbins, *Role of fiscal rules in determining fiscal performance*, 9 and 15; James Poterba, *Do budget rules work?* (Cambridge, MA: National Bureau of Economic Research, 1996), 8–9. For an argument that fiscal rules in

the United States functioned simply as an exercise in "political symbolism," see Peach, "Evolution of the federal budget and fiscal rules," 218. For an argument that causality runs "from rules to behavior," see Xavier Debrun, Laurent Moulin, Alessandro Turrini, Joaquim Ayuso-i-Casals, and Manmohan S. Kumar, "Tied to the mast? National fiscal rules in the European Union," *Economic Policy* 23, no. 54 (2008): 297–362.

46. International Monetary Fund, *The state of public finances: Outlook and medium-term policies after the 2008 crisis* (companion paper), March 6 (Washington, DC: IMF, 2009), 17 and 63. For G-20 countries as a whole, stabilization and stimulus costs were roughly equal, at about 3.2 percent of GDP for each purpose: IMF, *The state of public finances: Outlook and medium-term policies after the 2008 crisis*, March 6 (Washington, DC: IMF, 2009), 7 and 14.

47. Chancellor of the Exchequer, *Building Britain's Future*, Economic and Fiscal Strategy Report 2009 (Budget 2009), HC 407, April 22 (London: Stationery Office, 2009), table 1.1; International Monetary Fund, *State of public finances*, 21.

48. Lori Montgomery, "House adopts pay-as-you-go rules," *Washington Post*, January 6, 2007; European Commission, *Economic forecast spring 2009*, May 4 (Brussels: European Commission, Directorate-General for Economic and Financial Affairs, 2009), 40–42; Elitsa Vucheva, "This week in the European Union," *EU Observer*, May 8, 2009; "India's country rating vulnerable to further setbacks: Moody's," *Press Trust of India*, April 26, 2009.

49. Chris Giles, "Transfer of rock debts destroys US fiscal rule," *Financial Times*, February 8, 2008; Alistair Darling, "Pre-budget report statement to the House of Commons," November 24 (London: HM Treasury, 2008); Chancellor of the Exchequer, *Building Britain's Future* 31.

Chapter 4

Sources for epigraphs: Odd-Helge Fjeldstad and Mick Moore, *Revenue authorities and state capacity in anglophone Africa*, Working Paper No. 2008/1 (Bergen, NO: Chr. Michelsen Institute, 2008), 5; Robert R. Taliercio Jr., "Administrative reform as credible commitment: The design, performance, and sustainability of semi-autonomous revenue authorities in Latin America" (PhD diss., Harvard University, 2000), 147.

1. Robert R. Taliercio Jr., *Designing performance: The semi-autonomous revenue authority model in Africa and Latin America*, Policy, Research Working Paper series No. 3423, October 27 (Washington, DC: World Bank, 2004), 2.

2. Sheetal Chand and Karl Moene, *Controlling fiscal corruption* (Washington, DC: IMF, 1997); Roumeen Islam and Deborah Wetzel, *The macroeconomics of public sector deficits* (Washington, DC: World Bank, 1991); Allan Meltzer, "There is a way to defuse the bomb," *Financial Times*, December 14, 1983; Henry F.

Jackson, "The African crisis: Drought and debt," *Foreign Affairs* 63, no. 5 (1985): 1081–1094, 1086.

3. Seth Terkper, *Ghana: Tax administration reforms (1985–1993)* (Cambridge: International Tax Program, Harvard University, 1994); Chand and Moene, *Controlling fiscal corruption*; Islam and Wetzel, *Macroeconomics of public sector deficits*. An advisor to the Ghanian govenrment says that the model for its reform was probably Canada, which for many years had a separate revenue ministry. Terkper, *Ghana*, 5.

4. Odd-Helge Fjeldstad, *Corruption in tax administration: Lessons from institutional reforms in Uganda* (Bergen, NO: Chr. Michelsen Institute, 2005), 4–5; Steve Kayizzi-Mugerwa, *Fiscal policy, growth, and poverty reduction in Uganda* (Helsinki: World Institute for Development Economics Research, 2002), table 1; Siri Gloppen and Lise Rakner, "Accountability through tax reform? Reflections from sub-Saharan Africa," *IDS Bulletin* 33, no. 3 (2002): 30–40, 34.

5. Francisco Durand and Rosemary Thorp, "Reforming the state: A Study of the Peruvian tax reform," *Oxford Development Studies* 26, no. 2 (1998): 133–151; Robert R. Taliercio Jr., "Administrative reform as credible commitment: The design, performance, and sustainability of semi-autonomous revenue authorities in Latin America" (PhD diss., Harvard University, 2000), 132, 151 and ch. 7; Rosario Manasan, "Tax administration reform: Semi-autonomous revenue authorities, anyone?" *Phillippine Journal of Development* 30, no. 2 (2003): 173–193, table 3.

6. Luc De Wulf and José B. Sokol, eds. *Customs modernization handbook*, Trade and Development series (Washington, DC: World Bank, 2005), 40; Odd-Helge Fjeldstad and Mick Moore, *Revenue authorities and state capacity in anglophone Africa*, Working Paper No. 2008/1 (Bergen, NO: Chr. Michelsen Institute, 2008), 4; Robert R. Taliercio Jr., "The design, performance, and sustainability of semi-autonomous revenue authorities in Africa and Latin America," in *Unbundled Government*, ed. Christopher Pollitt and Colin Talbot (London: Routledge, 2004), 264–282, 264; Maureen Kidd and William Crandall, *Revenue authorities: Issues and problems in evaluating their success*, IMF Working Paper No. 06/240, October (Washington, DC: IMF, 2006), 5.

7. Glen Jenkins, "Modernization of tax administrations: Revenue boards and privatization as an instrument for change," *Bulletin for International Fiscal Documentation* 48, no. 2 (1994): 75–81, 76 and 84. British proponents of ARAs sometimes said that they were the intellectual offspring of a reform project undertaken by the British government in the 1980s known as the "executive agency" scheme, which disaggregated many of its central government ministries into a number of special-purpose organizations known as executive agencies. In fact, the lineage is mistaken. Peru, which established the "most iconic" of the ARAs, undertook its reform before the Thatcher government unveiled the executive agency plan in 1988. Nick Devas, Simon Delay, and Michael Hubbard, "Revenue authorities: Are they the right vehicle for improved tax administration?"

Public Administration and Development 21 (2001): 211–222, 212; Simon Delay, Nick Devas, and Michael Hubbard, *The reform of revenue administration* (Birmingham, UK: School of Public Policy, University of Birmingham, 1998), 38; Office of Public Services Reform, *Better government services: Executive agencies in the 21st century* (London: Office of Public Services Reform, 2002), annex B; Taliercio, "Administrative reform as credible commitment," 134–138.

8. Taliercio, "Administrative reform as credible commitment," 146–147 and 157.

9. Taliercio, "The design, performance, and sustainability of semi-autonomous revenue authorities in Africa and Latin America," 268.

10. Taliercio, "Design, performance, and sustainability of semi-autonomous revenue authorities in Africa and Latin America," 267; Fjeldstad and Moore, *Revenue authorities and state capacity in anglophone Africa*, 4–5; De Wulf and Sokol, *Customs modernization handbook*, 40.

11. Fjeldstad and Moore, *Revenue authorities and state capacity in anglophone Africa*, 5. The authors note the danger that "informal power relations [might] completely over-ride formal arrangements." Of course, they are writing with the benefit of hindsight. A formal–legal definition is provided also by Jenkins in "Modernization of tax administrations" 77; and by Kidd and Crandall in *Revenue authorities*, 14. An "autonomy index" for ARAs that is modeled on the early measures of de jure central bank independence is developed by Taliercio in "Administrative reform as credible commitment," 312–316. For references to the early research on the effects of de jure central bank independence see Jenkins, "Modernization of tax administrations," 84.

12. World Bank, *Economic growth in the 1990s: Learning from a decade of reform* (Washington, DC: World Bank, 2005), 285–286; Kidd and Crandall, *Revenue Authorities*, 18; Taliercio, *Designing Performance*, 8.

13. Nicholas Kaldor, "Will underdeveloped countries learn to tax?" *Foreign Affairs* 4, no. 2 (1963): 410–419, 416; Taliercio, *Designing performance*, 9; John Gray and Emma Chapman, *Evaluation of revenue projects synthesis report volume 1*, February (London: Department for International Development, 2001), 20–23.

14. International Monetary Fund, *Peru: 2000 Article IV Consultation—Staff Report*, IMF Country Report No. 01/48, March 19 (Washington, DC: IMF, 2001), 24–30.

15. Michael Keen, *Changing customs: Challenges and strategies for the reform of customs administration* (Washington, DC: IMF, 2003), 1 and 13; Devas, Delay, and Hubbard, "Revenue authorities," 13.

16. Taliercio, *Designing performance*, 2; Gloppen and Rakner, "Accountability through tax reform?" 30; Fjeldstad and Moore, *Revenue authorities and state capacity in anglophone Africa*, 2–3; Kidd and Crandall, *Revenue authorities*, 11; Delay, Devas, and Hubbard, *Reform of revenue administration*, 38; Devas, Delay, and Hubbard, "Revenue authorities," 212.

17. Kidd and Crandall, *Revenue authorities*, 53.

18. Taliercio, "Administrative reform as credible commitment," 105, 154, 212–223, 228, 234–238; World Bank, *Autonomy and revenue boards* (Washington, DC: World Bank, 2002), 4; Taliercio, *Designing performance*, 62–65; Fjeldstad, *Corruption in tax administration*, 5.

19. Fjeldstad and Moore, *Revenue authorities and state capacity in anglophone Africa*, 1.

20. Delay, Devas, and Hubbard, *Reform of revenue administration*, 44; Fjeldstad and Moore, *Revenue authorities and state capacity in anglophone Africa*, 6; Arthur J. Mann, *Are semi-autonomous revenue authorities the answer to tax administration problems in developing countries?* (Washington, DC: USAID, 2004), 46–48.

21. Gray and Chapman, *Evaluation of revenue projects synthesis report volume 1*, 2 and 37; Odd-Helge Fjeldstad, "Fighting fiscal corruption: Lessons from the Tanzania Revenue Authority," *Public Administration and Development* 23, no. 2 (2003): 165–175; Fjeldstad, *Corruption in tax administration*; Mann, *Are semi-autonomous revenue authorities the answer to tax administration problems in developing countries?* 41–51.

22. Fjeldstad, "Fighting fiscal corruption," 171–172, and *Corruption in tax administration*, 8–14.

23. Mick Moore, *How does taxation affect the quality of governance?* (Brighton, UK: Institute of Development Studies, University of Sussex, 2007), 31–32; Devas, Delay, and Hubbard, "Revenue authorities," 221; World Bank, *Autonomy and revenue boards*.

24. Delay, Devas, and Hubbard, *Reform of revenue administration*, 3 and 21; Gray and Chapman, *Evaluation of revenue projects synthesis report volume 1*, 38; Department for International Development, *Revenue authorities and taxation in sub-Saharan Africa: A concise review of recent literature* (London: Department for International Development, 2005), 17. For a reference to the political economy considerations that affect ARA reform see Fjeldstad, *Corruption in tax administration*, 12. An attempt at a "political economy analysis" of the Rwandan Revenue Authority is provided by Foreign Investment Advisory Service, *Sector study of the effective tax burden: Rwanda* (Washington, DC: Foreign Investment Advisory Service, 2006), ch. 3.

25. Gloppen and Rakner, "Accountability through tax reform?" 37–38; Gray and Chapman, *Evaluation of revenue projects synthesis report volume 1*, 26–27; Department for International Development, *Revenue authorities and taxation in sub-Saharan Africa*, 27–28; Fjeldstad and Moore, *Revenue authorities and state capacity in anglophone Africa*, 1. Talierco does find a correlation between perceptions of ARA autonomy and perceptions of ARA performance, among a sample of corporate taxpayers in Latin America. However, there is no assessment of the impact on the propensity to comply. Robert R. Taliercio Jr., "Administrative reform as credible commitment: The impact of autonomy on revenue authority performance in Latin America," *World Development* 32, no. 2 (2004): 213–232.

Chapter 5

Source for epigraph: T. E. Notteboom and W. Winkelmans, "Reassessing public sector involvements in European seaports," *International Journal of Maritime Economics* 3, no. 2 (2001): 242–259, 247.

1. Edna Bonacich and Jake Wilson, *Getting the goods: Ports, labor, and the logistics revolution* (Ithaca, NY: Cornell University Press, 2008), 120; Kimberley Edds, "LA's other traffic jam; Ports, docks can't keep up with flood of goods," *Washington Post*, November 3, 2004; Alex Pulaski, "West Coast cargo glut," *Sunday Oregonian*, January 2, 2005; Lawrence Kaufman, "Considering the alternatives," *Journal of Commerce*, December 20, 2004.

2. Bill Mongelluzzo, "Chokepoints everywhere," *Journal of Commerce*, January 10, 2005; Helen Hill and Janet Porter, "Top container lines demand action to relieve port congestion," *Lloyd's List*, November 12, 2004; Katrin Berkenkopf, "Port congestion hits Duisburg services," *Lloyd's List*, September 3, 2004; "Government must spend to avoid port growing pains," *Lloyd's List*, November 22, 2004.

3. F. A. Howe, "The sensitiveness of the modern seaport," *Economic Journal* 22, no. 87 (1912): 410–420, 410–411.

4. "A mainport is a transport junction in a certain country which takes care of the physical distribution and the related logistic activities of the incoming and outgoing international (including intercontinental) flows of commodities and people over different modes of transport from (and to) the hinterland." Peter Nijkamp and Caroline Rodenburg, *Mainports and gateways in Europe* (Amsterdam: Free University, 1998). On congestion within the U.S. air transport system see U.S. General Accounting Office (U.S. GAO), *National airspace system: Long-term capacity planning needed despite recent reduction in flight delays*, GAO-02–185 (Washington, DC: U.S. GAO, 2001), 5–6; Office of Inspector General, *Top management challenges*, PT-2008–008, November 15 (Washington, DC: U.S. Department of Transportation, 2007), 13–14; U.S. GAO, *Federal Aviation Administration: Challenges facing the agency in fiscal year 2009 and beyond*, GAO-08–460T (Washington, DC: U.S. GAO, 2008), 11. Performance data for the air transport system is provided online by the U.S. Bureau of Transportation Statistics: http://www.transtats.bts.gov.

5. European Parliament, *Airport capacity and ground handling: Towards a more efficient policy*, September 27 (Brussels: Committee on Transport and Tourism, 2007); Robert Aaronson, "The airport capacity crunch is hurting business," *Financial Times*, November 5, 2007. Data on global passenger traffic were provided to the author by Airports Council International.

6. Jamil Anderlini, "Beijing aims to build 97 regional airports," *Financial Times*, January 30, 2008; Sandeep Unnithan, "Chaos at airports," *India Today*, April 25, 2008; Raphael Minder, "Bumpy ride for airport projects," *Financial Times*, May 1, 2008.

7. Robert Aaronson, "Forces driving industry change," in *Strategic managment in the aviation industry*, ed. Werner Delfmann, Herbert Baum, Stefan Auerbach, and Sascha Albers (Aldershot, UK: Ashgate, 2005), 345–361, 345.

8. Aronson, "Forces driving industry change"; World Bank, *Infrastructure for development: A policy agenda for the Caribbean* (Washington, DC: World Bank, 1996), 94; M. H. Juhel, "Globalization, privatization, and restructuring of ports," *International Journal of Maritime Economics* 3 (2001): 139–174, 149–150.

9. Alfred Baird and Vincent Valentine, "Port privatisation in the United Kingdom," in *Devolution, port governance, and port performance*, ed. Mary Brooks and Kevin Cullinane (Oxford: JAI, 2007), 55–84; Ian Humphreys, "Privatisation and commercialisation: Changes in UK airport ownership patterns," *Journal of Transport Geography* 7, no. 2 (1999): 121–134, 124.

10. J. A. A. Lovink, "Improving the governance of airport authorities," *Policy Options*, (April 2001); Mary Brooks, "Port devolution and governance in Canada," in Brooks and Cullinane, *Devolution, port governance, and port performance*, 237–258; Sophia Everett and Ross Robinson, "Port reform: The Australian experience," in Brooks and Cullinane, *Devolution, port governance, and port performance*, 259–284; Michael J. Enright and Flash Ng, *Airport privatisation in Australia*, August 15 (Hong Kong: School of Business, University of Hong Kong, 2001); David Lyon and Graham Francis, "Managing New Zealand's airports in the face of commercial challenges," *Journal of Air Transport Management* 12, no. 5 (2006): 220–226; "Waterfront for the people," *New Zealand Herald*, December 2, 2006.

11. Peter de Langen and Larissa van der Lugt, "Governance structures of port authorities in the Netherlands," in Brooks and Cullinane, *Devolution, port governance, and port performance*, 109–137; Miguel Pereira, Miguel Pina e Cunha, and Patricia Jardim da Palma, "Giving out but not giving up: The Port of Lisbon Authority (1907–2005)," *International Public Management Review* 8, no. 1 (2007): 33–55; Beatriz Tovar, Lourdes Trujillo, and Sergio Jara-D az, *Organization and regulation of the port industry: Europe and Spain* (Las Palmas de Gran Canaria, ES: Universidad de Las Palmas de Gran Canaria, 2004); Jan Hoffman, "Latin American ports: Results and determinants of private sector participation," *International Journal of Maritime Economics* 3 (2001): 221–241; Antonio Estache, Marianela González, and Lourdes Trujillo, "Efficiency gains from port reform and the potential for yardstick competition: Lessons from Mexico," *World Development* 30, no. 4 (2002): 545–560.

12. Kevin Cullinane and D. W. Song, "The administrative and ownership structure of Asian container ports," *International Journal of Maritime Economics* 3 (2001): 175–197; Anthony Cheung, "How autonomous are public corporations in Hong Kong? The case of the airport authority," *Public Organization Review* 6 (2006): 221–236; Anming Zhang and Andrew Yuen, "Airport policy and performance in mainland China and Hong Kong," in *Aviation infrastructure performance: A study in comparative political economy*, ed. Clifford Winston and Ginés de Rus (Washington, DC: Brookings Institution, 2008), 159–192.

13. On the tradition of decentralized governance in the United States see Steven Morrison and Clifford Winston, "Delayed: US aviation infrastructure at a crossroads," in Winston and de Rus, *Aviation infrastructure performance*, 7–35; James Fawcett, "Port governance and privatization in the United States: Public ownership and private operation," in Brooks and Cullinane, *Devolution, port governance, and port performance*, 207–235. On the large proportion of U.S. mainports organized as autonomous bodies see Steven P. Erie, *Globalizing LA: Trade, infrastructure, and regional development* (Stanford, CA: Stanford University Press, 2004), 31.

14. Morton Keller, *America's three regimes: A new political history* (New York: Oxford University Press, 2007), 174–200; Jon C. Teaford, *The twentieth-century American city*, The American moment (Baltimore, MD: Johns Hopkins University Press, 1993), 37–43; Robert H. Wiebe, *Self-rule: A cultural history of American democracy* (Chicago: University of Chicago Press, 1995), 162–165.

15. Jameson W. Doig, *Empire on the Hudson: Entrepreneurial vision and political power at the Port of New York Authority*, Columbia History of Urban Life (New York: Columbia University Press, 2001), 49.

16. Herbert Kaufman, "Gotham in the air age," in *Public administration and policy development*, ed. Harold Stein (New York: Harcourt, Brace, 1952), 151–162, 174; Jameson W. Doig, "'If I see a murderous fellow sharpening a knife cleverly': The Wilsonian dichotomy and the public authority tradition," *Public Administration Review* 43, no. 4 (1983): 292–304, 296.

17. T. E. Notteboom and W. Winkelmans, "Reassessing public sector involvements in European seaports," *International Journal of Maritime Economics* 3, no. 2 (2001): 242–259, 247–248; Sophia Everett, "Corporatization: A legislative framework for port inefficiencies," *Maritime Policy and Management* 30, no. 3 (2003): 211–219, 211.

18. World Bank, *Infrastructure for development*, 88; Hoffman, "Latin American ports," 233; Juhel, "Globalization, privatization, and restructuring of ports," 169.

19. Sophia Everett and Ross Robinson, "Port reform in Australia: Issues in the ownership debate," *Maritime Policy and Management* 25, no. 1 (1998): 41–62, 41; Notteboom and Winkelmans, "Reassessing public sector involvements in European seaports," 248; Michael Carney and Keith Mew, "Airport governance reform: A strategic management perspective," *Journal of Air Transport Management* 9 (2003): 221–232, 222; Scott E. Tarry, *Innovation in the administration of public airports*, grant report, March (Washington, DC: PriceWaterhouseCoopers Endowment for the Business of Government, 2000), 6.

20. James Weinstein, "Organized business and the city commission and manager movements," *Journal of Southern History* 28, no. 2 (1962): 166–182, and *The corporate ideal in the liberal state, 1900–1918* (Westport, CT: Greenwood, 1981), ix; Howard Zinn, *The twentieth century: A people's history* (New York: Perennial, 2003), 349–254.

21. Erie, *Globalizing LA*, 31; Bonacich and Wilson, *Getting the goods*, 63; John Gulick, "Landside risks: The ecological contradictions of Port of Oakland globalism" (PhD diss., University of California, Santa Cruz, 2001), 278–279.

22. Barry C. Lynn, *End of the line: The rise and coming fall of the global corporation* (New York: Doubleday, 2005); Brian J. Cudahy, *Box boats: How container ships changed the world* (New York: Fordham University Press, 2006); Marc Levinson, *The box: How the shipping container made the world smaller and the world economy bigger* (Princeton, NJ: Princeton University Press, 2006).

23. Gary Rosenberger, "Reality check: US cargo," *Main Wire*, November 10, 2004; Peter Leach, "Global congestion to slow trade," *Journal of Commerce Online*, November 17, 2004.

24. "Top container lines demand action to relieve port congestion," *Lloyd's List*, November 12, 2004.

25. Christa Sys, *Measuring the degree of concentration in the container line shipping industry* (Ghent, BE: University College Ghent, 2007); Robert Wright, "Maersk overturns key strategies on size and vertical integration," *Financial Times*, May 27, 2008; Stéphane Hoste, Reginald Loyen, and Stephan Vanfraechem, "New perspectives on port competition: Antwerp and Rotterdam, 1945–1975," *Research in Maritime History*, No. 35 (2007): 57–84, 57; John W. Fischer, Bart Elias, and Robert S. Kirk, *US airline industry: Issues and role of Congress*, CRS Report for Congress, April 30 (Washington, DC: Congressional Research Service, 2008); Kevin Done, "Heathrow expansion plans backed," *Financial Times*, November 23, 2007.

26. "India ranks 39 on world goods transportation list," *Indian Express*, November 6, 2007. The Logistics Performance Index is located at http://go. worldbank.org/88X6PU5GV0.

27. Dan Olson, "MSP opens new runway as nation's air system edges toward gridlock," Minnesota Public Radio, October 27, 2005: http://news.minnesota. publicradio.org/features/2005/10/27_olsond_runway/.

28. Ronald Powell, "San Diego easing cargo backup at Port of Long Beach," Copley News Service, October 29, 2004; Reginald Loyen, Erik Buyst, and Greta Devos, eds, *Struggling for leadership: Antwerp–Rotterdam port competition between 1870–2000*, Contributions to Economics (New York: Physica-Verlag, 2003), 290; Bruce Barnard, "Rotterdam bites back," *Journal of Commerce*, July 19, 2004.

29. Jan Hoffman, "The process of concentration in port and shipping businesses," *Transport Newsletter*, no. 36 (2007): 6–8.

30. Jorge Gonzalez and Sasha Page, *Annual privatization report 2003: Emergence of a global airport industry* (Los Angeles: Reason Public Policy Institute, 2003); Anne Graham, *Managing airports: An international perspective* (Oxford: Butterworth–Heinemann, 2003), 37–47; Benjamin Koch and Sven Budde, "Internationalization strategies for airport companies," in Delfmann et al., *Strategic management in the aviation industry*, 378–406.

31. The author interviewed Sanjay Reddy, MIAL's managing director, in December 2007 and January 2008. See also Jockin Arputham, "An offer of partnership or a promise of conflict," Document ID No. G02314, May 30 (London: International Institute for Environment and Development, 2007): http://www.iied.org/pubs/pdfs/G02314.pdf; "Uddhav joins Raj; 'Outsiders in,'" *Times of India*, February 11, 2008.

32. Justin Stares, "Troops threat to striking truck drivers," *Lloyd's List*, July 30, 1999; Rekha Jain, G. Raghuram, and Rachna Gangwar, *Airport privatization in India: Lessons from the bidding process in Delhi and Mumbai* (Ahmedabad: Indian Institute of Management Ahmedabad, 2007); "Strikes against reform plans start at French ports," Reuters, April 23, 2008.

33. Roger Kerr, *Paying for parochialism: The costs of stalled port reform* (Auckland: New Zealand Business Roundtable, 1998); "Regional investment manager seeks all port company shares," media release, April 1 (Auckland, NZ: Auckland Regional Holdings, 2005). The author interviewed officials at the Port of Auckland and Auckland Regional Holdings in November 2007.

34. de Langen and van der Lugt, "Governance structures of port authorities in the Netherlands," 119; Alejandro Garcia Garcia de Paredes, "How to structure port management between government and market: A comparative study of the situation of Panama and Rotterdam" (M.Sc. thesis, Erasmus University of Rotterdam, 2006), 41.

35. Sarah Kelly, "Toward a more deliberative port planning: The 'vision and daring' of environmental NGOs in negotiations on the Second Maasvlakte, Port of Rotterdam, the Netherlands" (MCP thesis, Massachusetts Institute of Technology, 2005), 59; Helen Hill, "Rotterdam reaches a deal on Maasvlakte 2 project," *Lloyd's List*, June 22, 2004.

36. Alan Tiller, "Schiphol IPO hangs in the balance," *Daily Deal*, June 15, 2001; Martijn Boxtel and Menno Huys, *Unravelling decision making about the future development of Amsterdam's Schiphol Airport*, ERSA Conference Papers No. 05p179, August 2005: http://ideas.repec.org/p/wiw/wiwrsa/ersa05p179.html; Celeste Perri, "Amsterdam blocks share sale in airport," *International Herald Tribune*, October 2, 2006: http://www.highbeam.com/doc/1P1–129552525.html.

37. "Change urged in management of airports," *Times* (London), July 22, 1961.

38. Mark Benham, "The longest airport hold-up in history," *Evening Standard*, November 20, 200116; Department for Transport, *The future of air transport*, White Paper, December 16 (London: Department for Transport, 2003).

39. Steven Griggs and David Howarth, "Airport governance, politics, and protest networks," in *Democratic network governance in Europe*, ed. Martin Marcussen and Jacob Torfing (London: Palgrave Macmillan, 2006), 66–88.

40. On the influence of the Port Authority of New York and New Jersey on BAA see John M. Wilson, "The administrative problems of the long-term planning of airports," *Public Administration* 42, no. 1 (1964): 33–44, 41. The phrase

"development alliance" is used by John Gulick in "'It's all about market share': Competition among US West Coast ports for trans-Pacific containerized cargo," in *Space and transport in the world-system*, ed. Paul Ciccantell and Stephen Bunker (Westport, CT: Greenwood, 1998), 61–83. Harvey Molotch uses the phrase "growth coalition" to convey the same idea in "The city as growth machine: Toward a political economy of place," *American Journal of Sociology* 82, no. 1 (1976): 309–332.

41. Elliot J. Feldman and Jerome Milch, *Technocracy versus democracy: The comparative politics of international airports* (Boston: Auburn House, 1982), 265–268. On growth of passenger traffic see Dorothy Nelkin, *Jetport: The Boston airport controversy* (New Brunswick, NJ: Transaction, 1974), table 2.

42. Doig, *Empire on the Hudson*, 385–388; Alan A. Altshuler and David Luberoff, *Mega-projects: The changing politics of urban public investment* (Washington, DC: Brookings Institution Press, 2003), 137–139.

43. Nelkin, *Jetport*, 47.

44. Nelkin, *Jetport*, 84.

45. Nelkin, *Jetport*, 56, 130, and 133; "Boston debates airport growth," *New York Times*, November 15, 1970; John Kifner, "Power of Boston Airport Authority is under attack," *New York Times*, August 11, 1974.

46. Kifner, "Power of Boston Airport Authority is under attack"; Nelkin, *Jetport*, 131–139; John Kifner, "Massachusetts port head dismissed," *New York Times*, November 25, 1974; Yvonne Abraham, "1960s disagreements over transit persist in Boston area," *Boston Globe*, July 26, 1999; Peter Howe, "The 30-year saga of 14/32," *Boston Globe*, November 19, 2006.

47. Richard Carter, "A comparative analysis of United States ports and their traffic characteristics," *Economic Geography* 38, no. 2 (1962): 162–175, table 1; Donald Fitzgerald, "A history of containerization in the California maritime industry: The case of San Francisco" (PhD diss., University of California, Santa Barbara, 1986), 71 and 90; Mark Rosenstein, "The rise of maritime containerization in the Port of Oakland, 1950 to 1970" (M.A. thesis, New York University, 2000), 47, 81, 94–97; Yehuda Hayut, "Containerization and the load center concept," *Economic Geography* 57, no. 2 (1981): 160–176, table 2.

48. Robert Kagan, "Adversarial legalism and American government," *Journal of Policy Analysis and Management* 10, no. 3 (1991): 369–406, 369–370; Rosenstein, "Rise of maritime containerization in the Port of Oakland, 1950 to 1970," 69 and 72–73; Robert Kagan, "Adversarial legalism: Tamed or still wild?" *Journal of Legislation and Public Policy* 2, no. 2 (1999): 217–245, 230; Christopher Busch, David Kirp, and Daniel Schoenholz, "Taming adversarial legalism: The Port of Oakland's dredging saga revisited," *Journal of Legislation and Public Policy* 2, no. 2 (1999): 179–216; Gulick, "Landside Risks," ch. 4.

49. Busch, Kirp, and Schoenholz, "Taming adversarial legalism," 196–197; Gulick, "'It's all about market share,'" 64; Gulick, "Landside risks"; Diane Bailey, Thomas Plenys, Gina M. Solomon, Todd R. Campbell, Gail Ruderman Feuer,

Julie Masters, and Bella Tonkonogy, *Harboring pollution: The dirty truth about U.S. ports*, NRDC Report, March (New York: Natural Resources Defense Council, 2004), 33–36.

50. Doig, "'If I see a murderous fellow sharpening a knife cleverly'"; James D. Thompson, *Organizations in action: Social science bases of administrative theory* (New York: McGraw-Hill, 1967); Mary Fennell and Jeffrey Alexander, "Organizational boundary spanning in institutionalized environments," *Academy of Management Journal* 30, no. 3 (1987): 456–476; Martin Meznar and Douglas Nigh, "Buffer or bridge? Environmental and organizational determinants of public affairs activities in American firms," *Academy of Management Journal* 38, no. 4 (1995): 975–996.

51. Erie, *Globalizing LA*, 123; South Coast Air Quality Management District, *Multiple air toxics exposure study in the south coast air basin (Mates-II): Final report and appendices*, March (Diamond Bar, CA: South Coast Air Quality Management District, 2000).

52. Bonacich and Wilson, *Getting the Goods*, 66–67; Barbara Whitaker, "Deal clears way for Los Angeles port project," *New York Times*, March 7, 2003; Patrick McGreevy and Deborah Schoch, "L.A. port director resigns," *Los Angeles Times*, September 18, 2004; Bill Mongelluzzo, "Shake-up at Los Angeles: Keller's resignation underscores the balancing act ports face," *Journal of Commerce*, September 27, 2004, 19.

53. Port of Los Angeles and Port of Long Beach, *Clean Air Action Plan* (Long Beach, CA: Port of Long Beach, 2006), 41; interview with Michael Vanderbook, manager of strategic planning, Port of Long Beach, February 15, 2008.

54. Port of Long Beach, *White paper on green port policy*, August (Long Beach, CA: Port of Long Beach, 2005). Lobbying expenditure is obtained from the California secretary of state and the Center for Responsive Politics.

55. Los Angeles County Economic Development Corp., advertising supplement to *Hemispheres Magazine*, October 2007; Louis Sahagun, "Port complex aspires to be bustling, clean," *Los Angeles Times*, May 28, 2007.

56. Bill Mongelluzzo, "LA OKs TraPac terminal," *Journal of Commerce*, April 4, 2008.

57. "WTO sees 9% global trade decline in 2009," press release, March 23 (Geneva: World Trade Organization, 2009).

58. Andrew Ward, "Maersk hit by 'crisis of historic proportions,'" *Financial Times*, August 22, 2009; National Retail Federation, "Retail container traffic to fall 11.8 percent in first half of 2009," press release, February 6 (Washington, DC: National Retail Federation, 2009); Dave Hannon, "Container traffic continues to slow; Port of LA/Long Beach sees huge decline in February," *Purchasing.com*, April 8, 2009 (accessed May 12, 2009): http://www.purchasing.com/article/CA6650353.html; IATA, "Load factors drop as passenger demand falls; freight stabilises," press release, April 28 (Montreal: IATA, 2009).

59. Peter Pae, "As travel declines, aircraft boneyard in Victorville fills up," *Los Angeles Times*, March 15, 2009; Paul Watson, "Empty cargo ships wait out the economy in Philippine ports," *Los Angeles Times*, March 25, 2009; Keith Bradsher, "Cargo ships treading water off Singapore, waiting for work," *New York Times*, May 12, 2009.

60. For some discussion of the effects of decentralization and autonomization on operational efficiency see Hoffman, "Latin American ports," 222. For a summary of recent evaluations on airport privatization see Kenneth Button, "Air transportation infrastructure in developing countries: Privitization and Deregulation," paper prepared for the Fundación Rafael del Pino conference "Comparative Political Economy and Infrastructure Performance: The Case of Airports," Madrid, September 18–19, 2006. A cautious view about the salience of ownership is provided by Bijan Vasigh and Javad Gorjidooz, "Productivity analysis of public and private airports," *Journal of Air Transportation* 11, no. 3 (2006): 144–163. An older World Bank study observes that the "decisive question is not who has ownership of port equipment and properties, but if they are utilised on a commercial basis." World Bank, *Infrastructure for Development*, 80.

61. Doig, " 'If I see a murderous fellow sharpening a knife cleverly, '" 298.

Chapter 6

Source for epigraph: U.S. Congress, House of Representatives Committee on International Relations, Transcript of hearings on trade disputes in Peru and Ecuador, October 6, 2004.

1. Robert Smock, "Who's in a long-term decline?" *Power Engineering* 97 (1993): 17; Independent Power Report, "Chase funds $200-million for 1,420-MW hydro plan acquisition in Argentina," *Independent Power Report*, August 13, 1993, 11; David Woodruff, "Plugging into the power surge abroad," *Business Week*, August 15, 1994.

2. Fabrizio Gilardi, *Delegation in the regulatory state* (Cheltenham, UK: Edward Elgar, 2008), 43.

3. World Bank, *Natural gas: Private sector participation and market development* (Washington, DC: World Bank, 1999), 25–26.

4. Treaty between the United States of America and the Argentine Republic concerning the reciprocal encouragement and protection of investment; signed November 14, 1991, and entered into force October 20, 1994.

5. Gilardi, *Delegation in the regulatory state*, 1; Fabrizio Gilardi, "Policy credibility and delegation to independent regulatory agencies: A comparative empirical analysis," *Journal of European Public Policy* 9, no. 6 (2002): 873–893, 881–883; "Mark Thatcher, "Delegation to independent regulatory agencies: Pressures, functions, and contextual mediation," *West European Politics* 25, no. 1 (2002): 125–147, 127.

6. David Vogel, *The politics of risk regulation in Europe*, Center for Responsible Business Working Paper No. 6, January 1 (Berkeley, CA: Center for Responsible Business, University of California, Berkeley, 2003), 15; Claire Weill, "Can consultation of both experts and the public help developing public policy? Some aspects of the debate in France," *Science and Public Policy* 30, no. 3 (2003): 199–203, 199–200.

7. Gavin Little, "BSE and the regulation of risk," *Modern Law Review* 64, no. 5 (2001): 730–756; Kevin Jones, "BSE, risk, and the communication of uncertainty: A review of Lord Phillips' report from the BSE inquiry," *Canadian Journal of Sociology* 26, no. 4 (2001): 655–666; Sir John Krebs, "Protecting consumers in the future world market," City Food Lecture, London, January 14, 2003: http://www.freshinfo.com/index.php?s=n&ss=nd&sid=3046.

8. Giandomenico Majone, "The regulatory state and its legitimacy problems," *West European Politics* 22, no. 1 (1999): 1–24, 4–5, 9; Fabrizio Gilardi, Jacint Jordana, and David Levi-Faur, *Regulation in the age of globalization: The diffusion of regulatory agencies across Europe and Latin America* (Barcelona, ES: Institut Barcelona d'Estudis Internacionals, 2006), 4.

9. Gilardi, *Delegation in the regulatory state*, 58 and 117; Lene Holm Pedersen, "Transfer and transformation in processes of Europeanization," *European Journal of Political Research* 45, no. 6 (2006): 985–1021; Stephen Wilks and Ian Bartle, "The unanticipated consequences of creating independent competition agencies," *West European Politics* 25, no. 1 (2002): 148–172, 157.

10. John S. Cubbin and Jon Stern, *Regulatory effectiveness and the empirical impact of variations in regulatory governance*, World Bank Policy Research Working Paper No. 3535, March (Washington, DC: World Bank, 2005), 5; Gilardi, "Policy credibility and delegation to independent regulatory agencies," 880, and *Delegation in the regulatory state*, 57.

11. Gilardi, *Delegation in the regulatory state*, appendix 4; Witold Henisz, Bennet Zelner, and Mauro Guillén, "The worldwide diffusion of market-oriented infrastructure reform, 1977–1999," *American Sociological Review* 70, no. 6 (2005): 871–897, table 1; David Levi-Faur, "The politics of liberalisation: Privatisation and regulation-for-competition in Europe's and Latin America's telecoms and electricity industries," *European Journal of Political Research* 42, no. 5 (2003): 705–740, 707–708.

12. Jacint Jordana, David Levi-Faur, and Xavier Marin, *The global diffusion of regulatory agencies: Institutional emulation and the restructuring of modern bureaucracy* (Haifa, IL: University of Haifa, 2007), 2–3; Jacint Jordana and David Levi-Faur, "Toward a Latin American regulatory state? The diffusion of autonomous agencies across countries and sectors," *International Journal of Public Administration* 29, no. 4–6 (2006): 335–366, 336.

13. Jordana and Levi-Faur, "Toward a Latin American regulatory state?" 336; Jordana, Levi-Faur, and Marin, *Global diffusion of regulatory agencies*, 35; Gilardi, *Delegation in the regulatory state*, 109, 113–114; Pedersen, "Transfer and transformation in processes of Europeanization," 995; Henisz, Zelner, and Guillén,

"Worldwide diffusion of market-oriented infrastructure reform, 1977–1999," 875–876; Organization for Economic Cooperation and Development (OECD), *Regulatory policies in OECD countries: From interventionism to regulatory governance* (Paris:OECD, 2002), 95; Martin Lodge, "The Importance of being modern: International benchmarking and national regulatory innovation," *Journal of European Public Policy* 12, no. 4 (2005): 649–667.

14. Jeswald Salacuse and Nicholas Sullivan, "Do BITs really work? An evaluation of bilateral investment treaties and their grand bargain," *Harvard International Law Journal* 46 (2005): 67–120, 69; Roberto C. de Albuquerque, "The disappropriation of foreign companies involved in the exploration, exploitation, and commercialization of hydrocarbons in Bolivia," *Law and Business Review of the Americas* 14 (2008): 21–52, 24; Ibironke Odumosu, "The law and politic of engaging resistance in investment dispute settlement," *Penn State International Law Review* 26 (2007): 251–286.

15. Salacuse and Sullivan, "Do BITs really work?" 68–69 and 75; Eric Gottwald, "Leveling the playing field: Is it time for a legal assistance center for developing nations in investment treaty arbitration?" *American University International Law Review* 22 (2007): 237–275, 241–242; Christopher Ryan, "Meeting expectations: Assessing the long-term legitimacy and stability of international investment law," *University of Pennsylvania Journal of International Law* 29 (2008): 725–761; Thomas W. Wälde, "The 'umbrella' clause in investment arbitration," *World Investment and Trade* 6, no. 2 (2005): 183–236.

16. Edwin L. Dale Jr., "World Bank pact is signed by US," *New York Times*, August 28, 1965.

17. Stanley Metzger, "Private foreign investment and international organizations," *International Organization* 22, no. 1 (1968): 288–309, 300.

18. Salacuse and Sullivan, "Do BITs really work?" 77; Zachary Elkins, Andrew Guzman, and Beth Simmons, "Competing for capital: The diffusion of bilateral investment treaties, 1960–2000," in *The Global Diffusion of Markets and Democracy*, ed. Beth Simmons, Frank Dobbin, and Geoffrey Garrett (New York: Cambridge University Press, 2008), 220–260, 247; Ryan, "Meeting expectations," 735.

19. Susan Franck, "Integrating investment treaty conflict and dispute systems design," *Minnesota Law Review* 92 (2007): 161–229, 172; Salacuse and Sullivan, "Do BITs really work?" 88; Susan Franck, "The legitimacy crisis in investment treaty arbitration: Privatizing public international law through inconsistent decisions," *Fordham Law Review* 73, no. 4 (2005): 1521–1625, 1538; Michael Moore, "International arbitration between states and foreign investors," *Stanford Law Review* 18, no. 7 (1966): 1359–1380, 1369–1376; Ryan, "Meeting expectations," 733; Luke Peterson, *Bilateral investment treaties and development policy-making* (Winnipeg, CA: International Institute for Sustainable Development, 2004), 21–22.

20. Jean Kalicki, *ICSID arbitration in the Americas* (Washington, DC: Arnold & Porter, 2007), 5; Andrew P. Tuck, "Investor–state arbitration revised: A critical

analysis of the revisions and proposed reforms to the ICSID and UNCITRAL arbitration rules," *NAFTA: Law and Business Review of the Americas* 13 (2007): 885–992, 886; Salacuse and Sullivan, "Do BITs really work?" 70; Jason Webb Yackee, "Conceptual difficulties in the empirical study of bilateral investment treaties," *Brooklyn Journal of International Law* 33 (2008): 405–462, 410.

21. Yves Dezalay and Bryant G. Garth, *Dealing in virtue: International commercial arbitration and the construction of a transnational legal order* (Chicago: University of Chicago Press, 1996), 48–51 and 95–97; Neil Kaplan, *The good, the bad and the ugly* (Hong Kong: Cannonway Consultants, 2004); Catherine Rogers, "The vocation of the international arbitrator," *American University International Law Review* 20 (2005): 957–1020, and "Regulating international arbitrators: A functional approach to developing standards of conduct," *Stanford Journal of International Law* 41 (2005): 53–120, 64–65; Susan Franck, "Empirically evaluating claims about investment treaty arbitration," *North Carolina Law Review* 86 (2007): 1–86, 76–83.

22. Thatcher, "Delegation to independent regulatory agencies," 139–140; David Coen and Mark Thatcher, "The new governance of markets and nonmajoritarian regulators," *Governance* 18, no. 3 (2005): 329–346, 336; Mark Thatcher, "The third force? Independent regulatory agencies and elected politicians in Europe," *Governance* 18, no. 3 (2005): 347–373.

23. Martino Maggetti, "De facto independence after delegation: A fuzzy-set analysis," *Regulation & Governance* 1, no. 4 (2007): 271–294; Thatcher, "The third force?" 365, and "Delegation to independent regulatory agencies" 139; José A. Gómez-Ibáñez, *Regulating infrastructure: Monopoly, contracts, and discretion* (Cambridge: Harvard University Press, 2003), 227; Maria Martens, *Voice or loyalty? The evolution of the European Environmental Agency* (Oslo: Center for European Studies, University of Oslo, 2008), 18.

24. David Coen and Mark Thatcher, *After delegation: The evolution of European networks of regulatory agencies* (London: University College London, 2006); Maggetti, "De facto independence after delegation"; Pedersen, "Transfer and transformation in processes of Europeanization," 995; Stephen Wilks, "Agency escape: Decentralization or dominance of the European Commission in the modernization of competition policy?" *Governance* 18, no. 3 (2005): 431–452, 438; Mark Thatcher and David Coen, "Reshaping European regulatory space: An evolutionary analysis," *West European Politics* 31, no. 4 (2008): 806–836.

25. Jon Stern and John Cubbin, *Regulatory effectiveness: The impact of regulation and regulatory governance arrangements on electricity industry outcomes*, Policy Research Working Paper No. 3536, March 1 (Washington, DC: World Bank, 2005), 21–22; Ioannis Kessides, *Reforming infrastructure: Privatization, regulation, and competition* (Washington, DC: World Bank, 2004), 18; Margaret Pearson, "The business of governing business in China: Institutions and norms of the emerging regulatory state," *World Politics* 57, no. 2 (2005): 296–322, 297; emphasis in original.

26. Mauricio Dussauge-Laguna, *Regulatory agencies in Mexico: Between independence and control* (London: London School of Economics and Political Science, 2008); Stern and Cubbin, *Regulatory effectiveness*, 14; Nicola Phillips, "States and modes of regulation in the global political economy," in *Regulatory governance in developing countries*, ed. Martin Minogue and Ledivina V. Cariño, (Cheltenham, UK: Edward Elgar, 2006), 17–38, 34.

27. Derek Eldridge and Brian Goulden, "A diagnostic model for capacity building in regulatory agencies and competition commissions," in Minogue and Cariño, *Regulatory governance in developing countries*, 303–326, 311; Jon Stern, "Electricity and telecommunications regulatory institutions in small and developing countries," *Utilities Policy* 9 (2000): 131–157, 144 and table 141; Stern and Cubbin, *Regulatory effectiveness*, 23–24; Martin Lodge, "Regulatory reform in small developing states: Globalisation, regulatory autonomy, and Jamaican telecommunications," *New Political Economy* 7, no. 3 (2002): 415–433, 428; Martin Lodge, "Embedding regulatory autonomy in Caribbean telecommunications," *Annals of Public and Cooperative Economics* 73, no. 4 (2002): 667–693, 681–687; Rahul Mukherji, "Promoting competition in India's telecom sector," in *Reinventing Public Service Delivery in India*, ed. Vikram K. Chand (Delhi: Sage, 2006), 57–94; Margaret Pearson, "Governing the Chinese economy: Regulatory reform in the service of the state," *Public Administration Review* 67, no. 4 (2007): 718–730.

28. CMS Energy Form 10-K filing with Securities and Exchange Commission for fiscal year 2002; and CMS Gas Transmission Co. v. Argentine Republic, ICSID case no. ARB/01/8; decision of the tribunal on objections to jurisdiction (July 17, 2003); award (May 12, 2005).

29. Gottwald, "Leveling the playing field," 250 and 263; Mercedes Ales, Leonardo Granato, and Carlos Oddone, "Argentina facing international claims over foreign investments," *Law and Business Review of the Americas* 14 (2008): 481–492, 481.

30. CMS Gas Transmission Co. v. Argentine Republic. Also Tuck, "Investor–state arbitration revised," 907–908; James Fry, "International human rights law in investment arbitration," *Duke Journal of Comparative and International Law* (2007): 77–148, 101.

31. Enron Corp. v. Argentine Republic, ICSID case no. ARB/01/3; decision on the Argentine Republic's request for a continued stay of enforcement of the award (October 7, 2008). Also "Lavagna says court could declare ICSID ruling null," BBC Monitoring, May 16, 2005; Ryan, "Meeting expectations," 747–748.

32. Kathryn Botham, "Bolivia's legal gamble: Negotiating nationalization," *Wisconsin International Law Journal* 26 (2008): 507–549; de Albuquerque, "The disappropriation of foreign companies involved in the exploration, exploitation, and commercialization of hydrocarbons in Bolivia"; Lindsay S. Pinto, "Resolving the Bolivian gas crisis: Lessons from Bolivia's brush with international arbitration," *George Washington International Law Review* 39 (2007): 947–984.

33. U.S. Government Accountability Office (U.S. GAO), *Energy Security: Issues related to potential reductions in Venezuelan oil production*, GAO-06–668, June 27 (Washington, DC: U.S. GAO, 2006); Tuck, "Investor–state arbitration revised," 909; Kalicki, *ICSID arbitration in the Americas*, 4; Benedict Mander, "Statoil signs deal to survey Venezuela reserves," *Financial Times*, January 24, 2008.

34. Milagros Aguirre, "Ecuador: Political campaign starts with kicking out oil company," Inter Press Service, May 25, 2006; Kate Joynes, "President of Ecuador adds to business woes by renouncing nine bilateral investment treaties," *Global Insight*, January 30, 2008.

35. Webb Yackee, "Conceptual difficulties in the empirical study of bilateral investment treaties," 419–420; Franck, "Legitimacy crisis in investment treaty arbitration," 1587–1589.

36. Wälde, "'Umbrella' Clause in Investment Arbitration," 190 and 194; Jeswald Salacuse, "Is there a better Way? Alternative methods of treaty-based, investor–state dispute resolution," *Fordham International Law Journal* 31 (2007): 138–185, 142 and 147; Tuck, "Investor–state arbitration revised," 886; Jack J. Coe Jr., "Toward a complementary use of conciliation in investor–state disputes," *UC Davis Journal of International Law* 12 (2005): 7–46, 8–9.

37. CMS Gas Transmission Co. v. Argentine Republic. Also Franck, "Legitimacy crisis in investment treaty arbitration," 1558; Pinto, "Resolving the Bolivian gas crisis," 963–964.

38. Franck, "Legitimacy crisis in investment treaty arbitration," 1559–1568; Fry, "International human rights law in investment arbitration," 84.

39. Franck, "Legitimacy crisis in investment treaty arbitration," 1559; Gabriel Egli, "Don't get bit: Addressing ICSID's inconsistent application of most-favored nation clauses to dispute resolution provisions," *Pepperdine Law Review* 34 (2007): 1046–1083; Barnali Choudhury, "Recapturing public power: Is investment arbitration's engagement of the public interest contributing to the Democratic deficit?" *Vanderbilt Journal of Transnational Law* 41 (2008): 775–832, 797.

40. Dezalay and Garth, *Dealing in virtue*, 58; Egli, "Don't get bit," 1060.

41. Doe v. United States, 253 F.3d 256, 262 (6th Cir. 2001).

42. ICSID Secretariat, *Possible improvements of the framework for ICSID arbitration* (Washington, DC: International Centre for Settlement of Investment Disputes, 2004), 10; Tuck, "Investor–state arbitration revised," 897–900.

43. Rogers, "Regulating international arbitrators"; Tuck, "Investor–state arbitration revised," 900; Joseph Brubaker, "The judge who knew too much: Issue conflicts in international adjudication," *Berkeley Journal of International Law* 26 (2008): 111–152.

44. Tecnias Medioambientales Tecmed S.A. v. The United Mexican States, ICSID case no. ARB (AF)/00/2; award (May 29, 2003). See also Odumosu, "Law and politic of engaging resistance in investment dispute settlement."

45. Elkins, Guzman, and Simmons, "Competing for capital," 253; Choudhury, "Recapturing public power," 784.

46. David Levi-Faur, "The global diffusion of regulatory capitalism," *Annals of the American Academy of Political and Social Science* 598, no. 1 (2005): 12–32, 13; Thomas Zweifel, *Democratic deficit? Institutions and regulations in the European Union, Switzerland, and the United States* (Lanham, MD: Rowman & Littlefield, 2002), 70.

47. Dwight Waldo, *The administrative state* (New York: The Ronald Press, 1948), 118; David Rosenbloom, "Retrofitting the administrative state to the Constitution," *Public Administration Review* 60, no. 1 (2000): 39–46.

48. Gregory Palast, Jerrold Oppenheim, and Theo MacGregor, *Democratic regulation: A guide to the control of privatized public services through social dialogue* (Geneva: International Labour Office, 2000); Peter Vass, "Regulatory governance and accountability: A UK perspective on improving the regulatory state," in Minogue and Cariño, *Regulatory governance in developing countries,* 82–113; Thatcher, "Delegation to independent regulatory agencies," 140; Coen and Thatcher, "New governance of markets and non-majoritarian regulators," 341; Gómez-Ibáñez, *Regulating infrastructure,* 227; OECD, *Regulatory policies in OECD countries,* 74–76.

49. Giandomenico Majone, *Regulating Europe,* European Public Policy series (New York: Routledge, 1996), 284–300, and "The regulatory state and its legitimacy problems"; Select Committee on Constitution, *The Regulatory state: Ensuring its accountability* (London: House of Lords, 2004), introduction; Thatcher, "Delegation to independent regulatory agencies," 140; Mathew McCubbins, Roger Noll, and Barry Weingast, "Administrative procedures as instruments of political control," *Journal of Law, Economics and Organization* 3, no. 2 (1987): 243–277, 244; Susan Webb Yackee, "Sweet-talking the fourth branch: The influence of interest group comments on federal agency rulemaking," *Journal of Public Administration Reseach and Theory* 16, no. 1 (2006): 103–124.

50. Brian Levy and Pablo T. Spiller, eds., *Regulations, institutions, and commitment: Comparative studies of telecommunications* (New York: Cambridge University Press, 1996), 9 and 29; Martin Minogue, "Apples and oranges: Comparing international experiences in regulatory reform," in Minogue and Cariño, *Regulatory Governance in Developing Countries,* 61–81, 77; Gerard Clark, "An introduction to the legal profession in China in the year 2008," *Suffolk University Law Review* 41, no. 4 (2008): 833–850, 833–837.

51. Jon Stern, "What makes an independent regulator independent?" *Business Strategy Review* 8, no. 2 (1997): 67–74, 73; Jon Stern and Stuart Holder, "Regulatory governance: Criteria for assessing the performance of regulatory systems," *Utilities Policy* 8, no. 1 (1999): 33–50, 42; Minogue, "Apples and oranges," 75–76; Karl P. Sauvant and Lisa E. Sachs, *The effect of treaties on foreign direct investment* (New York: Oxford University Press,

2009); Jason Webb Yackee, "Do we really need BITs? Toward a return to contract in international investment law," *Asian Journal of WTO & International Health Law and Policy* 3, no. 1 (2008): 121–146, 122–123.

Chapter 7

Source for epigraph: Ray Rivera, "Bloomberg creates a task force to advocate for U.S. infrastructure needs," *New York Times*, January 20, 2008.

1. U.S. Census Bureau, *Historical statistics of the United States, colonial times to 1970* (Washington, DC: U.S. Census Bureau, 1976), series B413, H700, N427, Q456, Q152, S436, Y290.

2. Christophe Kamps, *The dynamic macroeconomic effects of public capital: Theory and evidence for OECD countries* (Berlin: Springer, 2004), 2, and *New estimates of government net capital stocks for 22 OECD countries 1960–2001* (Washington, DC: IMF, 2004), 21–22 and 24–25; Charles Hulten and George E. Peterson, "The public capital stock: Needs, trends, and performance," *American Economic Review* 74, no. 2 (1984): 166–173, table 1; Organization for Economic Cooperation and Development (OECD), *Infrastructure policies for the 1990s* (Paris: OECD, 1993), 7–8 and 23, 26–29; Roland Straub and Ivan Tchakarov, *Assessing the impact of a change in the composition of public spending*, IMF Working Paper No. 07/168, July (Washington, DC: IMF, 2007), 4 and 37.

3. Stephen Flynn, "A crack in the dam: America's infrastructure problems are growing worse," *Popular Mechanics*, November 1, 2007,; Burt Solomon, "The real infrastructure crisis," *National Journal*, July 5, 2008; "Mayor Bloomberg joins Governors Rendell and Schwarzenegger to create *non-partisan* coalition for federal infrastructure investment," press release (New York: Office of the Mayor, January 19, 2008); American Society of Civil Engineers, *Report card for America's infrastructure* (Reston, VA: American Society of Civil Engineers, 2005); Kamps, *The dynamic macroeconomic effects of public capital*, 3.

4. Joseph Zikmund, "Sources of the suburban population: 1955–1960 and 1965–1970," *Publius* 5, no. 1 (1975): 27–43; Mike Davis, *Planet of slums* (New York: Verso, 2006); Angus Maddison, "A comparison of levels of GDP per capita in developed and developing countries, 1700–1980," *Journal of Economic History* 43, no. 1 (1983): 27–41; Kalpana Kochhar, "The 500 billion dollar question," *Business Standard* (India), May 4, 2008; Delhi Planning Commission, *Eleventh five year plan* (Delhi: Planning Commission, 2007), 255. Urbanization data are provided by the Department of Economic and Social Affairs of the United Nations Secretariat: http://esa.un.org/unup. Data on per capita GDP growth for India and China are provided in the International Monetary Fund's *World Economic Outlook* database: http://www.imf.org/external/pubs/ft/weo.

5. William Easterly, "When is fiscal adjustment an illusion?" *Economic Policy* 14, no. 28 (1999): 57–76, 59–62; Marianne Fay and Mary Morrison,

Infrastructure in Latin America and the Caribbean: Recent developments and key challenges, Directions in Development: Infrastructure (Washington, DC: World Bank, 2005), iii.

6. Deloitte Touche Tohmatsu, *Closing the infrastructure gap: The role of public–private partnerships* (Washington, DC: Deloitte Touche Tohmatsu, 2006); Fay and Morrison, *Infrastructure in Latin America and the Caribbean*, iii; Darrin Grimsey and Mervyn Lewis, *Public private partnerships: The worldwide revolution in infrastructure provision and project finance* (Northampton, MA: Edward Elgar, 2007).

7. Ryan Orr, "The privatisation paradigm," *Infrastructure Journal*, September–October (2006): 16–18.

8. Macquarie Bank Ltd., "Why Macquarie manages infrastructure funds," March 3 (Sydney: Macquarie Bank Ltd., 2006): http://www.macquarie.com.au/au/about_macquarie/media_centre/20060303a.htm; Emily Thornton, "Roads to riches: Why investors are clamoring to take over America's highways, bridges, and airports," *Business Week*, May 7, 2007; Ryan Orr, "The rise of infra funds," in *Global Infrastructure Report 2007*, ed. Project Finance International (London: Project Finance International, 2007), 2–12, 2; Robert N. Palter, Jay Walder, and Stian Westlake, "How investors can get more out of infrastructure," *McKinsey Quarterly*, February 2008: www.mckinseyquarterly.com/How_investors_can_get_more_out_of_infrastructure_2105; Macquarie Europe Ltd., *Macquarie Global Insfrastructure Securities Fund* (London: Macquarie Europe Ltd., 2007), 2.

9. Alasdair Roberts, "Transborder service systems: Pathways for innovation or threats to accountability?" Market-based Government series, March (Arlington, VA: IBM Endowment for the Business of Government, 2004).

10. See http://www.ncppp.org (National Council on Public–Private Partnerships); http://www.pppcouncil.ca (Canadian Council for Public–Private Partnerships); and http://www.partnershipsuk.org.uk (Partnerships UK).

11. M. Fouzul Kabir Kahn and Robert Parra, *Financing large projects* (New York: Prentice Hall, 1997), 161–175; Public–Private Infrastructure Advisory Facility (PPIAF), *Annual report 2000* (Washington, DC: PPIAF, 2000); Orr, "The privatisation paradigm," 16.

12. Tom Clark, Mike Elsby, and Sarah Love, *Twenty-five years of falling investment* (London: Institute for Fiscal Studies, 2001); John Hall, "Private opportunity, public benefit?" *Fiscal Studies* 19, no. 2 (1998): 121–140.

13. Hall, "Private opportunity, public benefit?" 122; Michael G. Pollitt, *The declining role of the state in infrastructure investments in the UK* (Cambridge: Cambridge University, 2000), 3–4 and 12–13; Allyson Pollock and David Price, "Has the NAO audited risk transfer in operational private finance initiative schemes?" *Public Money & Management* 28, no. 3 (2008): 173–178, 173; Declan Gaffney, Allyson M. Pollock, David Price, and Jean Shaoul, "NHS capital expenditure and the private finance initiative," *British Medical Journal* 319, (July 3, 1999): 48–51.

14. Graeme A. Hodge and Carsten Greve, "Public–private partnerships: An international performance review," *Public Administration Review* 67, no. 3 (2007): 545–558, 553; J. Luis Guasch, Jean-Jacques Laffont, and Stéphane Straub, *Renegotiation of concession contracts in Latin America* (San Diego: University of California, San Diego, 2003), 2.

15. Commonwealth Business Council, *An Agenda for growth and livelihoods: Public–private partnerships for infrastructure* (London: Commonwealth Secretariat, 2006), 2; Maxim Boycko, Andrei Shleifer, and Robert Vishny, "A theory of privatisation," *Economic Journal* 106, no. 434 (1996): 309–316, 318.

16. Howard Frant, "High-powered and low-powered incentives in the public sector," *Journal of Public Administration Reseach and Theory* 6, no. 3 (1996): 365–381, 367; Jean-Etienne de Bettignies and Thomas Ross, "The economics of public–private partnerships," *Canadian Public Policy* 30, no. 2 (2004): 135–154, 139.

17. Partnerships Victoria, *Public sector comparator technical note* (Melbourne: Department of Treasury and Finance, 2001), 20–21; Peter MacMahon, "Minister defends the 8bn bill for PPP programme," *The Scotsman*, March 26, 2005; Arthur Andersen and Enterprise LSE, *Value for money drivers in the private finance initiative*, report to the Private Finance Initiative Treasury Taskforce, January 26 (London: Arthur Anderson and Enterprise LSE, 2000), 25.

18. Martin Ricketts, "The use of contract by government and its agents," *Economic Affairs* 29, no. 1 (2009): 7–12, 11; Mitch Daniels, "For whom the road tolls," *New York Times*, May 27, 2006.

19. U.S. Government Accountability Office (U.S. GAO), *Highway public–private partnerships: Securing potential benefits and protecting the public interest could result from more rigorous up-front analysis*, GAO-08–1052T, July 24 (Washington, DC: U.S. GAO, 2008), 6.

20. Efraim Sadka, *Public–private partnerships: A public economics perspective*, IMF Working Paper No. 06/77, March (Washington, DC: IMF, 2006), 3–4.

21. Graham Allen, *The private finance initiative (PFI)*, Economic Policy and Statistics section, House of Commons Library research paper 01/117, December 18 (London: House of Commons Library, 2001), 20–23; Alasdair Roberts, "Lockbox government: Segmented funding strategies and the erosion of governmental flexibility," *Governance* 15, no. 2 (2002): 105–134, 256–258; Allyson Pollock and Mark Hellowell, "The private financing of NHS Hospitals: Politics, policy, and practice," *Economic Affairs* 29, no. 1 (2009): 13–19, 14; Mark Hellowell, "Is PFI on the critical list?" *Public Finance*, August 29, 2008: http://www.public-finance.co.uk/features_details.cfm?News_id=58722 (accessed September 18, 2008); Ricketts, "The use of contract by government and its agents," 11.

22. Pollitt, *Declining role of the state in infrastructure investments in the UK*, 20; Rob Ball, Maryanne Heafey, and David King, "The private finance initiative in the UK," *Public Management Review* 9, no. 2 (2007): 289–310; Allen, *Private finance initiative*, 39–43; J. Laurence, "Consortium condemned over 100m windfall profit from NHS," *Independent*, May 3, 2006; Graeme A. Hodge and Carsten

Greve, "PPPs: The passage of time permits a sober reflection," *Economic Affairs* 29, no. 1 (2009): 33–39, 37.

23. Trefor Williams, *Moving to public–private partnerships: Learning from experience around the world* (Arlington, VA: IBM Endowment for the Business of Government, 2003), 6.

24. Paul Maltby and Tim Gosling, "Opening it up: Accountability and partnerships," in *3 steps forward, 2 steps back: Reforming PPP policy*, ed. Tim Gosling (London: Institute for Public–Private Partnerships, 2004), 81–110, 114.

25. Matthew Flinders, "The politics of public–private partnerships," *British Journal of Politics and International Relations* 7, no. 2 (2005): 215–239, 19; Organization for Economic Cooperation and Development (OECD), *Modernising government: The way forward* (Paris: OECD, 2005), 28; United Kingdom, *Your right to know: The government's proposals for a freedom of information act*, Cm 3818, December (London: HM Stationery Office, 1997), para. 1.1.

26. "Fiscal 'stunned' at tolls denial," BBC News, January 4, 2006 (accessed September 16, 2008): http://news.bbc.co.uk/1/hi/scotland/4578308.stm; Alasdair Roberts, *Blacked out: Government secrecy in the information age* (New York: Cambridge University Press, 2006), ch. 7; Jean Shaoul, Anne Stafford, and Pamela Stapleton, "Highway robbery? A financial analysis of design, build, finance, and operate (DBFO) in UK roads," *Transport Reviews* 26, no. 3 (2006): 257–274, 270; Valarie Sands, "The right to know and obligation to provide: Public private partnerships, public knowledge, public accountability, public disenfranchisement, and prison cases," *University of New South Wales Law Journal* 29, no. 3 (2006): http://www.austlii.org/au/journals/UNSWLJ/2006/57.html.

27. Graeme A. Hodge, "Corporates in the driving seat," *The Age*, July 6, 2006, 8; George Monbiot, *Captive state: The corporate takeover of Britain* (London: Macmillan, 2000); Graeme A. Hodge, "The risky business of public–private partnerships," *Australian Journal of Public Administration* 63, no. 4 (2004): 37–49, 45; Fay and Morrison, *Infrastructure in Latin America and the Caribbean*, 22; Carles Boix, *Privatization and public discontent in Latin America* (Chicago: University of Chicago, 2005), 11.

28. Thornton, "Roads to riches," 56; Christian Wolmar, *Down the tube: The battle for London's Underground* (London: Aurum, 2002), 117.

29. Allen, *The private finance initiative*, 36; Pollitt, *The declining role of the state in infrastructure investments in the UK*, 26; "Fiscal 'stunned' at tolls denial."

30. Maude Barlow and Tony Clarke, *Blue gold: The fight to stop the corporate theft of the world's water* (New York: New Press, 2002); William Finnegan, "Leasing the rain," *New Yorker*, April 8, 2002.

31. J. Luis Guasch and Stéphane Straub, *Infrastructure concessions in Latin America: Government-led renegotiations* (Washington, DC: World Bank, 2005), 4; "BIAL defends user fee, cuts rates," *Financial Express*, March 7, 2008.

32. Labour Party, *Manifesto 1997* (London: Labour Party, 1997); Ryan Orr, *Investment in foreign infrastructure: The legacy and lessons of legal-con-*

tractual failure (Palo Alto, CA: Collaboratory for Research on Global Projects, Stanford University, 2006), 5; Ryan Orr and Barry Metzger, *The legacy of failed global projects: A review and reconceptualization of the legal paradigm* (Palo Alto, CA: Collaboratory for Research on Global Projects, Stanford University, 2005), 12; Don E. Eberly, *The rise of global civil society: Building communities and nations from the bottom up* (New York: Encounter Books, 2008).

33. Flinders, "Politics of public–private partnerships," 12–14; Nick Cohen, "The taxpayer always foots the bill," *New Statesman*, July 9, 2001; Jean Shaoul, "A financial analysis of the National Air Traffic Services PPP," *Public Money & Management* 23, no. 3 (2003): 185–194, 192; Ball, Heafey, and King, "Private finance initiative in the UK," 300–301; Commission on Public Private Partnerships, *Building better partnerships* (London: Institute for Public Policy Research, 2001), 84; Pollock and Price, "Has the NAO audited risk transfer in operational private finance initiative schemes?" 177–178; Anthony Boardman, Finn Poschmann, and Aidan Vining, "North American infrastructure P3s: Examples and lessons learned," in *The challenge of public–private Partnerships*, ed. Graeme A. Hodge and Carsten Greve (Cheltenham, UK: Edward Elgar, 2005), 162–189; Aidan Vining, Anthony Boardman, and Finn Poschmann, "Public–private partnerships in the US and Canada: There are no free lunches," *Journal of Comparative Policy Analysis* 7, no. 3 (2005): 199–220.

34. Orr, "Privatisation paradigm," 18; J. Luis Guasch, *Granting and renegotiating infrastructure concessions: Doing it right*, WBI Development Studies (Washington, DC: World Bank, 2004), 13; Eduardo Engel, Ronald Fischer, and Alexander Galetovic, "Privatizing highways in Latin America: Fixing what went wrong," *Economa* 4, no. 1 (2003): 129–164, 131.

35. Guasch, *Granting and renegotiating infrastructure concessions*, 18; Engel, Fischer, and Galetovic, "Privatizing highways in Latin America" 131; David Martimort and Stéphane Straub, *The political economy of private participation, social discontent, and regulatory governance* (Toulouse, FR: University of Toulouse, 2005), 14–18.

36. Engel, Fischer, and Galetovic, "Privatizing highways in Latin America," 147.

37. Louis Uchitelle, "Mexico's toll roads not taken," *New York Times*, February 22, 1993; Sam Dillon, "Mexico's privately run highways prove a costly failure," *New York Times*, August 23, 1997; J. Luis Guasch and Stéphane Straub, "Renegotiation of infrastructure concessions," *Annals of Public and Cooperative Economics* 77, no. 4 (2006): 479–493, 484.

38. Clive Harris, *Private participation in infrastructure in developing countries* (Washington, DC: World Bank, 2003), 2, 6, and 10.

39. Fay and Morrison, *Infrastructure in Latin America and the Caribbean*, 20; John Rossant, "Shoring up Suez," *Business Week*, March 17, 2003; Ranjit Lamech and Kazim Saeed, *Private power investors in developing countries: Survey*

2002—Preliminary findings (Washington, DC: World Bank, 2002), 2. Veolia was known as Vivendi in 2002.

40. Clemencia Torres de Mästle and Ada Karina Izaguirre, "Recent trends in private activity in infrastructure," *Gridlines*, May, 2008; Thornton, "Roads to riches," 52; Palter, Walder, and Westlake, "How investors can get more out of infrastructure."

41. Stephen Barber, *Infrastructure, that solid and safe refuge, Financial Times*, September 15, 2008: http://www.ftadviser.com/InvestmentAdviser/ Investments/Comment/article/20080915/9a272e1e-7f1b-11dd-9dcc-00144f2af8e8/Infrastructure-that-solid-and-safe-refuge.jsp (accessed September 28, 2008); Sandeep Tucker, "Infrastructure funds lose out in a scramble to divest their assets," *Financial Times*, August 25, 2008; Freshfields Bruckhaus Deringer, *Outlook for infrastructure: 2008 and beyond* (London: Freshfields Bruckhaus Deringer, 2008); "Latin American projects on hold as credit dries up," *Financial Times*, October 24, 2008; World Bank Public–Private Infrastructure Advisory Facility (PPIAF), *Assessment of the impact of the crisis on newPPI projects*, news note, March 5 (Washington, DC:PPIAF, 2009); Leslie Wayne, "Politics and the financial crisis slow the drive to privatize," *New York Times*, June 5, 2009.

42. KPMG International, *The changing face of infrastructure* (London, KPMG International, 2009), 3; "Safeguarding government infrastructure investment," press notice, March 3 (London: HM Treasury, 2009); PPIAF, *Assessment of the impact of the crisis on New PPI projects*, 4–5; "World Bank group launches multi-billion infrastructure initiatives to help developing countries weather crisis," press release, April 25 (Washington, DC: International Finance Corp., 2009).

43. Hodge and Greve, "PPPs"; Luis Andres and World Bank, *The impact of private sector participation in infrastructure: Lights, shadows, and the road ahead* (Washington, DC: World Bank, 2008), 32–34; Fay and Morrison, *Infrastructure in Latin America and the Caribbean*, iv–v; Martimort and Straub, *Political economy of private participation, social discontent, and regulatory governance*, 3; Corporac on Corporac on Latinobarómetro, *2008 Report*, March 26 (Santiago, CL: Corporac on Latinobarómetro, March 26, 2009), 36.

44. Erik Woodhouse, *The political economy of international infrastructure contracting: Lessons from the IPP experience* (Stanford, CA: Spogli Institute for International Studies, Stanford University, 2005), 8; Orr and Metzger, *Legacy of failed global projects*, 6; Orr, "Privatisation paradigm," 18.

45. Harris, *Private participation in infrastructure in developing countries*, 12–14; Fay and Morrison, *Infrastructure in Latin America and the Caribbean*, viii–ix.

46. Orr, *Investment in foreign infrastructure*, 12–13; Torres de Mästle and Karina Izaguirre, "Recent trends in private activity in infrastructure," 4.

Chapter 8

Source for epigraph: "The value of bank independence," *Financial Times*, August 2, 2009.

1. Irving L. Janis, *Victims of groupthink: A psychological study of foreign-policy decisions and fiascoes* (Boston: Houghton, 1972).

2. More recent work on the development of "governance indicators" has recognized the need to move beyond formal–legal measures, though this has proved a difficult task. Many key indexes still heavily rely on them. See Daniel Kaufmann and Aart Kraay, *Governance indicators: Where are we, where should we be going?* World Bank Policy Research Working Paper No. 4370, October 1 (Washington, DC: World Bank, 2007), 8 and table 1; Christiane Arndt and Charles Oman, *Uses and abuses of governance indicators* (Paris: OECD, 2006); Steven Van de Walle, "The state of the world's bureaucracies," *Journal of Comparative Policy Analysis* 8, no. 4 (2006): 437–448.

3. Robin Bade and Michael Parkin, *Central bank laws and monetary policy* (London, CA: University of Western Ontario, 1985), 2 and 25.

4. Kenneth Rogoff, "The optimal degree of commitment to an intermediate monetary target," *Quarterly Journal of Economics* 100, no. 4 (1985): 1169–1189, 1180; Carlos Santiso, *Budget institutions and fiscal responsibility: Parliaments and the political economy of the budget process in Latin America* (Washington, DC: World Bank Institute, 2005), 2.

5. "Historians and many social scientists prefer nuanced, layered explanations.... But economists like parsimony." Dani Rodrik, Arvind Subramanian, and Francesco Trebbi, "Institutions rule: The primacy of institutions over geography and integration in economic development," *Journal of Economic Growth* 9, no. 2 (2004): 131–165, 133.

6. Harold D. Lasswell, *Politics: Who gets what, when, how* (New York: McGraw Hill, 1936); World Bank, *The political economy of reform: Issues and implications for policy dialogue and development operations*, Report No. 44288-GLB, June 19 (Washington, DC: World Bank, 2008), 9.

7. Maurice Duverger, *The idea of politics: The uses of power in society* (London: Methuen & Co., 1978), 3–5; Leslie Lipson, *The great issues of politics* (Upper Saddle River, NJ: Prentice-Hall, 1981), 25.

8. Robert J. Samuelson, *The great inflation and its aftermath: The transformation of America's economy, politics, and society* (New York: Random House, 2008), 112; José A. Gómez-Ibáñez, *Regulating infrastructure: Monopoly, contracts, and discretion* (Cambridge: Harvard University Press, 2003), 227.

9. Colin Talbot, Carole Johnson, and Jay Wiggan, *Exploring performance regimes* (Manchester, UK: University of Manchester Business School, 2005), 4.

10. Edward Luttwak, *Coup d'état, a practical handbook* (New York: Knopf, 1969).

11. Michael Freeman, *Freedom or security: The consequences for democracies using emergency powers to fight terror* (Westport, CT: Praeger, 2003).

12. Seymour Martin Lipset and Jason M. Lakin, *The democratic century* (Norman: University of Oklahoma Press, 2004), 209–211.

13. Pierre Bourdieu, "Cultural reproduction and social reproduction," in *Knowledge, education, and cultural change*, ed. Richard Brown (London: Taylor and Francis, 1973), 71–112.

14. Bade and Parkin, *Central bank laws and monetary policy*, 24; Alberto Alesina and Lawrence Summers, "Central bank independence and macroeconomic performance," *Journal of Money, Credit, and Banking* 25, no. 2 (1993): 151–162, 159.

15. Douglass C. North, *Institutions, institutional change, and economic performance: The political economy of institutions and decisions* (New York: Cambridge University Press, 1990), 6 and 89.

Index